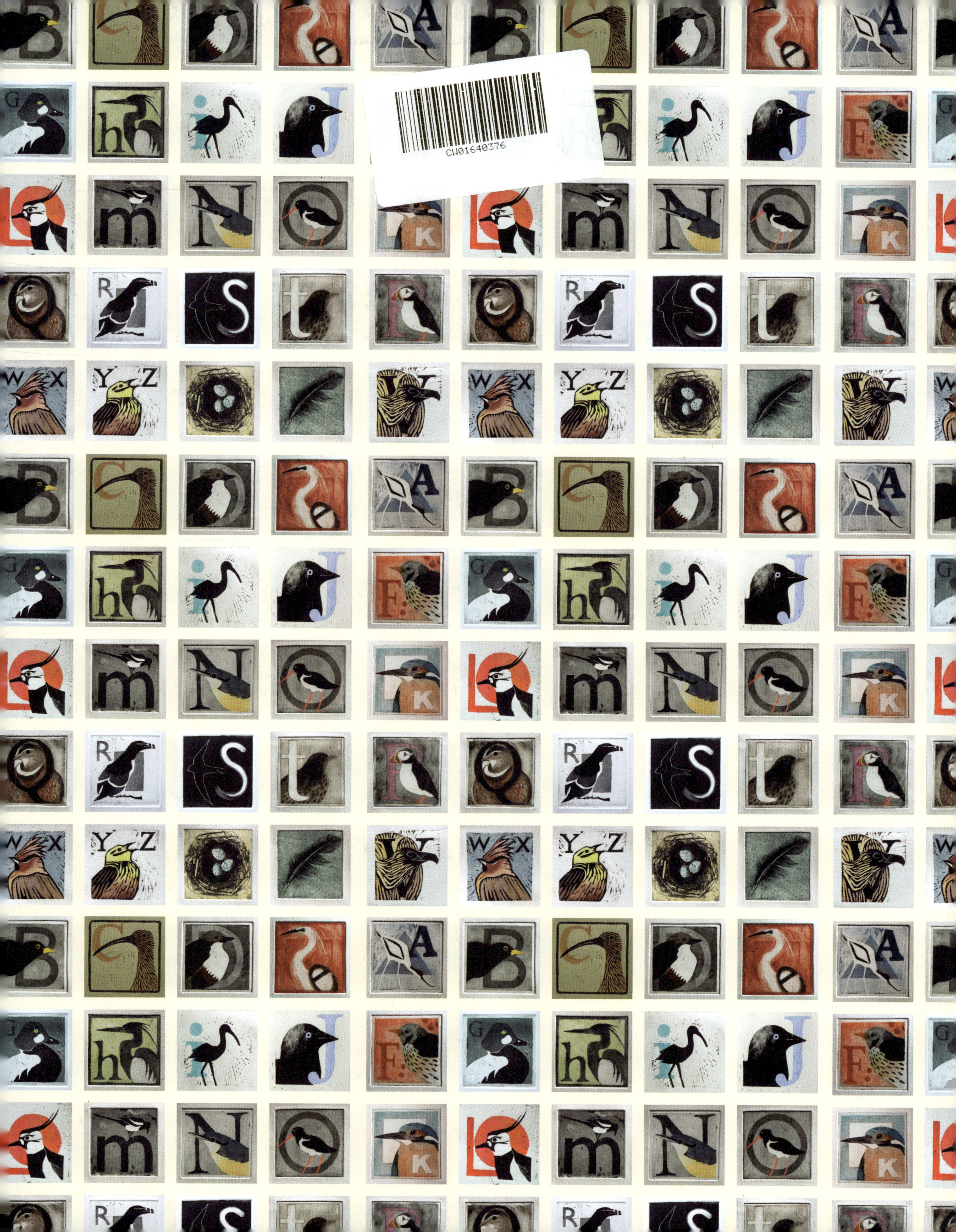

First Impressions

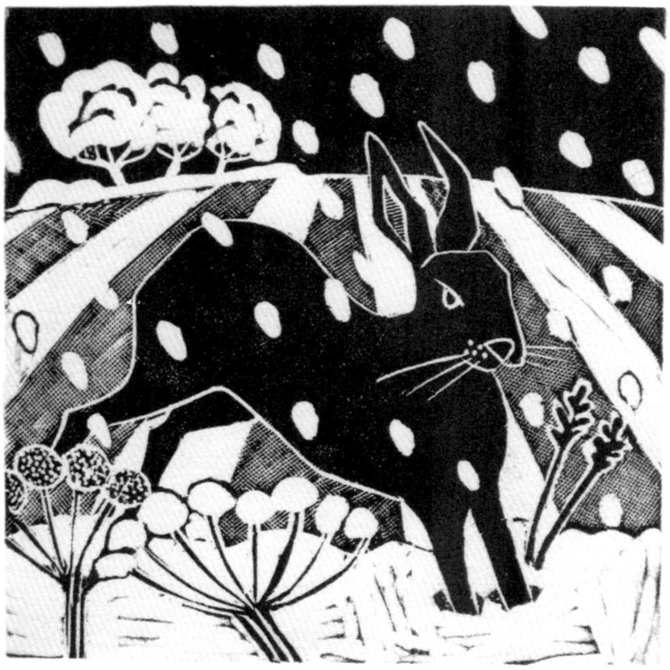

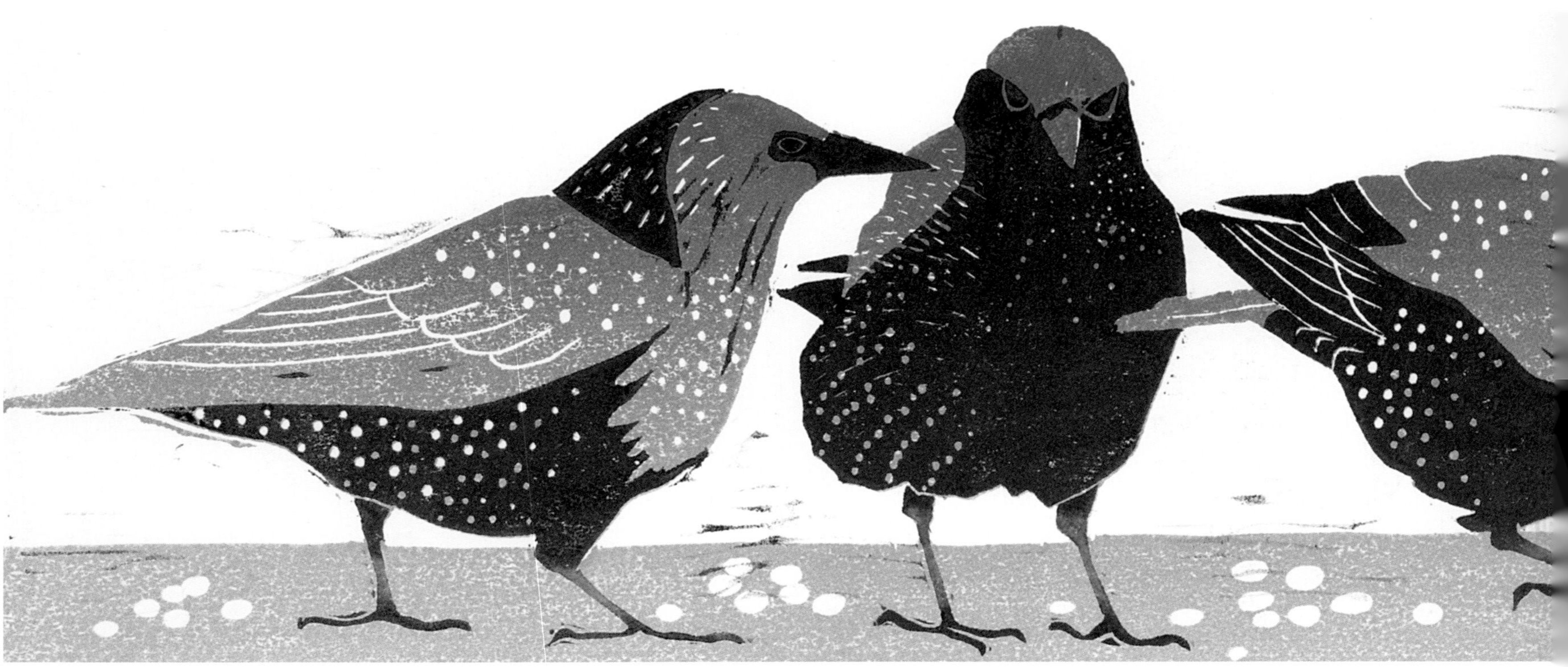

First Impressions: hand made prints inspired by nature

Lisa Hooper

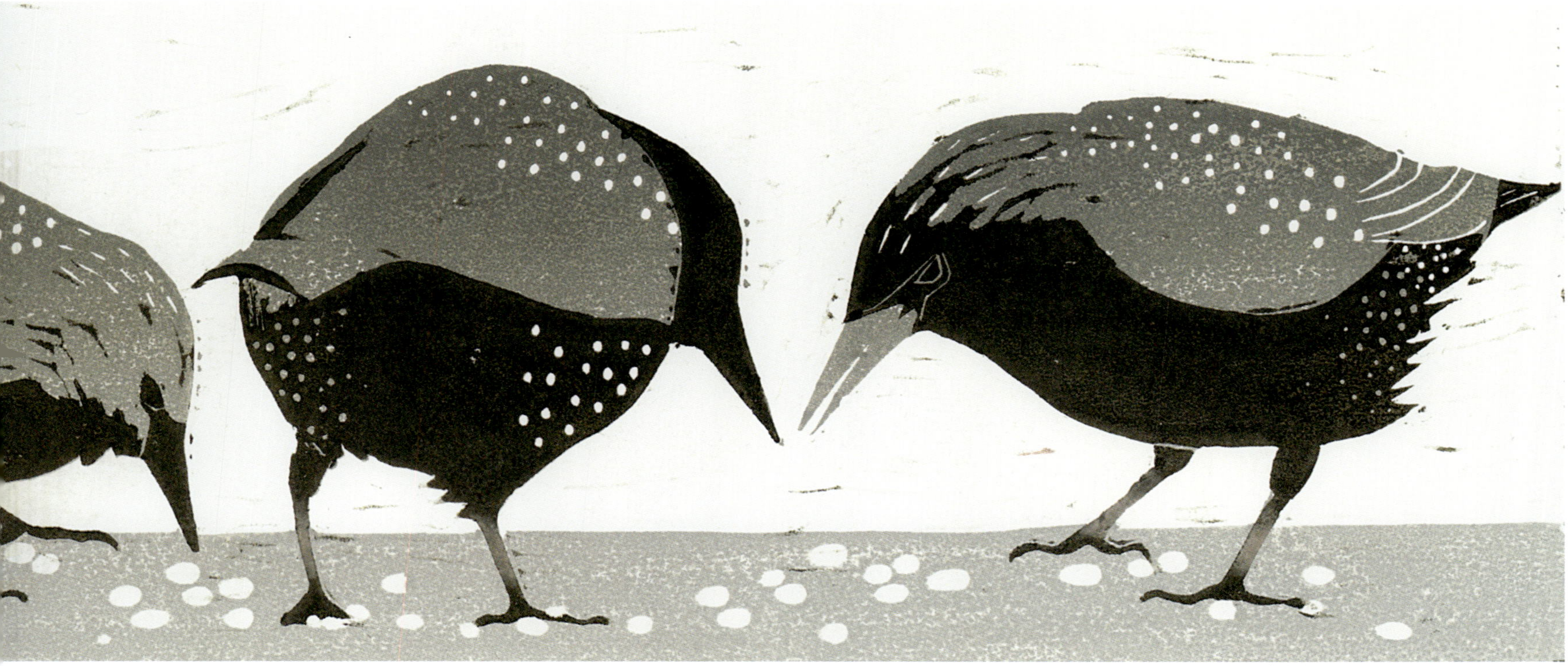

First published in 2014 by
Langford Press, 10 New Road, *Langtoft*
Peterborough PE6 9LE
www.langford-press.co.uk
Email sales@langford-press.co.uk

ISBN 978-1-904078-63-0

A CIP Record for this book is available
from the British Library

Editorial consultant, Rob Hume
Origination design and typeset in Optima and Utopia by,
MRM Graphics Ltd, Winslow, Bucks
Printed in Spain

Front cover: *Friends from the north,* 51 cm x 48 cm, 2013
Half title page: *Winter Hare,* 11 cm x 11 cm, 2011
Title page: *Invited Guests,* 60 cm x 13 cm, 2013

In loving memory of my father, Jim Hooper (1935 – 1996), who taught me to paint and whose untimely death taught me to get on with it

Contents

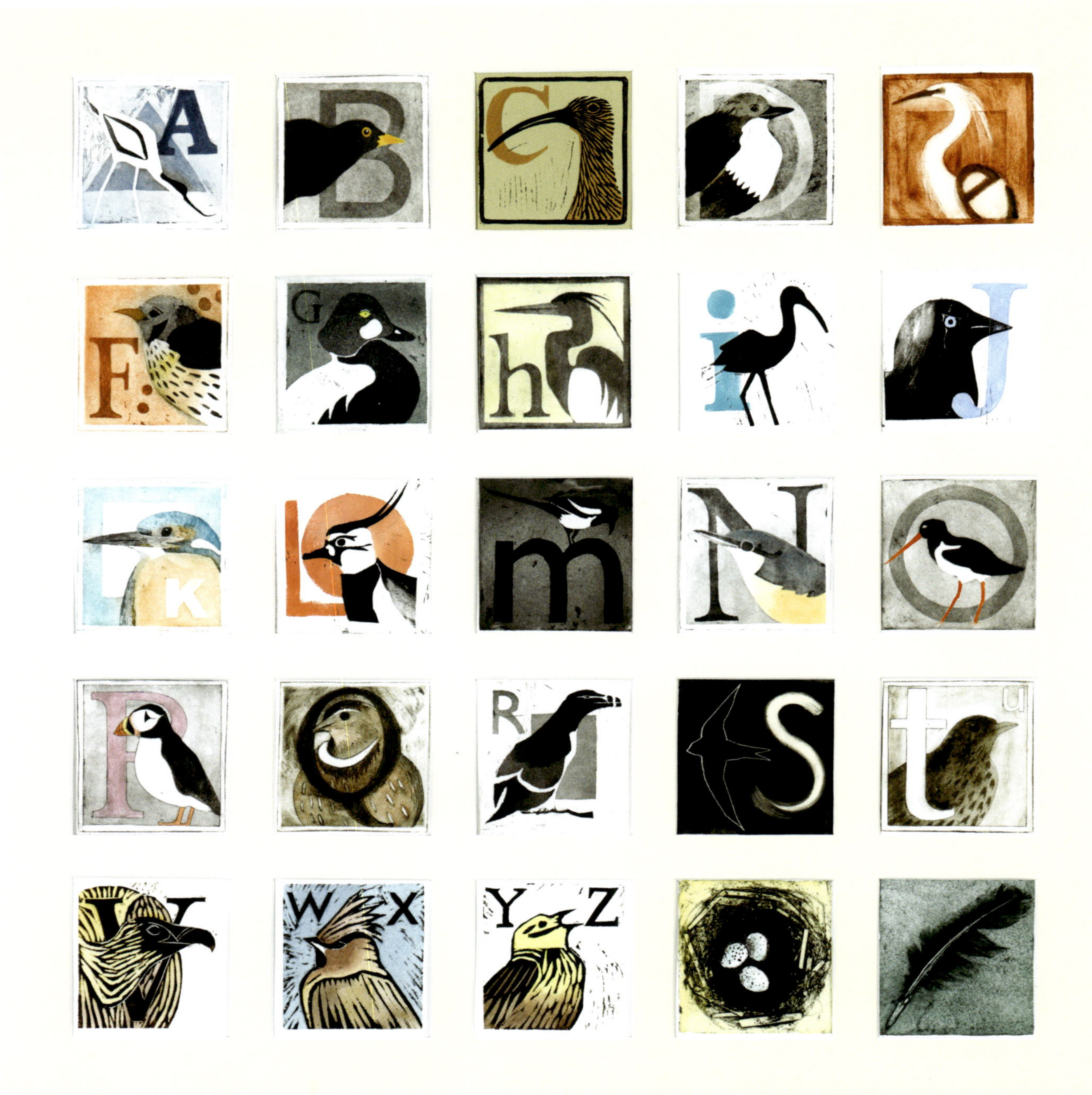

BIRD ALPHABET, composite print assembled from 25 11 cm x 11 cm prints in a variety of print media, completed 2006.

ACKNOWLEDGEMENTS

Many people have helped me on the way with this book. I am indebted to Ian Langford for giving me the chance to pursue this and for his guidance and encouragement. Thanks are due to Keith Allison at MRM Graphics and Stuart Fortune for their design input and to Rob Hume for reading and editing the text. I'm also grateful to Euan Adamson, photographer, for all the high resolution images in this book.

On a more personal level I owe much to friends, family and (let's not forget) customers, all of whom have supported me in different ways. I'd like to thank John Threlfall for his generous and warm support from the moment I washed up on his patch. Zoë and Jill Blamire at the McGill Duncan Gallery and Liz and Steve Harris at the Birdscapes Gallery I thank, for their excellent and consistent representation.
I am also grateful to Gracefied Arts Centre for the Visual Arts Grant which enabled me to attend a joyous Summer School in Japanese woodblock printing in 2012 at Edinburgh Printmakers, and to the village of Port William, for taking me under its wing. Finally, specific thanks are due to my Mum who made it all possible by taking my relocation to Scotland in her stride and to my husband Alan who makes everything possible, every day, by simply being there.

Introduction

"Success depends not on learning to do what is difficult, but in finding out what is easy", Phyllis Barton from Walking the block, 2008, Jane Weir.

Phyllis Barton was a textile artist, printing onto cloth, which is a technique I am still getting round to. But she clearly understood something fundamental about printmaking and perhaps about art. There is great strength in simplicity. Complexity in printmaking can all too quickly land you in a muddle and the dilemma with printmaking is that, as your technical skills develop, the temptation to add more colours or more detail grows. So there is a tension, and a constant inner battle to keep the images simple and direct. My artistic ambition has always been to move towards simplicity, without losing integrity or expression. I want my images to communicate and to endure.

My early artistic career was cut short at 16, when I was told that if I wanted to go to university I would have to drop art. I carried on painting in adult life, as a pastime, and tried to go to evening classes whenever I could. I developed a love of craft and turned my hand to all sorts of things from basket making to mosaics. In 1991, living in Cheltenham, and working full time for the Countryside Commission, I tried to join an evening class in pottery at the local college of Higher Education. In one of those strange quirks of life, it was perennially full, and I was encouraged by a friend to try the etching class instead.

I don't come from a family of artists or birdwatchers, but have had to plough my own furrow. We were, I suppose, averagely interested in birds when I was growing up. We fed them in the garden and my father owned a pair of binoculars, but none of us ever went out specifically to watch birds. As I child I loved and excelled at art, but I gave it up for more academic subjects at 16, after which it became a pastime. Nor have I ever felt inclined to sketch birds in the field. So where does the passion come from?

An early love of the countryside as I grew up on the edge of the New Forest, and an intense curiosity about the natural world, are part explanations. An interest in the politics of the environment prompted me to try to learn a bit more about the British countryside by joining a natural history society and learning to identify wild flowers and plants. In turn this led to employment, first on a rather precarious series of contracts with what was then the Nature Conservancy Council, and latterly in a series of roles over 17 years with the Countryside Commission (and its successor bodies). Just as those two organisations were merged into Natural England, I was made redundant. Sometime in between I had become a printmaker, and was then free to pursue art full time.

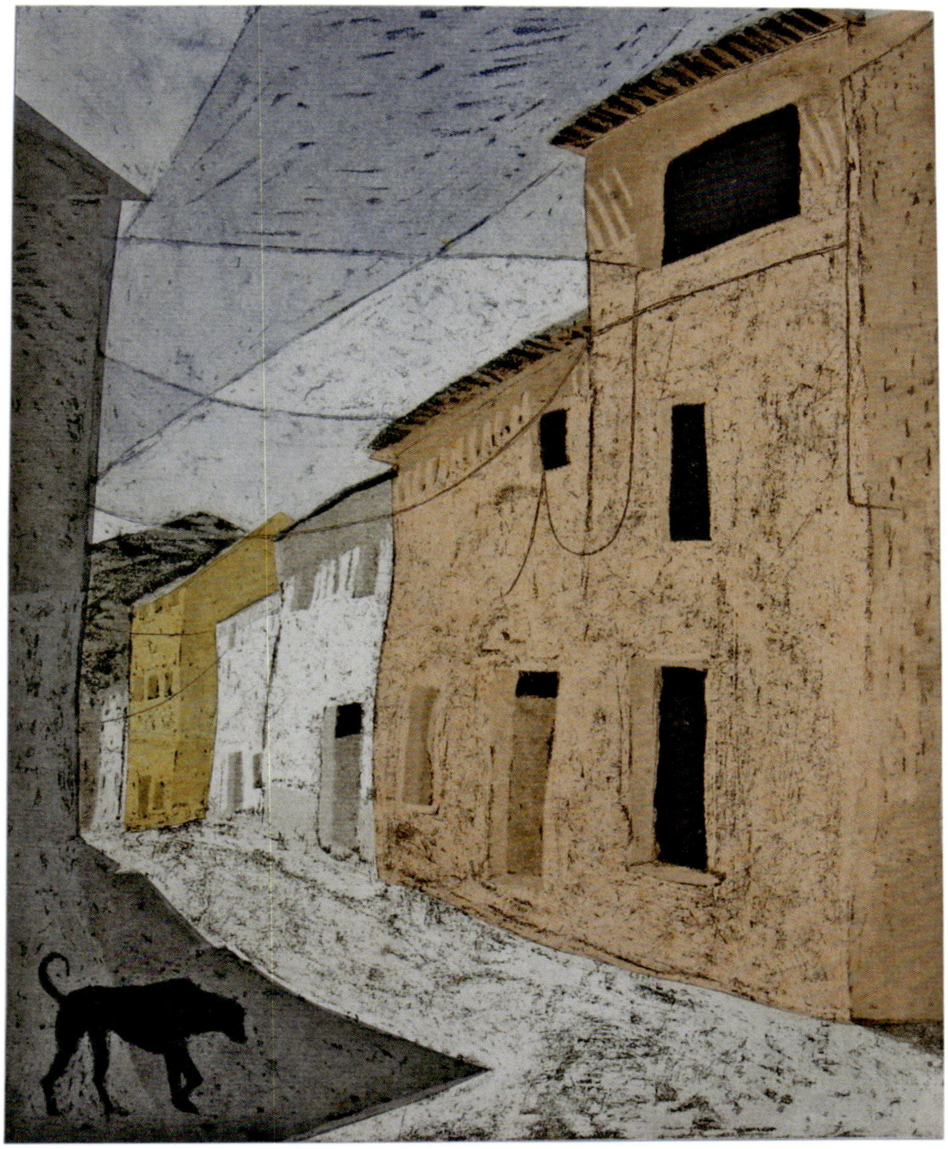

Black dog, Quesada,
26 cm x 32 cm, 2004

This is one of a series of prints of Spanish villages (this one in the Cazorla National Park in Jaen), undertaken at the etching studios at the Cheltenham and Gloucester College of Higher Education. This is an example of Chine Collée, where shapes are cut out of coloured paper and their reverse is coated with glue. The paper pieces are then laid face down on the inked plate in the right position. When the print is passed through the press the pressure sticks the tissue to the print, ahead of the ink which prints onto the tissue face. This is a way of providing blocked areas of colour, but it is very difficult to keep the pieces in exactly the right spot. In this case the tissue was salmon coloured.

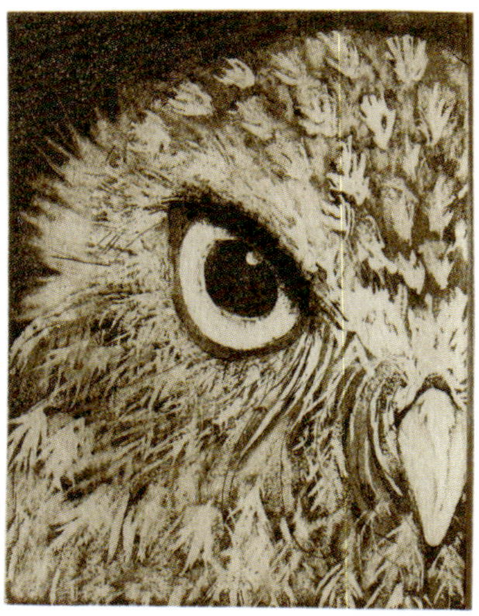

Little Owl,
6 cm x 8 cm, 2001

A relatively simple aquatint, designed for a personal Christmas card. I decided to avoid the obvious full face approach to this subject. The bird was drawn from an old photograph taken by my husband's brother-in-law who was an A Class bird ringer.

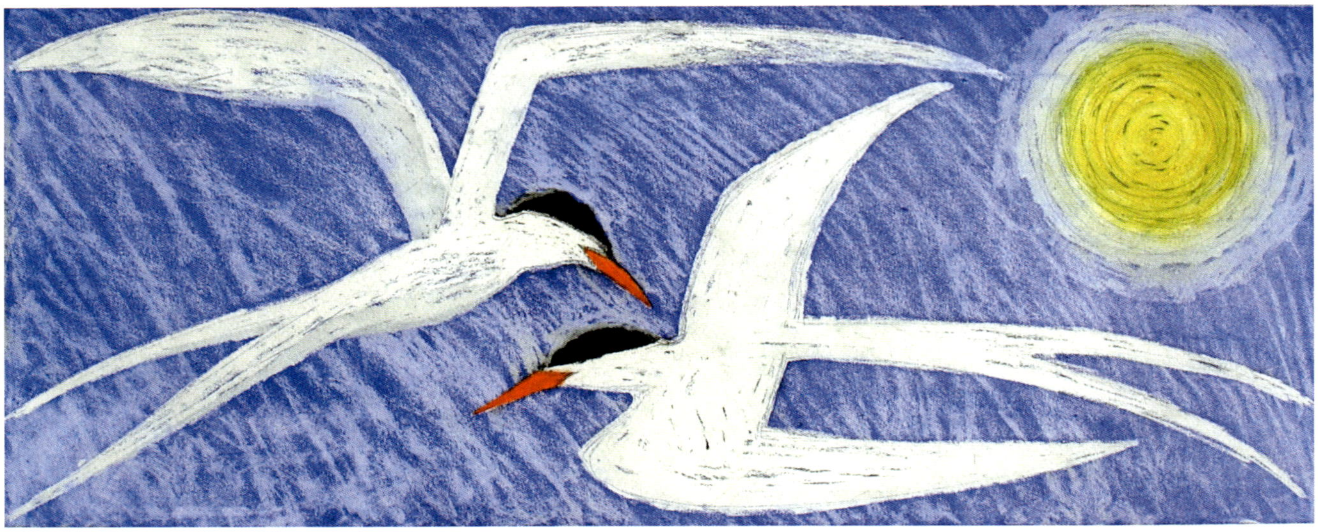

Arctic Terns,
50 cm x 25 cm, 2003

These birds were drawn from imagination. The plate was hand coloured on the block and also colour was added afterwards.

From the moment I walked into the etching studio in Cheltenham with its sharp smells of acid and white spirit and its jumble of wonderful old Albion and etching presses, I was hooked. I loved everything about it - the strange and seemingly mediaeval processes: degreasing the plate using chalk and ammonia; smoking the hard ground onto it with tapers; etching the metal away in acid baths and wiping the ink from the plate with such care and skill, prior to printing with these giant mangles. It was a medium that completely thrilled me.
At the time I was very much in love with southern Europe, particularly Spain, and I embarked on a number of prints of white, sun soaked villages.
I was interested in birds and landscape at that time too, and I did try to do a couple of prints of birds and flowers.

Although I was becoming more interested in birds, I found the medium difficult to adapt to these subjects and, not being a great sketcher, nor having access to modern digital photography, I didn't have much material to work from. In 2001, I won an award called the AA2A, which gave me 100 hours' access to the printmaking facilities in order to pursue a particular project. I chose to produce a series of prints of barns, as there are a number of glorious Tithe barns in the Midlands. This was also when I started to make my first woodcuts.

Between 1991 and 2005 I probably spent 400

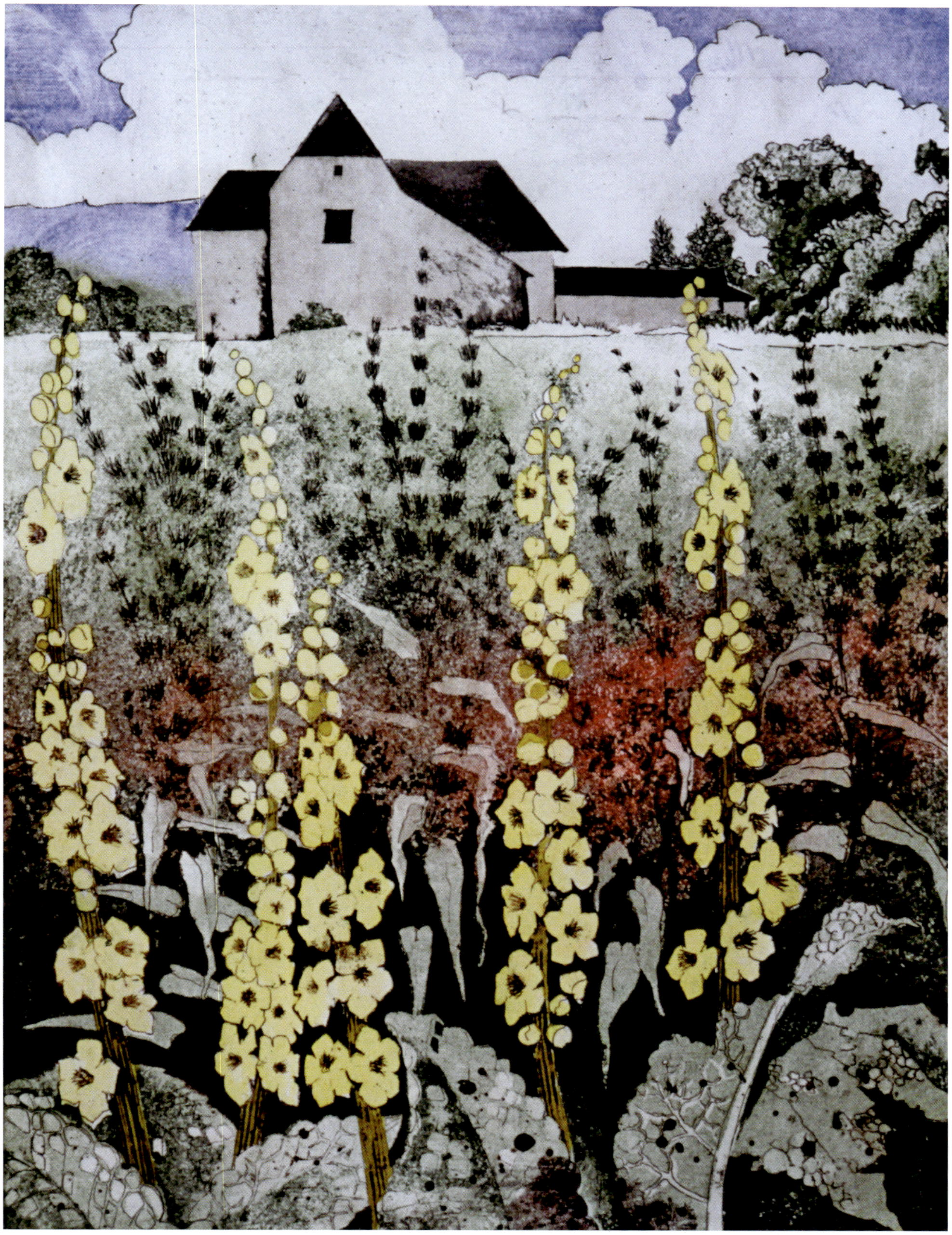

HAY LANE BARN, ABLINGTON,
36 cm x 46 cm, 2002

This print was made from one plate. Some of the colours are printed "a la poupée", (the sky and the warm red in the dock plants), others are added by hand afterwards (the yellow flowers of the mullein). Many of my barn prints featured wild plants from the scene: at the time I was taking part in wild flower recording schemes and had a strong interest in plant life.

hours in the etching studios, and in 1998 I bought my own press and began to sell through art societies and galleries in the West Midlands. So etching was my introduction to printmaking and it proved to be a turning point. Since then I have tried most of the print media (lithography and silk screen are the two omissions), abandoned painting, and become a full time artist, relocating to Scotland in 2006.

This book concerns my artistic development since then, and is structured around various print media in the order in which I explored them. It is not a technical book, but it seeks to give the reader a good understanding of the processes involved in making original prints. Inevitably it is also about my own journey from career conservationist to wildlife artist. And it is about the sources of my own inspiration both natural (the plants, landscapes and birds of Scotland) and prosaic - the textile artists of the 20th Century, Inuit art, bird poetry, Edward Bawden and a number of contemporary wildlife artists, many of whom feature in this series of books.

When, in a pre-digital age, I was interested in photographing wild flowers, wet weather, low light, and the winter were all times when I would turn to birds. Holidays in the Spanish interior where there were strikingly different birds to watch in comfortable temperatures also drew me to birdlife. Seeing new birds was exciting, but seeing familiar birds was also reassuring, even comforting.

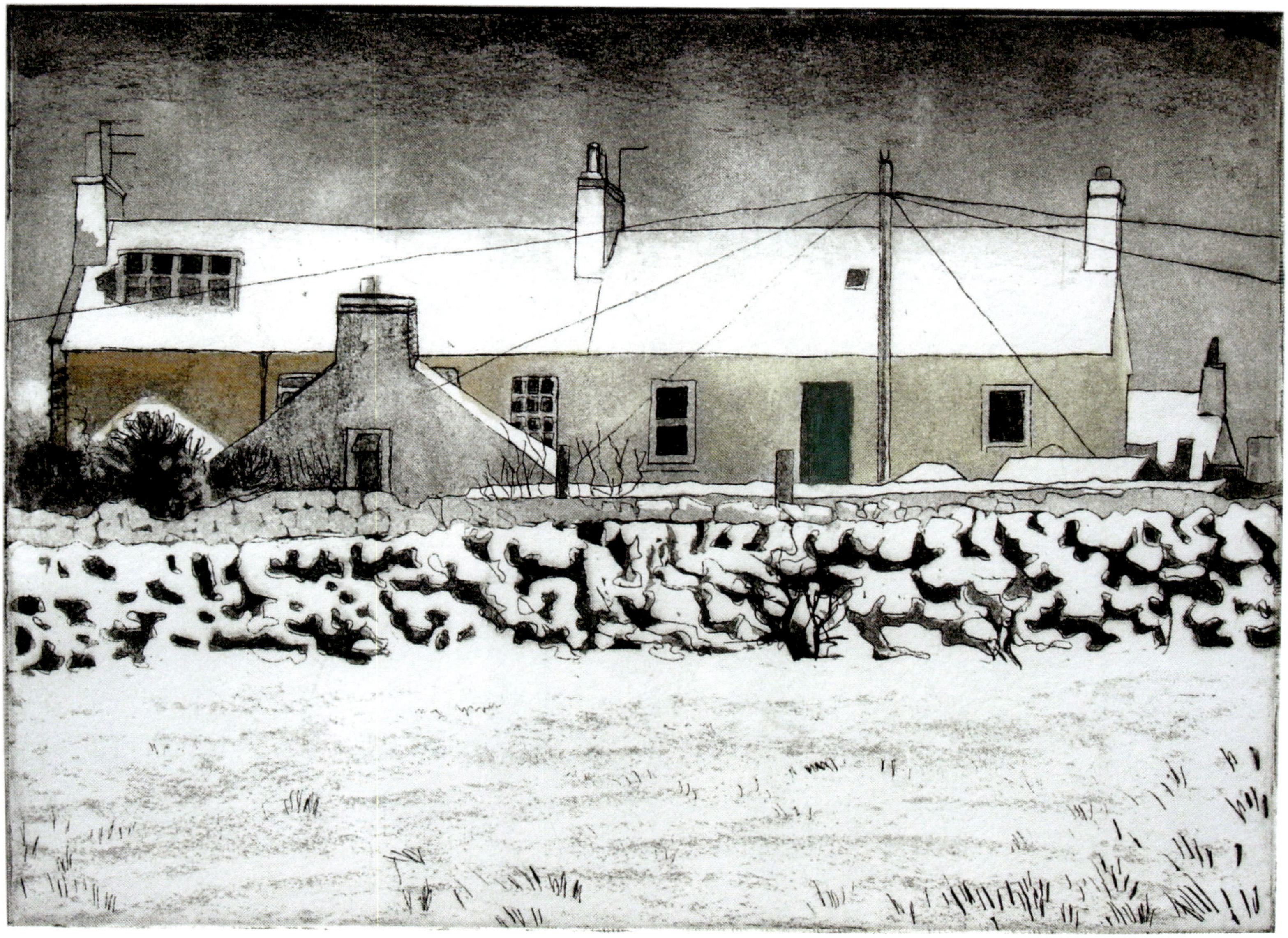

Snow, Port William,
22 cm x 16 cm, 2006

This is an etching which depicts the village in south west Scotland to which we moved in February 2006. It was made during the first winter but was inspired by a significant snowfall the week we moved into our large and numbingly cold Victorian house. Said to be the first snow for eleven years, it was certainly not the last. I went on to produce many pictures of the harbour area of Port William, and some, like this, of the backs and back-yards of seaside cottages, with their stone walls, vegetable plots and fishing tackle.

Etching - Intaglio printing

'Rooks flew across the sky, bright February watched
Their steady course straight on, like an etcher's line scratched.'

February Dawn, by Ivor Gurney

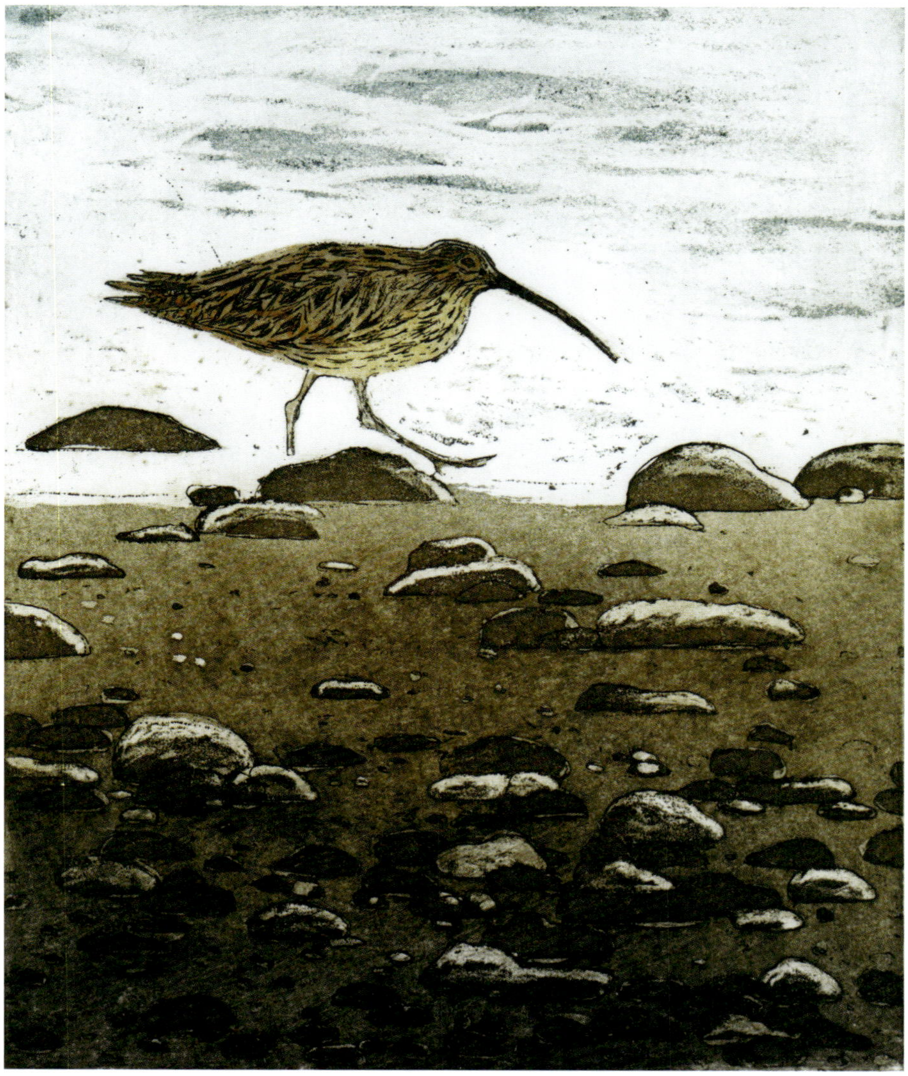

Beach Patrol,
14 cm x 17 cm, 2010

A curlew on patrol near to Port William. The colours in this are printed from the plate with the exception of the ochre highlight on the bird's body, which is added by hand using watercolour.

There is one fundamental distinction in printmaking, which is worth explaining at the outset: the difference between relief printing and intaglio printing. Relief printing is the simplest form of printing, where the printmaker cuts away areas of the flat surface from which she or he is going to print, and then rolls ink onto the remaining raised parts and prints from them. The ink is carried on the top surface, and the cut away areas, carrying no ink, print white. Potato prints, rubber stamp prints, linocuts, woodcuts and wood engravings are all made like this.

Etchings are intaglio prints, made on zinc or copper plates. In the case of an intaglio print, the artist creates grooves in the plate by etching, for instance lines, into it. Etching is achieved by coating the metal plate in an acid-resistant wax or varnish, and then scraping the lines through the varnish onto the metal plate using a sharp tool. By dipping the plate in acid, these lines are etched into the metal, while the rest of the plate remains smooth and untouched. The varnish is then removed and the plate is ready for inking.
The artist inks the plate by forcing glutinous ink into the grooves or depressions (and in the process getting it all over the surface as well). The surplus ink must be wiped carefully from the surface. To do this you have to use lint free cloths, known as scrim, to remove most of the ink, and then polish the top surface with tissue. The aim is to leave ink only in the depressions in the plate (where the lines were etched) and to remove it from unbitten areas.

Etchings can be printed only by using great force and damp paper. An etching press, which delivers a line of high pressure (imagine a heavy duty mangle), forces a dampened piece of paper to squeeze into the grooves, picking up the ink. Metal engravings are printed in the same way, but the grooves are engraved by hand rather than chemically etched. It is almost impossible to print an etching without a press. I have always used zinc plates, which are slightly softer than copper but are perhaps easier to work with. I still use oil-based etching inks, but there are water-based substitutes nowadays which produce acceptable results.

Relief printing, of course, generates white lines very easily. Etching then, unlike relief printing, allows you to create black lines very easily. You simply coat the de-greased plate in a resistant wax, draw a blunt needle through it to expose the metal, and etch it for ten minutes. I use a solution of copper sulphate to etch my plates at

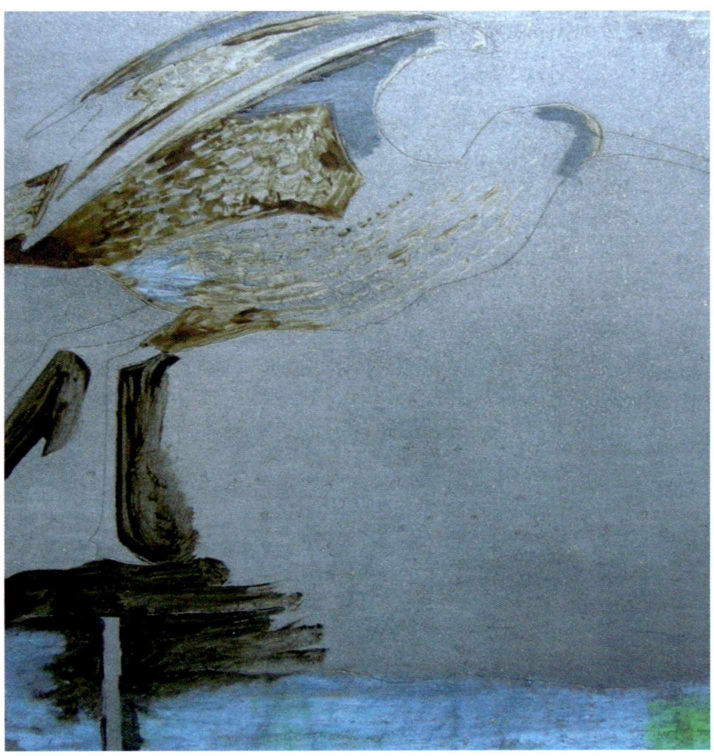

This picture shows a plate which is part-etched, with some areas of resist applied. The brown 'stop-out' is painted on and offers a complete resist, preventing the acid from biting into the plate. The coloured areas are marks made with oil-based crayons. The colour is irrelevant, but the crayons create a broken resist, in this case used for the more subtle variations in tone in the reflection of the bird.

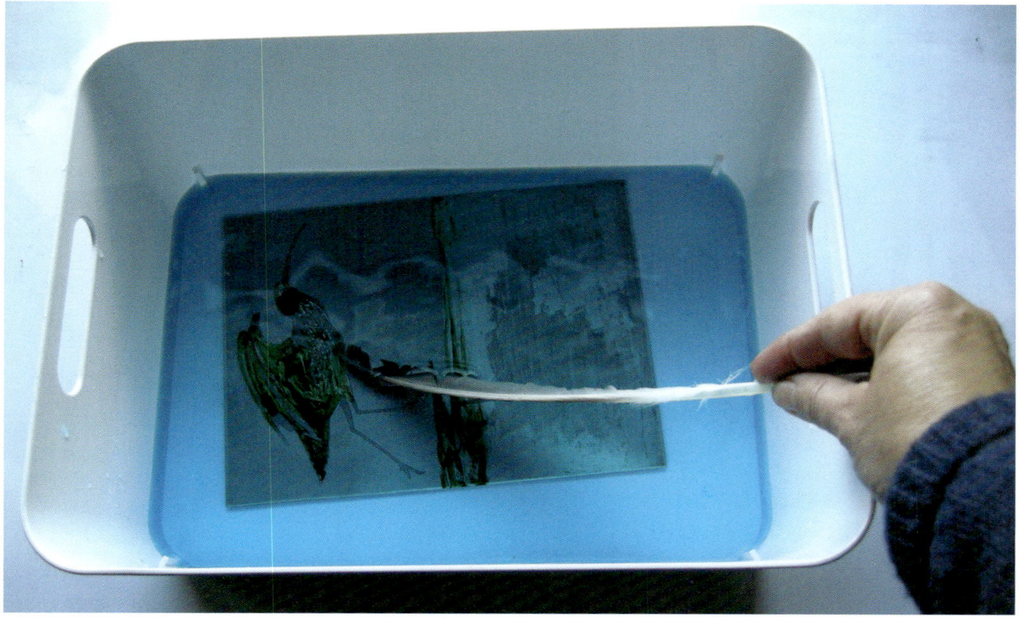

The plate is immersed in a solution of copper sulphate and etched for a few seconds. The feather is a traditional tool, used to agitate the solution, and to shift etched particles which can block the bite, without scratching the resist.

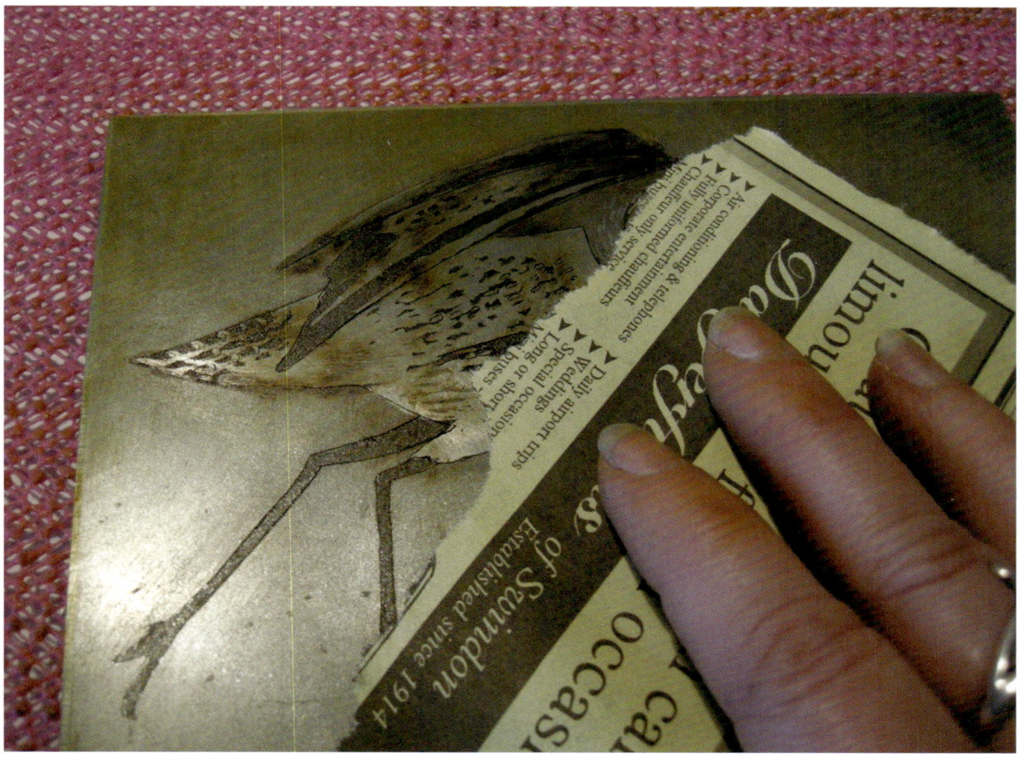

Wiping surplus ink from the surface of the plate using paper.

home, as it is a relatively safe chemical and it is easy to obtain. The cleaned plate will bear a printable groove.You can vary the depth of the groove and therefore the strength of the printed line, by etching it for more or less time. You can also create a softer line by using a different type of resist and you can create tones by cross hatching or open biting.

Complex tonal ranges can only be made by using a technique called aquatint. The cleaned plate is dusted with a thin film of rosin (this is powdered resin), or commonly nowadays with an acrylic aerosol. Either technique will produce a microscopic field of tiny dots. Rosin has to be bonded to the plate by heating with a Bunsen burner. The process for etching a tone is to use a painted on resist to protect any areas of the plate which are to remain white, and then dip the plate in the etching solution for a few seconds. The solution will etch a tiny moat around each dot of rosin or acrylic paint, and when that is inked up it will print as a pale tone (grey). Then, if you paint over the areas that you want to remain this colour with the resist, and re-etch the plate, the remaining exposed areas will print a darker tone (as the moats are a little deeper). You can keep doing this until the last tone is black. An experienced etcher will be able to get a good range of tones (say 10) quite easily, but the timing is not linear (the tones take longer and longer to etch) nor is it foolproof: over biting will reduce the darkest tone to grey.
A colour plate has to be bitten with colour in mind, as more deeply etched areas of aquatint are needed to trap the colour pigment.

There is something about the strangeness of birds which draws me. First, their otherness. Glance quickly at a flock of barnacle geese grazing and they become a single organism with snake like heads kinked and eyed, moving as one in an organized, Medusa-like whole. Who can fail to see the reptile in a cormorant or be astounded by a coot's elaborate footware, or a curlew's bill? Who hasn't wondered at the drumming of a snipe in some beautiful northern landscape or the trilling fall of a rock pipit, or the astonishing mimicry of starlings (curlew calls are our local speciality)? Can the skylark's song and the elaborate chatter of swallows really be empty of meaning (except to say 'push off unless you're a mate') when their messages seem so clearly to be much more complex if only we could crack the code.

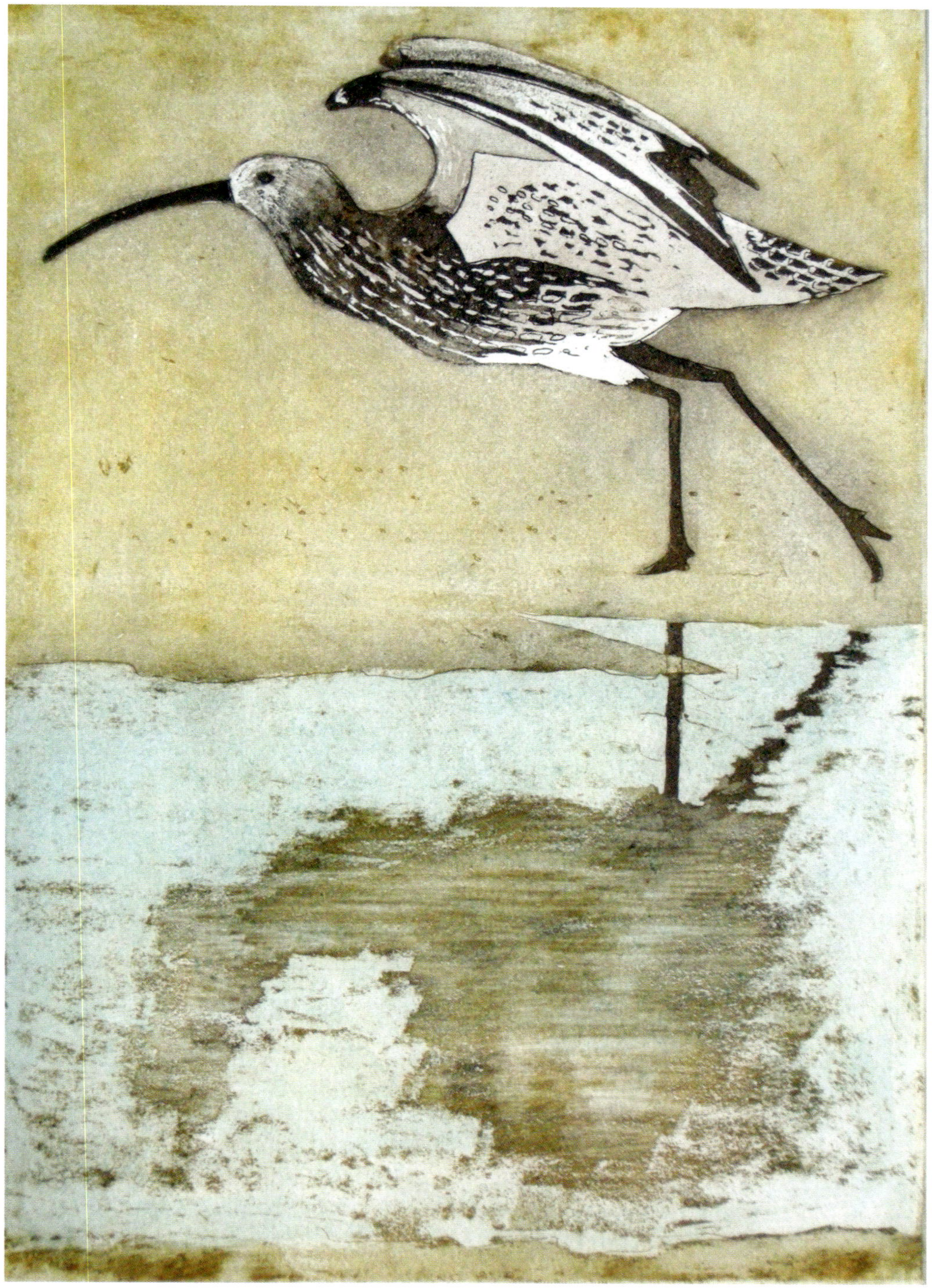

Curlew, Sanday,
17.5 cm x 24 cm, 2012

The finished print. This print shows quite subtle use of aquatint. The broken effect on the water is achieved by oil-based pastels to give an incomplete resist. In contrast, on the bird itself, liquid ground has been used to define precise areas of tone. The sand has been quite deeply bitten in order to pick up enough of the ochre pigment to yield good printed colour intensity.
This is a recent print of a bird seen on Sanday in Orkney in 2012. On the same day we saw two whooper swans, two or three arctic terns and a great skua, all sitting together on a sandy spit in North Loch, in June!

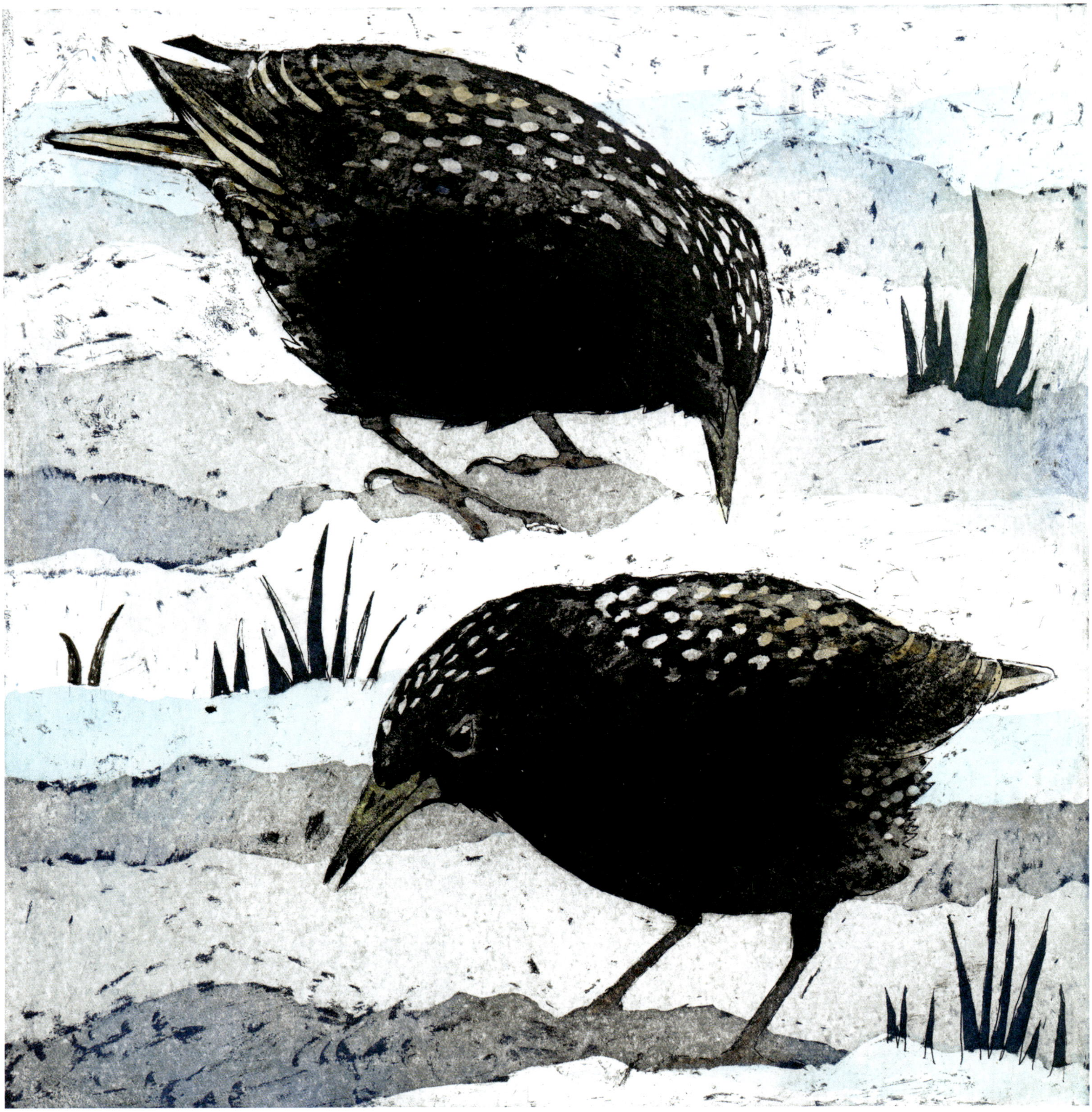

Starlings in Snow,
20 cm x 20 cm, 2013

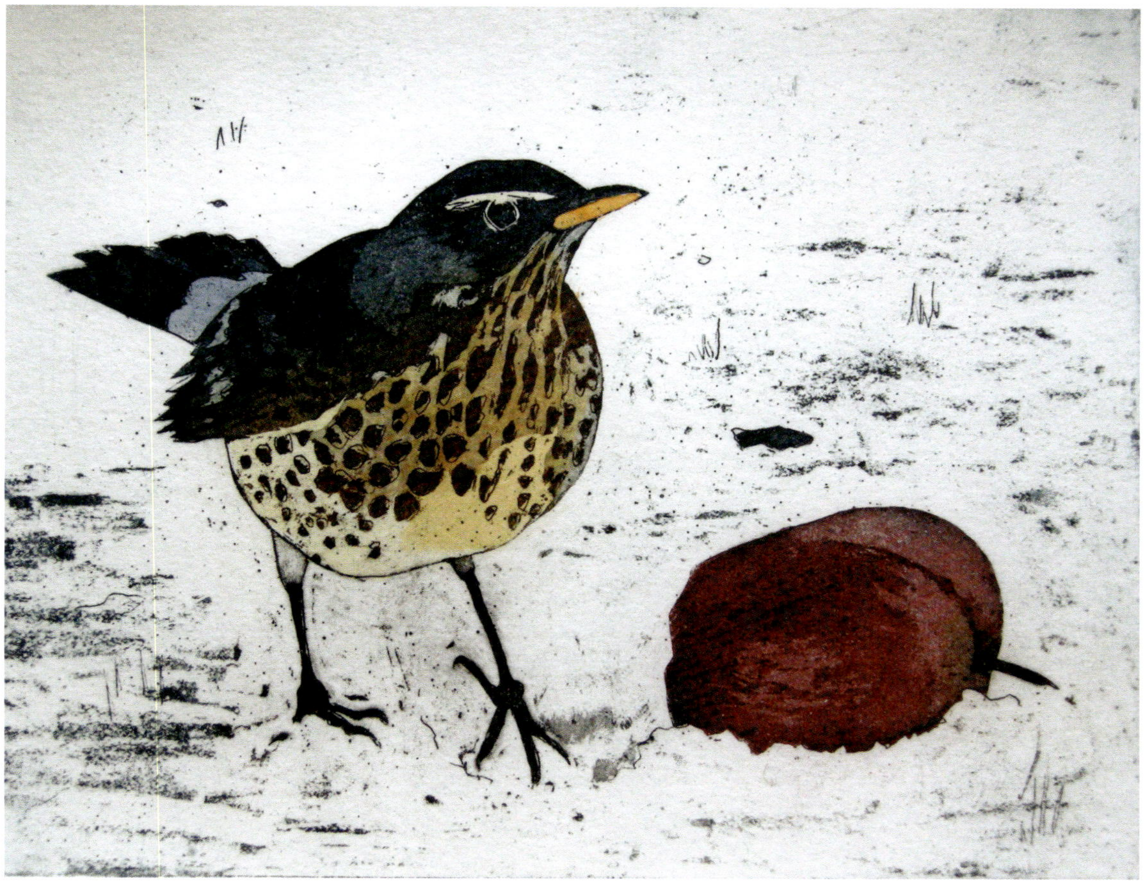

FIELDFARE
16 cm x 13 cm, 2011

This print is both hand coloured (the bill and the breast of the bird) and coloured on the plate (the apple and the blue/black elsewhere). This image was reproduced as a Christmas card by the RSPB in 2012.

Etching is a very versatile medium for monochrome work as it delivers line and tone very successfully. One of its limitations though, is colour. It is quite hard to introduce colour to etching plates. You can use more than one plate (ie one per colour) but, because you are using damp paper which alters in size as it dries, you need to work very quickly to achieve perfect registration.

You can also add different colours to a single plate by using a dolly of some sort (cotton buds are good) to limit colour application to a certain area. This is known as "à la poupée". However, the process of cleaning back the surface ink inevitably spreads the colours, so they need to be applied one at a time and cleaned carefully at each stage to avoid getting muddy mixtures.

Of course etchings can also be hand coloured, when they are dry, with watercolour. Although purists frown at hand colouring I believe it is a versatile, skilled, and perfectly respectable way to achieve an end result. After all, a plate which is to be hand coloured has to be planned just as carefully as one which has printed colours.

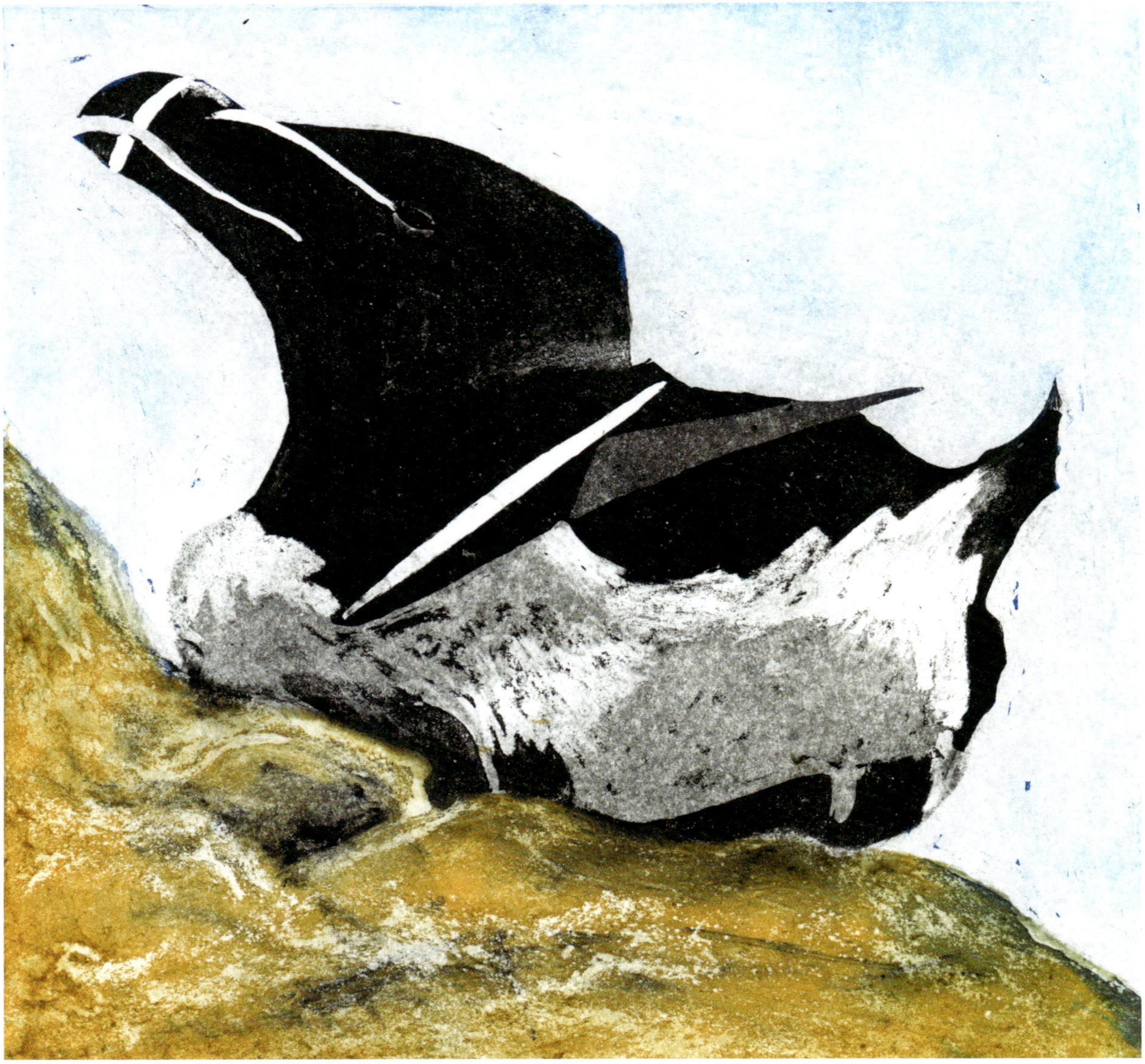

Razorbill,
17.5 cm x 17 cm, 2013

Another interesting technique involves under-wiping the plate. The picture of a razorbill was designed as a colour print, using the technique of applying several colours to one plate. This is the result, printed conventionally.

By inking the plate in black/brown ink and then under-wiping the surface (using a lint free rag to clean the plate but halting the process before the plate would normally be considered printable), you can achieve a more moody look from the same plate, *opposite*.

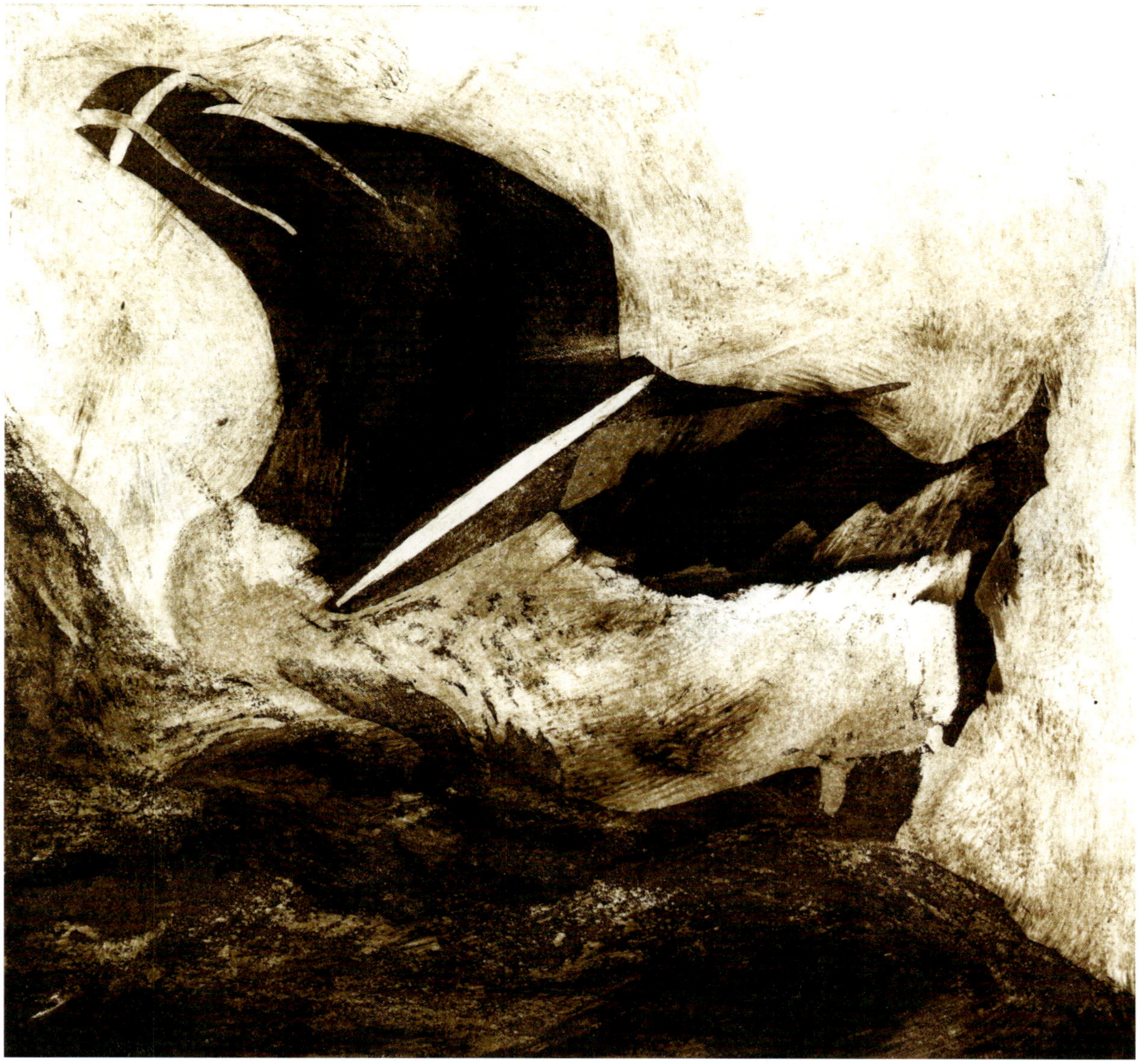

The under-wiped razorbill,

Then there is the resilience of birds. There they are, hot little machines (with bodies hotter than ours), feather light, out there in all weathers, scratching a living through British winters out of seemingly nothing and enduring it all with an apparently chipper attitude. House sparrows still finding the energy for vocal bust ups, Blackbirds singing at dawn on cold March mornings when spring seems never to want to come, all of them going about their business with energy and enthusiasm. Living in the moment is one thing, but remembering how to make a nest with unpromising materials and no arms, knowing how to fly to and from Africa, knowing without language or memory how to raise their young – these are awe-inspiring and incredibly endearing qualities.

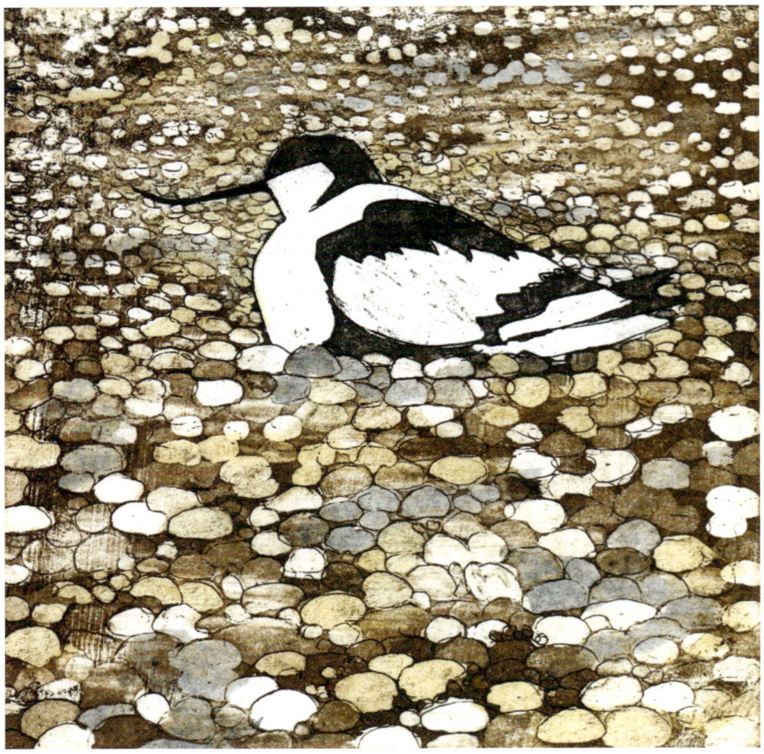

Avocet, Cley,
10 cm x 11 cm, 2012

This bird was observed at Cley marshes, in spring. A very typical pose. The only hand colouring is on the stones.

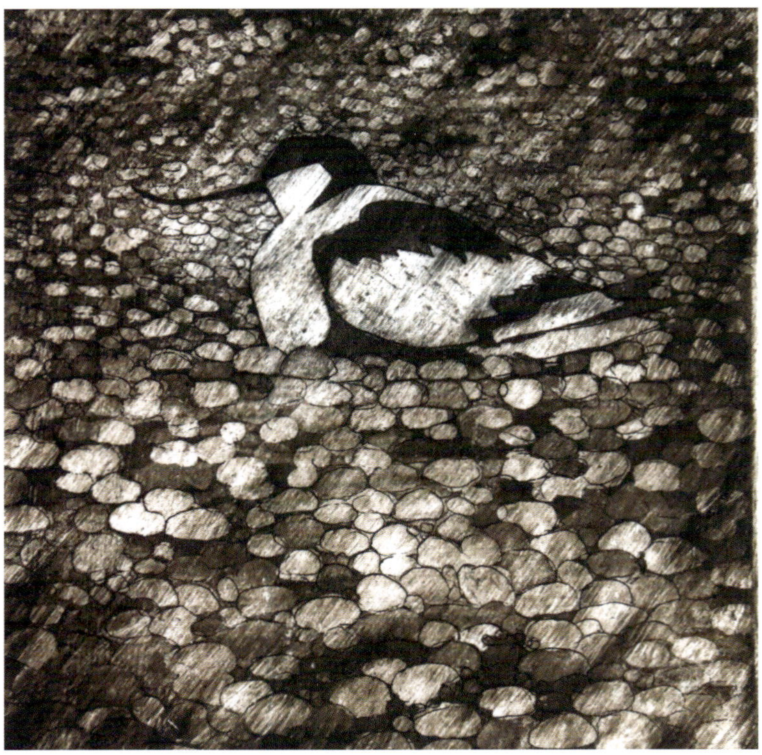

The under-wiped avocet
in the rain!

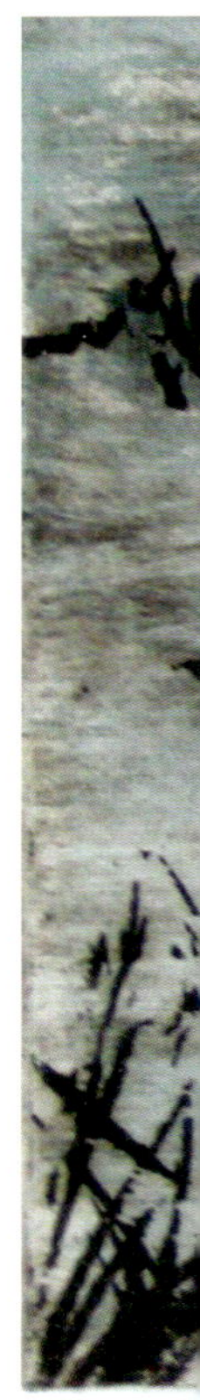

Of course it is difficult to achieve consistent results from this method, but it is nevertheless sometimes quite effective. I have done the same thing with the avocet print. This is the fully wiped version (also hand coloured).

And the under-wiped version is shown as well – note that the under-wiping can look like rain if it is directional.

One further technique is worth discussing. Sometimes it can be difficult to produce an image with complex areas of dark tone. For instance, if you wanted to put grass or reeds into the foreground of a picture using aquatint, you would have to etch the dark silhouette for longer than any other part of the plate, so you would have to paint the resist onto the background, leaving thin lines showing, which is very difficult. A technique called sugar lift allows you to etch in reverse. The basic method is quite straightforward. You prepare a plate with an aquatint ground. Then you use a sugar solution (you can buy this or make it out of sugar, ink and washing up liquid) to paint on the dark elements – grass or other shapes. Then you coat the plate in a liquid ground (a resist). If you then immerse the plate in warm water and gently rub it, the sugar solution will dissolve and lift off the ground in the areas that you painted. These can then be bitten in the acid for as long as necessary.

Here are two prints made using the sugar-lift technique:

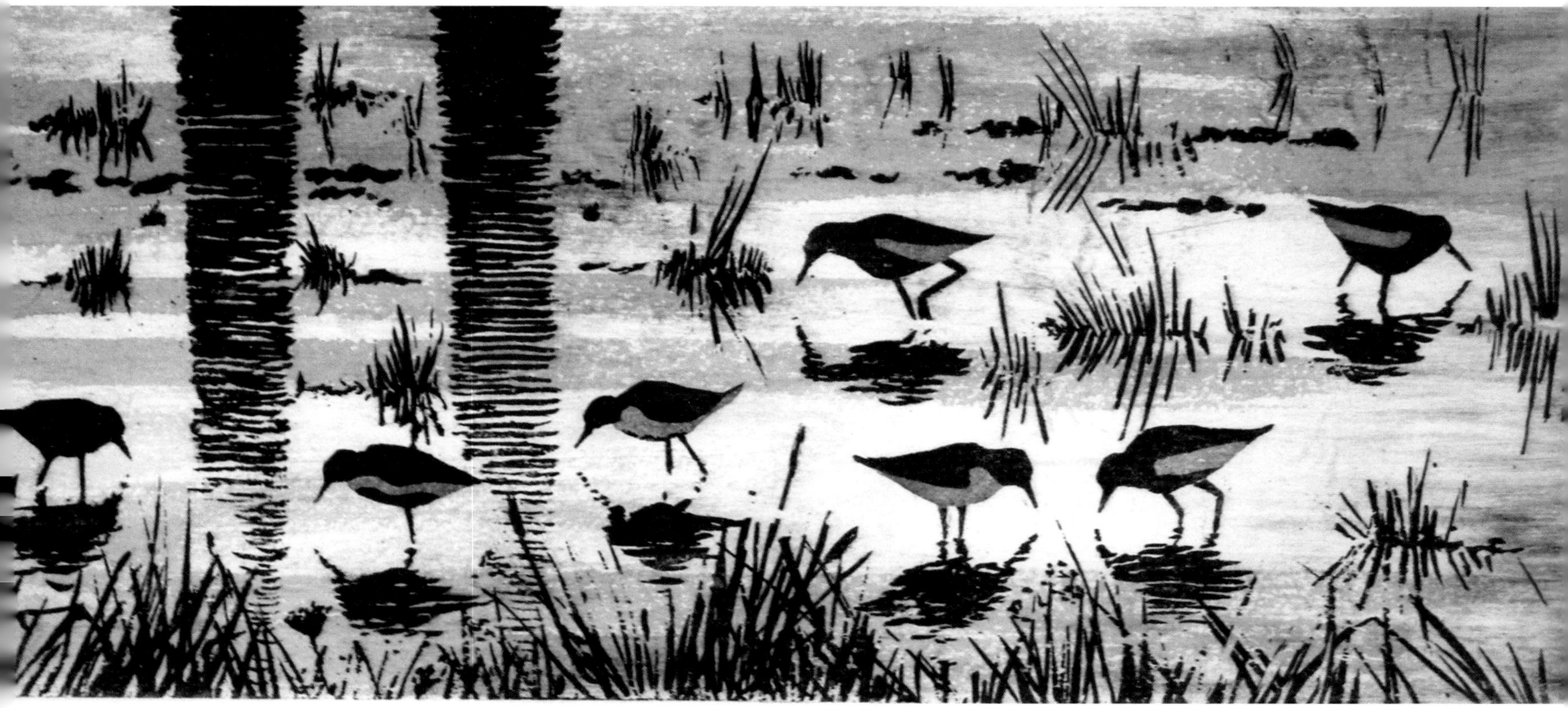

Dunlins, Prestonpans,
31.5 cm x 13.5 cm, 2012

These birds were observed at one of the Longniddry Bents hides on the East Lothian coast. The chimneys are from the Cockenzie power station and are quite a dominant feature on this coast. It seemed important to include their reflections. Note that to etch the grasses conventionally you would need to paint around each leaf with the resist to protect the water and bite the leaf: a very tedious operation. This is the final picture, which has been hand-coloured with a light blue/green wash.

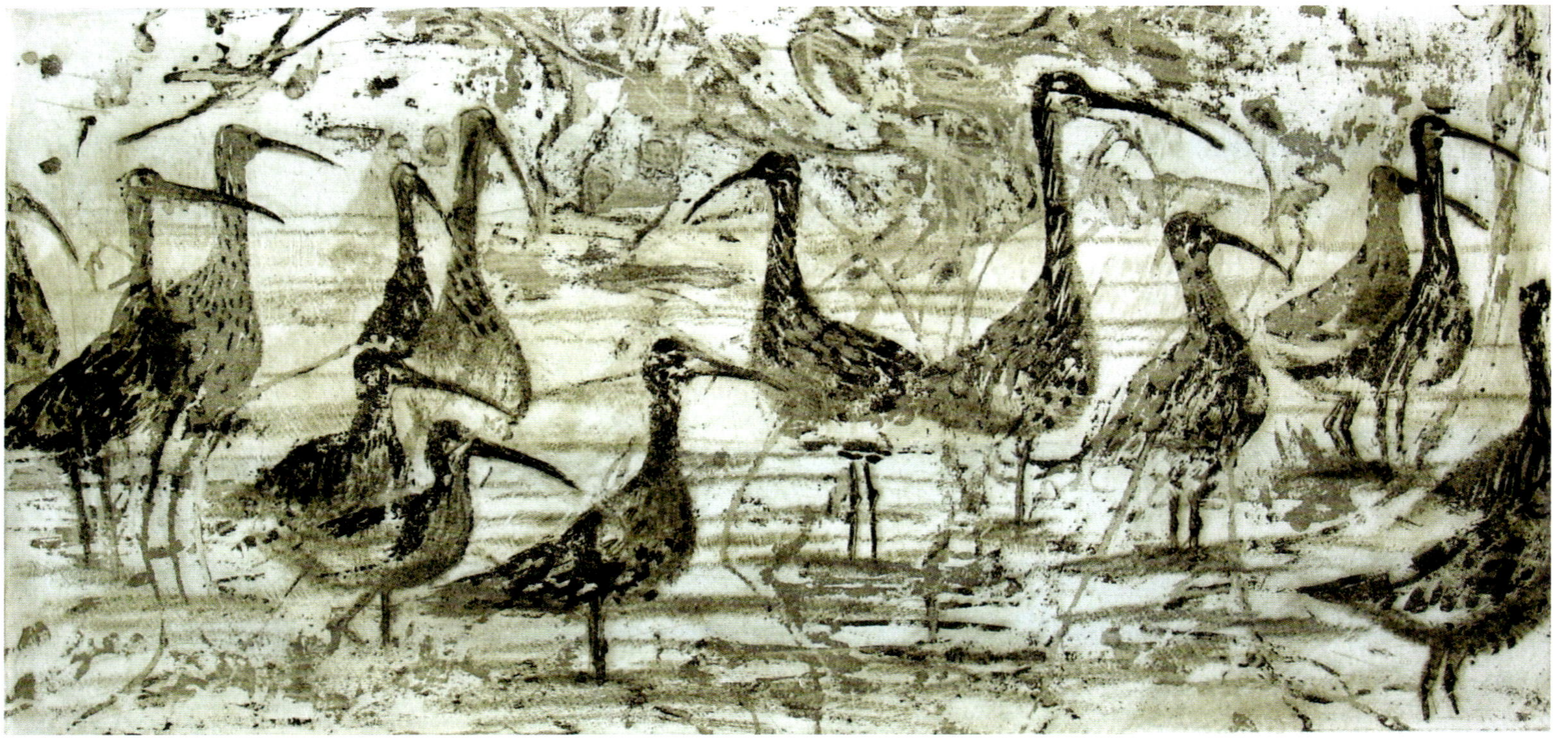

CURLEWS AT DAWN,
48 cm x 24 cm, 1999

This early etching was a sugarlift. I actually started to blow the sugar solution with a straw to enliven the result as I was preparing the plate. The blue background to this print was added by surface rolling with pale blue ink. That means a very large diameter roller was used to roll ink, in one pass, onto the unbitten surface of the etching plate, after the birds had been inked and wiped, and before taking a print. The plate thus becomes both an intaglio and a relief printing surface.

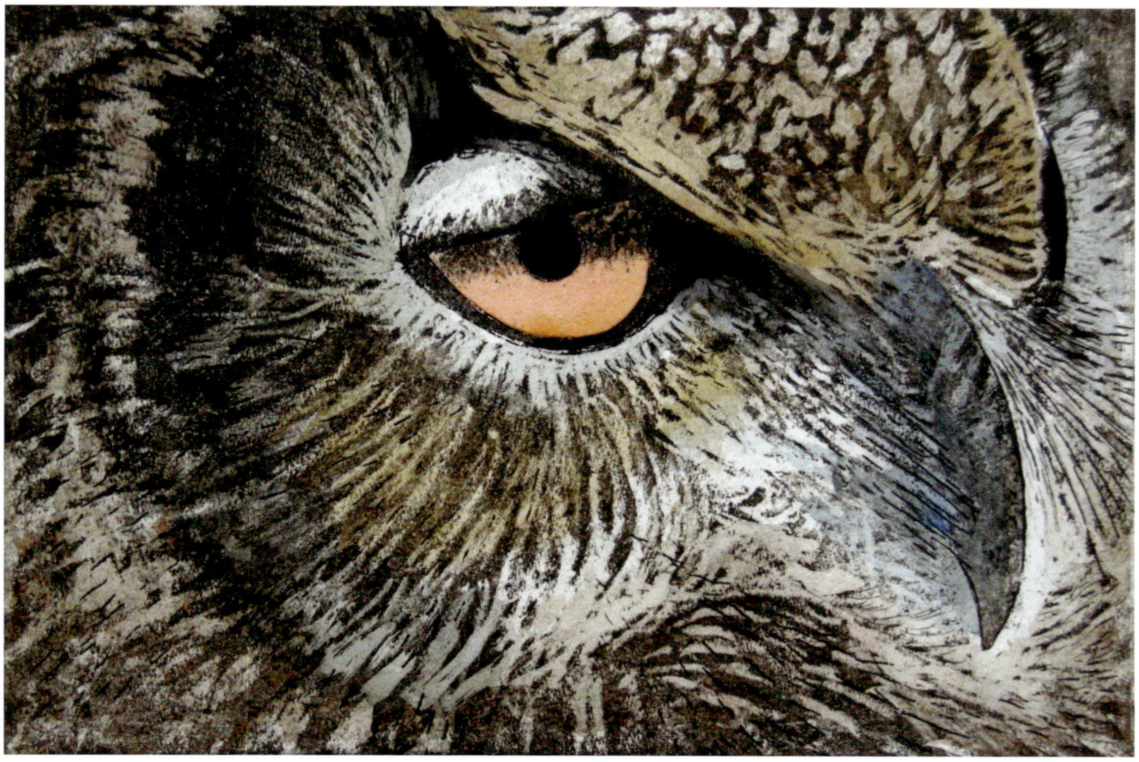

Eagle owl,
15 cm x 11 cm, 2013

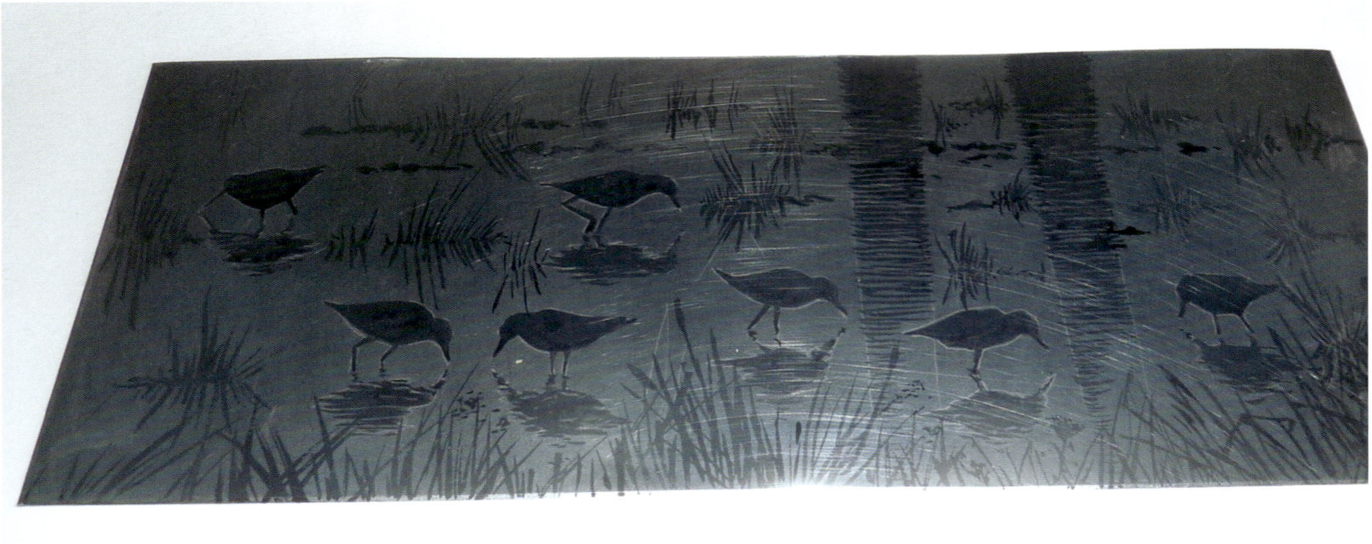

The sugar solution is just visible where it has been applied to the aquatinted plate.

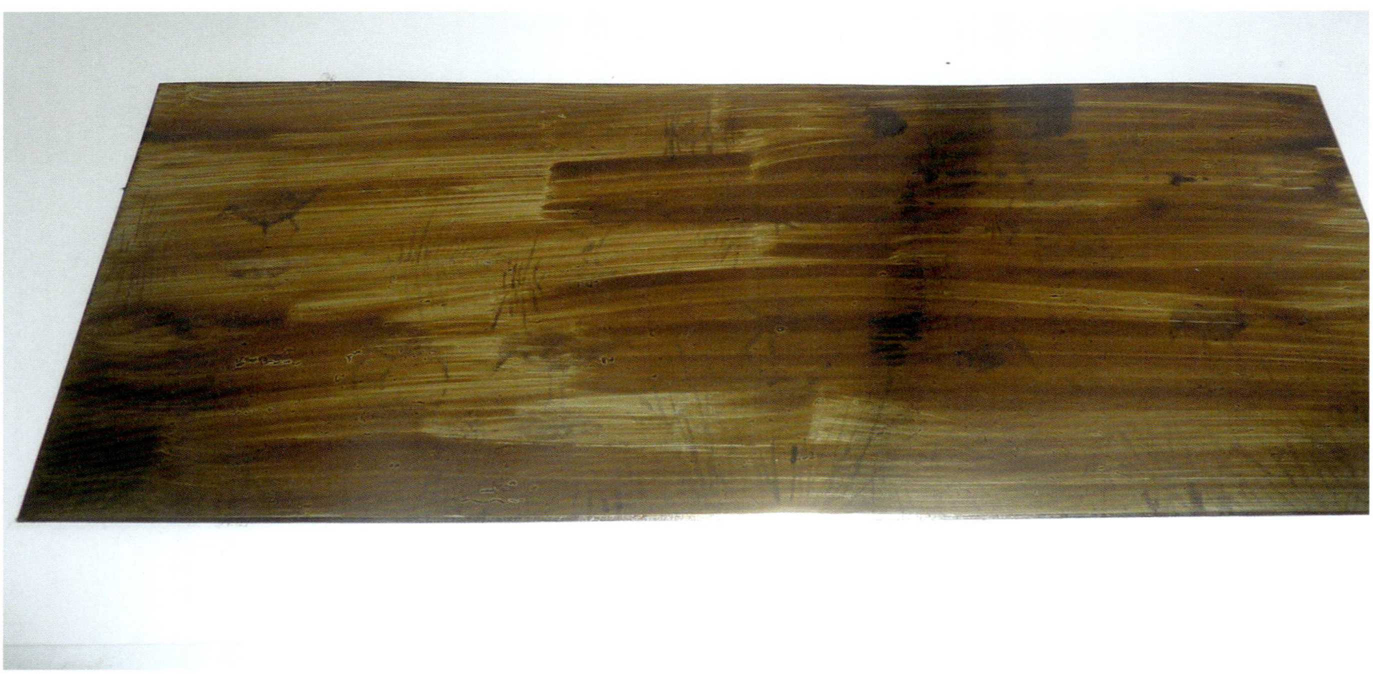

The plate is covered in liquid ground. You can just see the sugar painting underneath the ground, particularly the bird, top left.

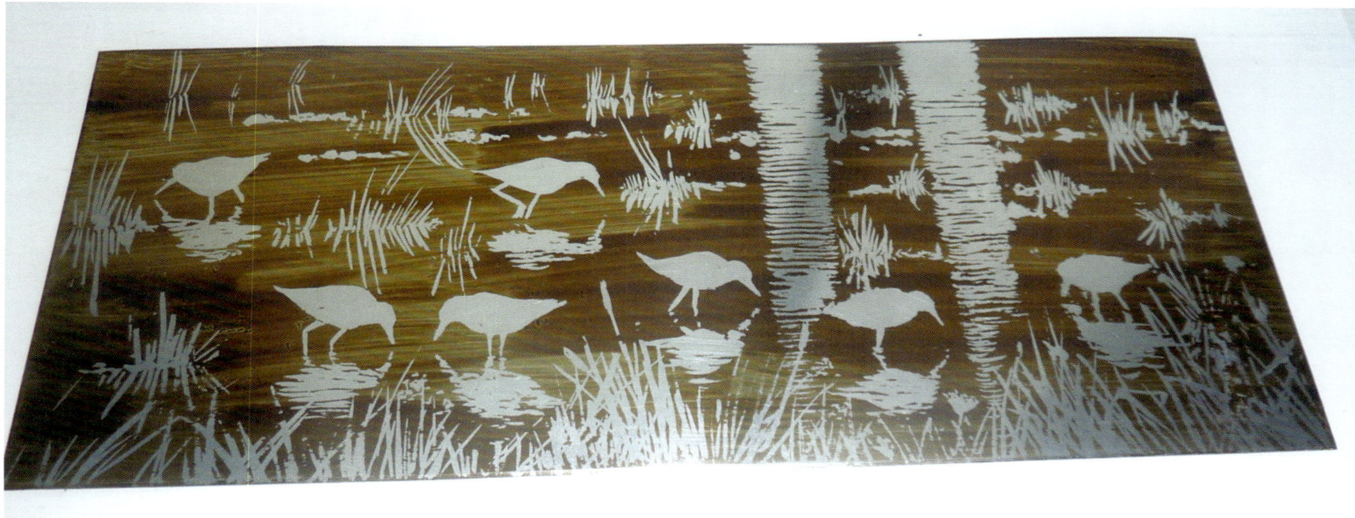

This shows the plate after immersion in warm water. The sugared areas have lifted off the resist, exposing the metal. The resist is in place, perfectly defining the negative areas to be bitten.

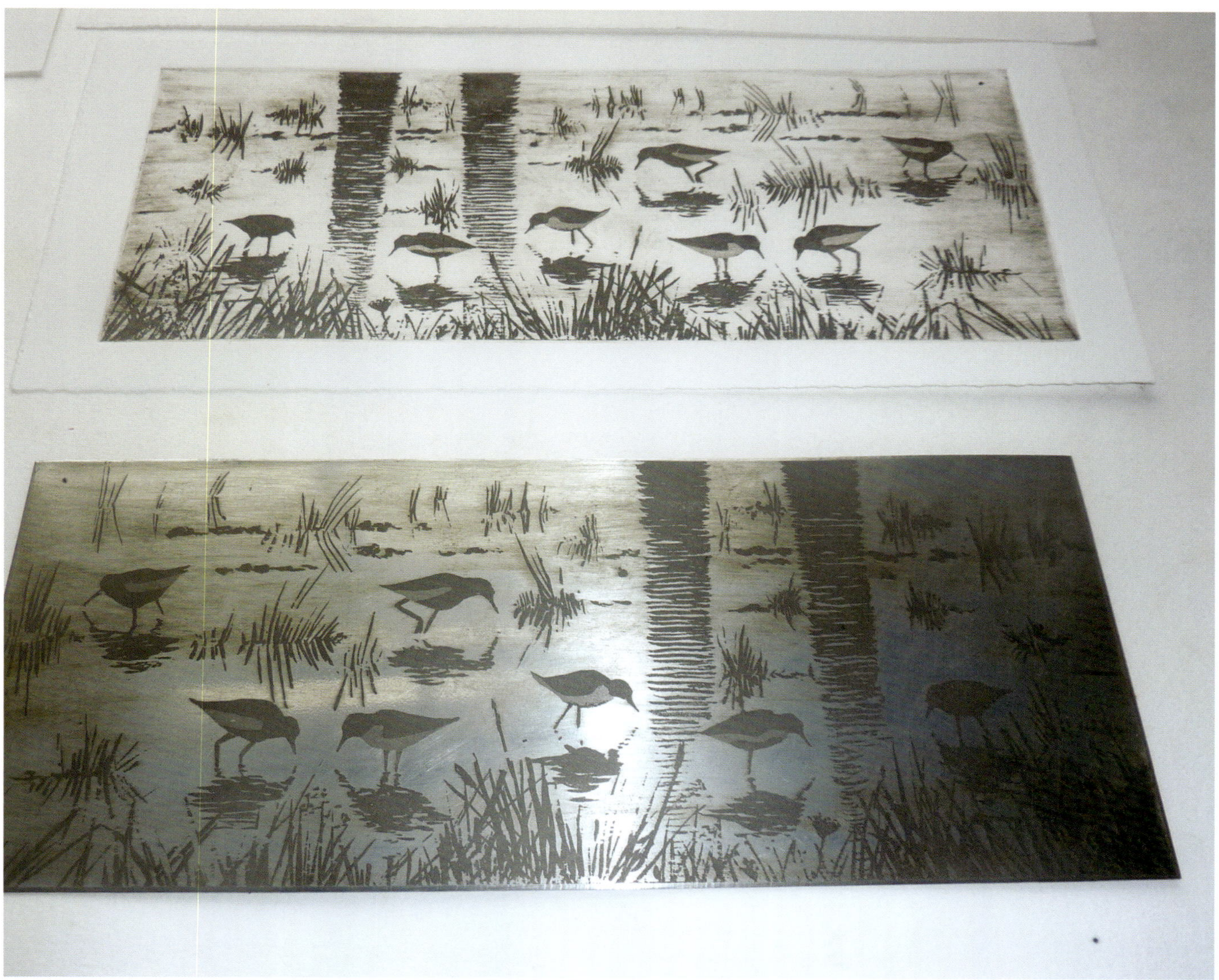

The finished plate, with an unpainted proof above it.

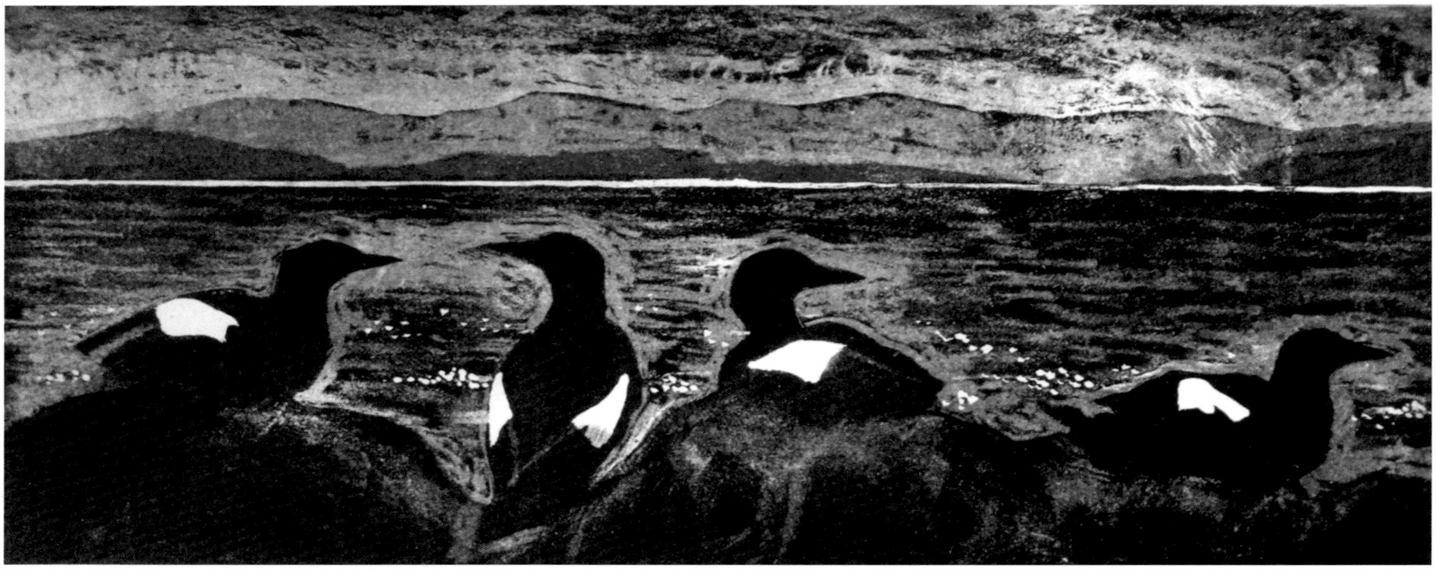

Black guillemots, Arran,
17 cm x 6 cm, 2008

Another picture inspired by a holiday on Arran, this typical pose of black guillemots with the rather moody view caught my eye. This is an aquatint, coloured on the plate and using areas of oil-based crayon resist as well as liquid ground.

Shovelers,
17 cm x 24 cm, 2011

I have always liked shovelers and I also find water and reflections irresistible. This is an aquatint, with very little line work, using soft and hard resists. The eyes are the only hand coloured element.

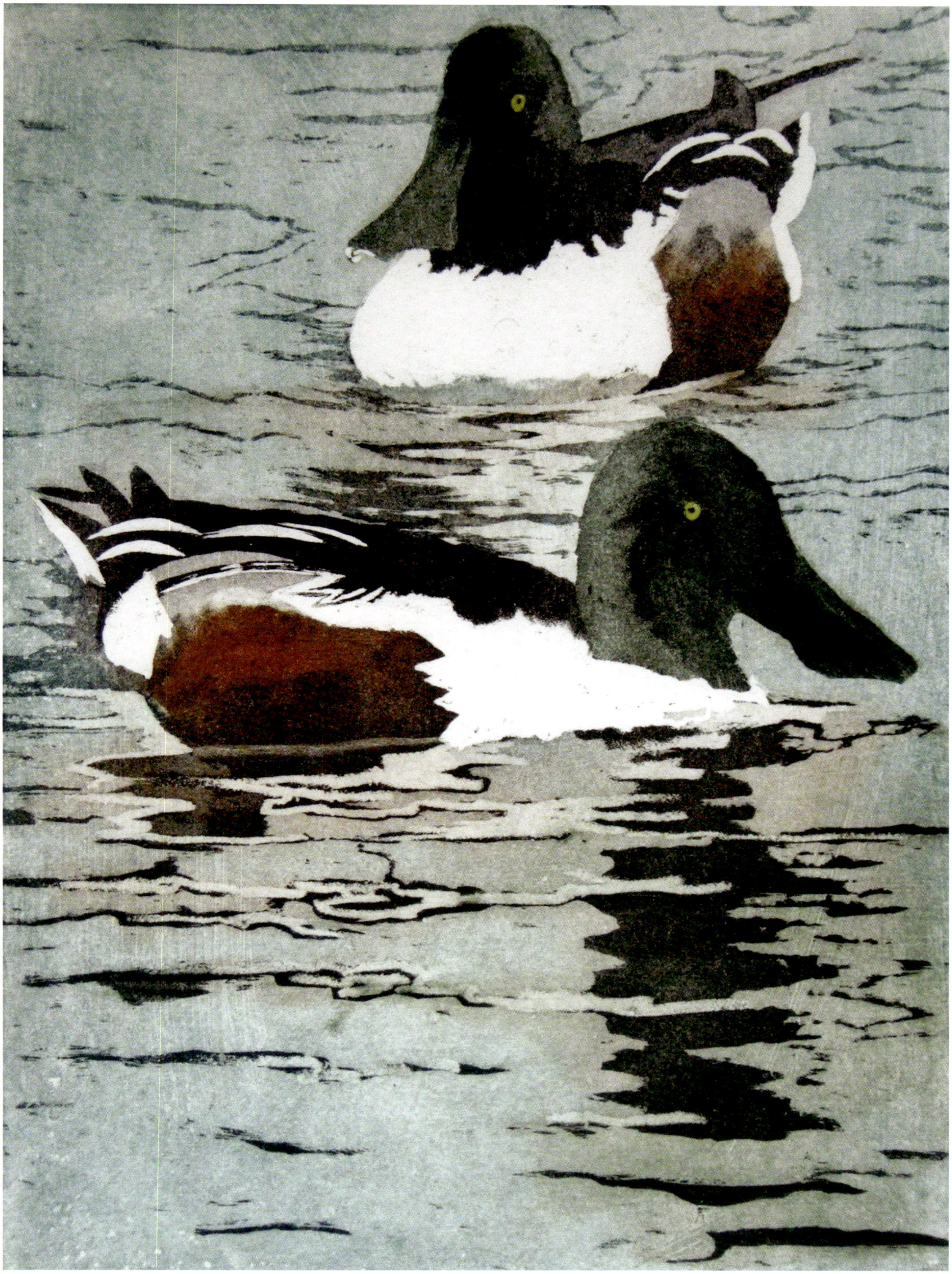

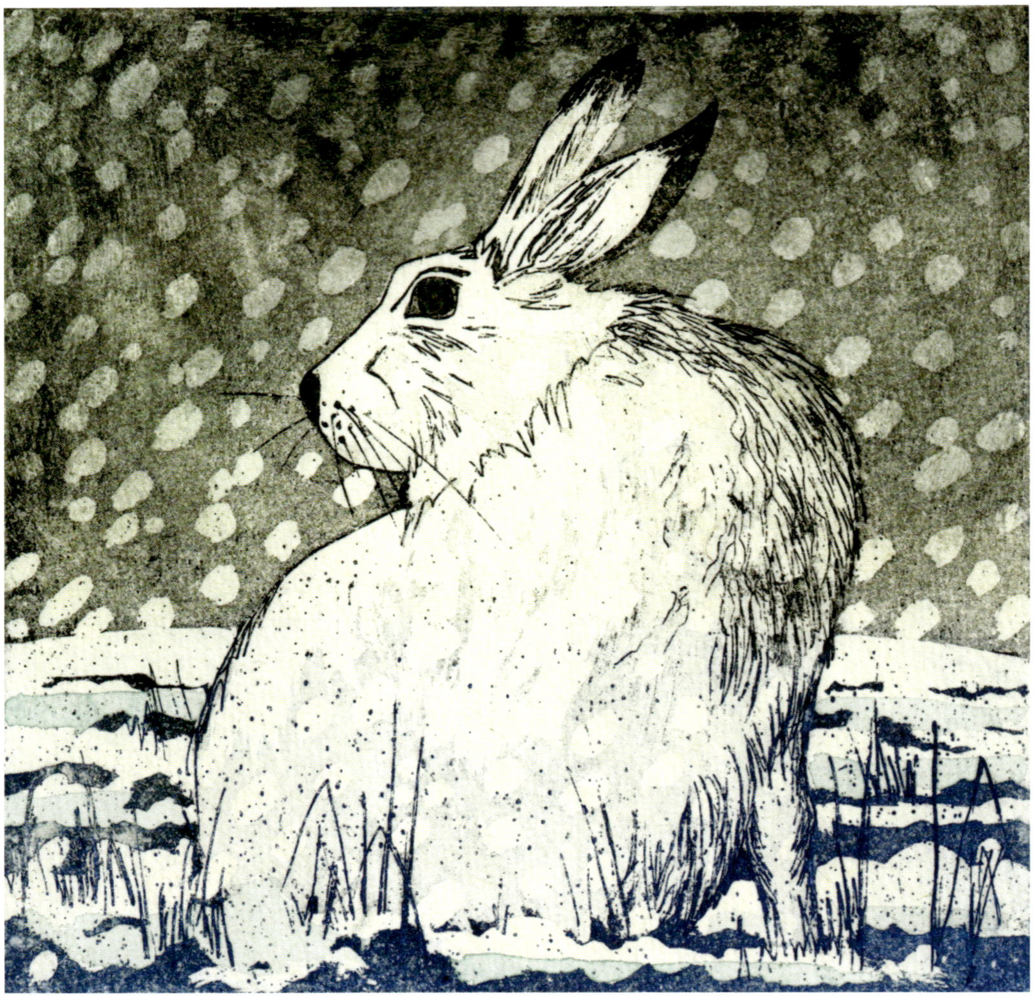

Mountain Hare,
14 cm x 14 cm, 2009

This is printed from a hard ground/aquatint plate, with a small amount of hand colouring: inspired by mountain hares seen in Ayrshire. It has been reproduced commercially as a greetings card.

Wood and linocut - relief printing in black and white

'The hardest thing of all to see is what is really there.'

The Peregrine, J A Baker

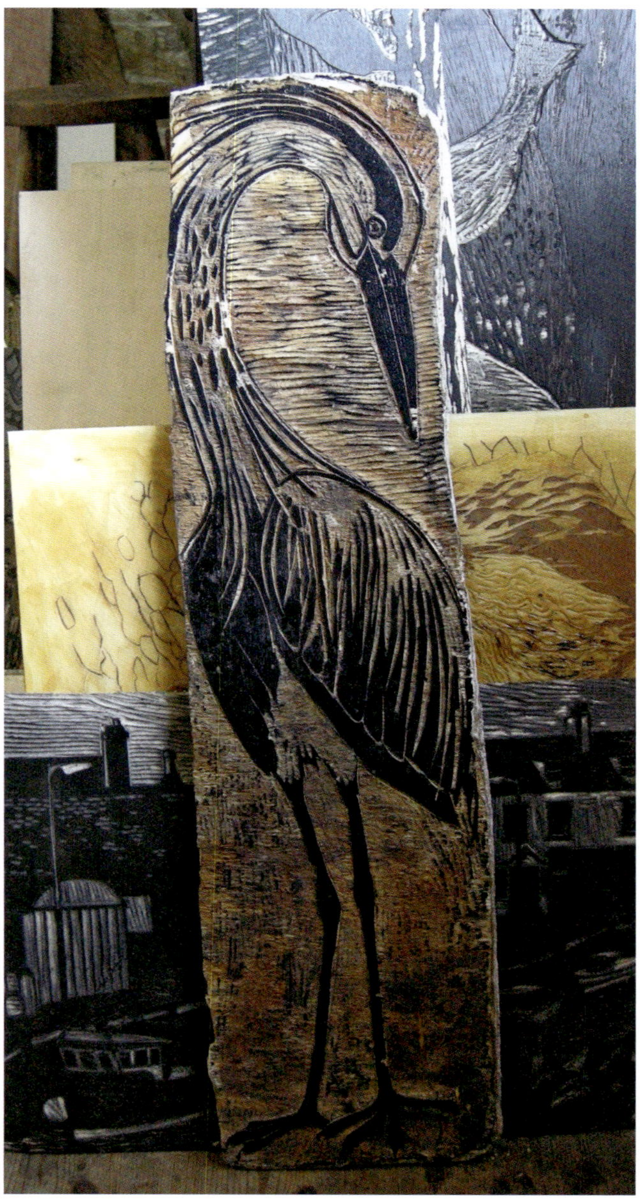

Printing plates.

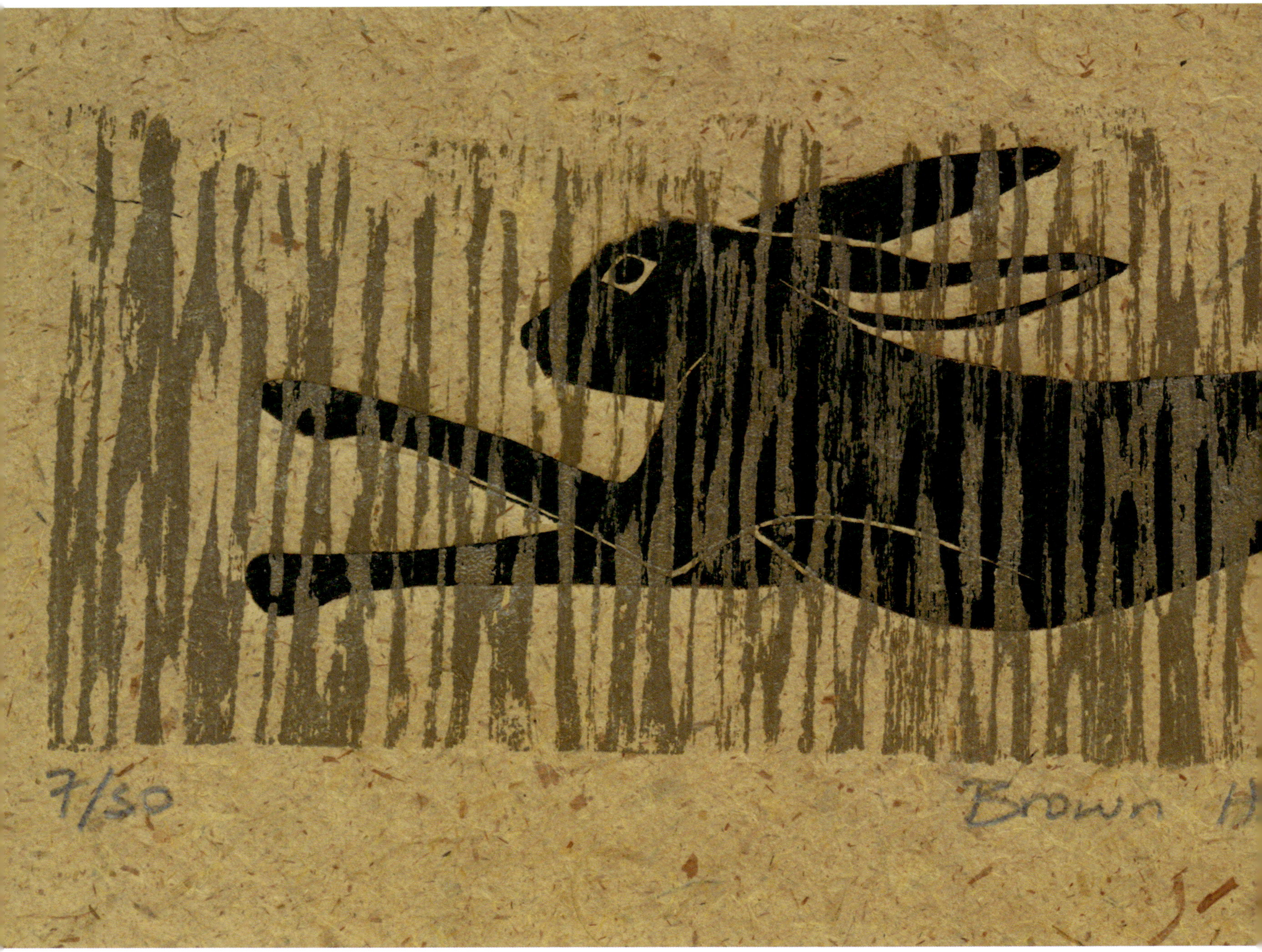

BROWN HARE,
49 cm x 22 cm, 2008

The linocut has been overprinted with driftwood to suggest grass.

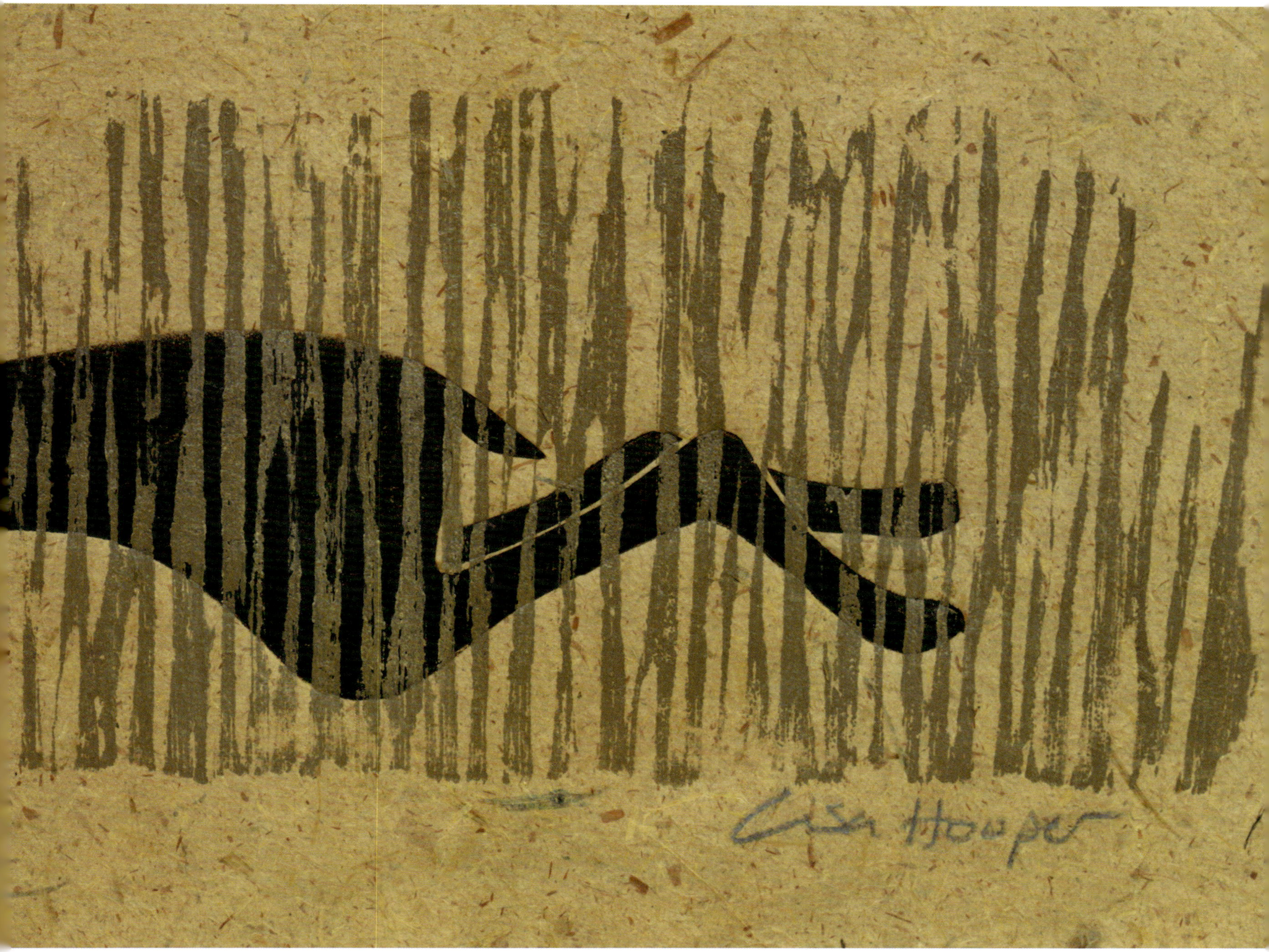

Basic techniques

The technique of cutting into a flat surface to create a relief print must be the most ancient form of printmaking. Imagine a hand, inked with ochre, pressed against the wall of a cave: you are seeing a relief print. Perhaps the most commonly used material from which to make early prints would have been wood. The first woodcuts were probably cut by Chinese monks in the 6th Century and cannot, at any rate, have pre-dated the invention of paper in about the second century AD. The lure of being able to print multiple repetitions must have been seductive, but it was a thousand years before movable type was invented first in China, and later in Europe. The craft of hand cutting blocks is therefore very old indeed, and as a craft activity it has survived the developments of print technology which have made it commercially redundant. The materials are readily available, the tools simple and printing can be carried out without machinery.

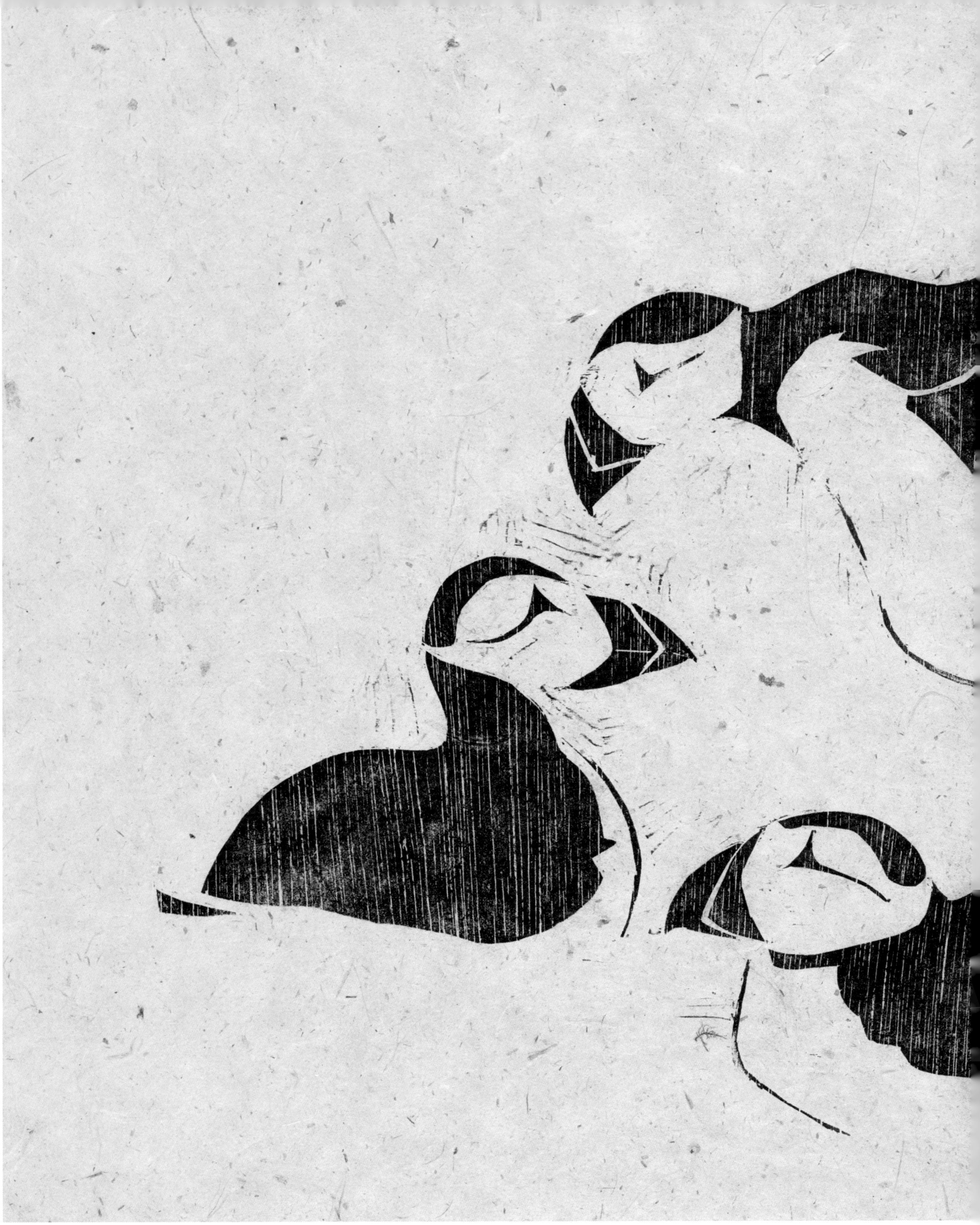

Two's Company,
38 cm x 34 cm, 2012

The use of flooring hardboard in this print results in a strong grain, which unifies and enhances the image.

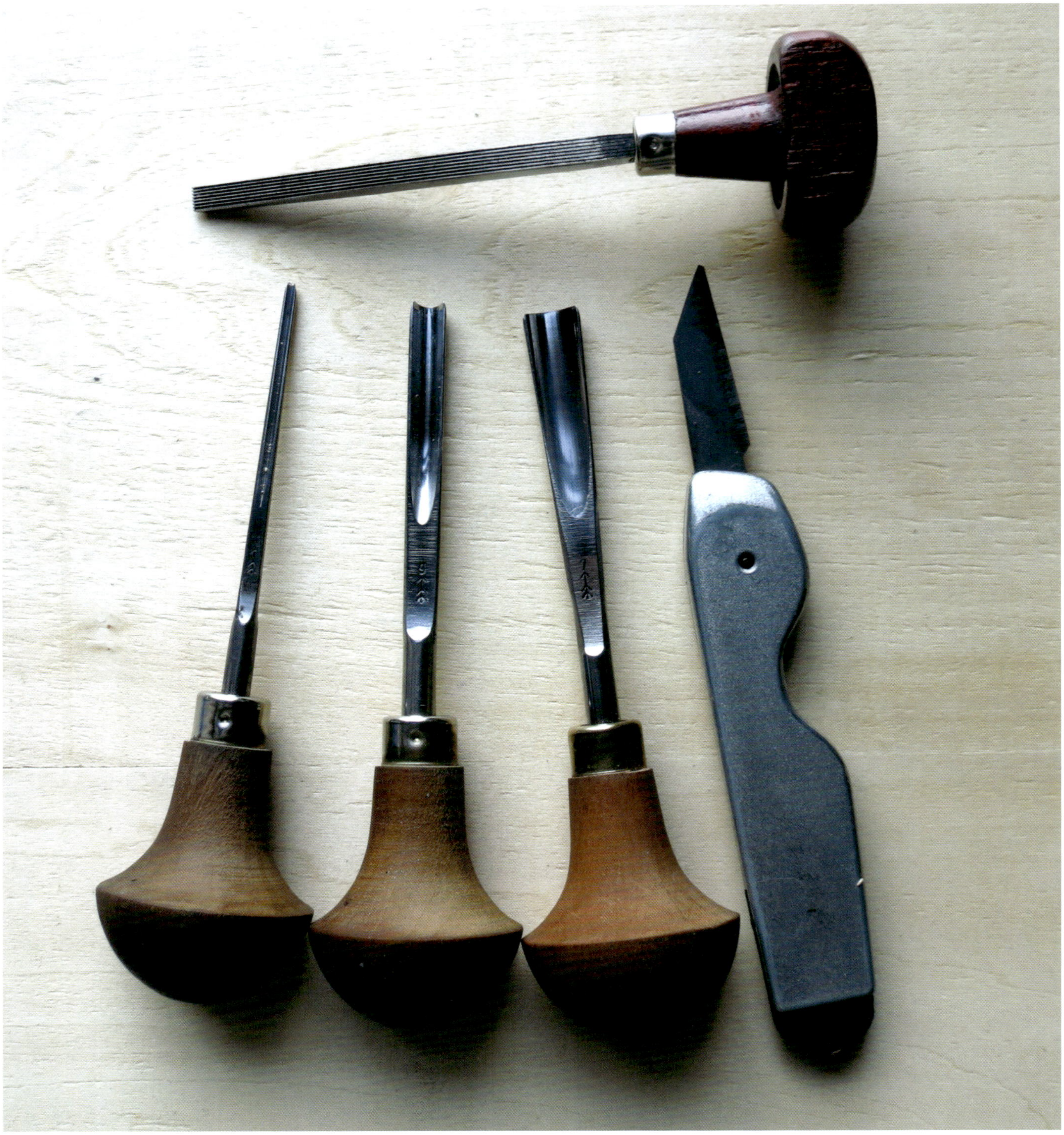

Tools for lino and woodcutting: V and U shaped cutters, a wider flatter chisel for clearing, a sharp knife and (across the top) a multiple line engraver.

At this point I should explain the difference between woodcuts and wood engravings. Woodcuts are made on side grain woodblocks, usually fruitwoods or other relatively soft woods, occasionally even on ply, hardboard or MDF. They can therefore be large. The tools used are the same as lino cutting tools and they make fairly crude marks. Wood engravings are made on end grain boxwood. The material is hard and expensive so they are often very small (commonly used as bookplates) and very intricate. The wood is gouged out (engraved) using very fine engraving tools and a completely different technique. They are relief prints too, and the medium is fascinating, but it is not something I have ever done, and I won't be describing it further here. I should also explain that I don't use a relief printing press as I started off as an etcher, and I have an etching press. It is not really practicable to have two presses in the studio, and for that reason the techniques I describe here are mainly hand printing techniques.

Having a drawing in mind I select a piece of wood and draw round it. Then I compose a sketch on the paper, using the space as best I can. Less often the wood, particularly if it is a piece of driftwood, suggests a drawing all by itself! If I am composing an image of birds, I will often draw a number of birds in different poses and spend quite a lot of time arranging the composition before finishing the drawing.

When the drawing is right, I will take a tracing and decide whether or not to reverse it. This is because the print comes out back to front and sometimes, even with a bird as opposed to a recognisable landscape (which of course always has to be reversed), the image can work one way round better than the other. Then I use carbon paper to transfer the drawing to the wood. For the moment I am describing the process for printing a block in a single colour, so there is only one block to consider.

As I have hinted, one of the reasons I use so many different media is that sometimes - most of the time - an idea for a picture comes to me complete with the preferred medium. Some pictures have to be woodcuts, others have to be etchings. For instance an image with a lot of tonal subtlety and detailed line work would translate readily into an etching. But a bold, simple design would suggest a wood- or linocut. Because half tones are difficult to achieve with woodcut, it lends itself to bold, black and white images. Later, there was a more prosaic reason for developing my relief printing skills: when I came to set up an etching studio at home in Scotland I struggled for three years to find an etching solution which I could buy easily and which I could use safely and successfully at home. In the meantime I could only work by developing alternative printing methods, which is how I came to try out so many print media.

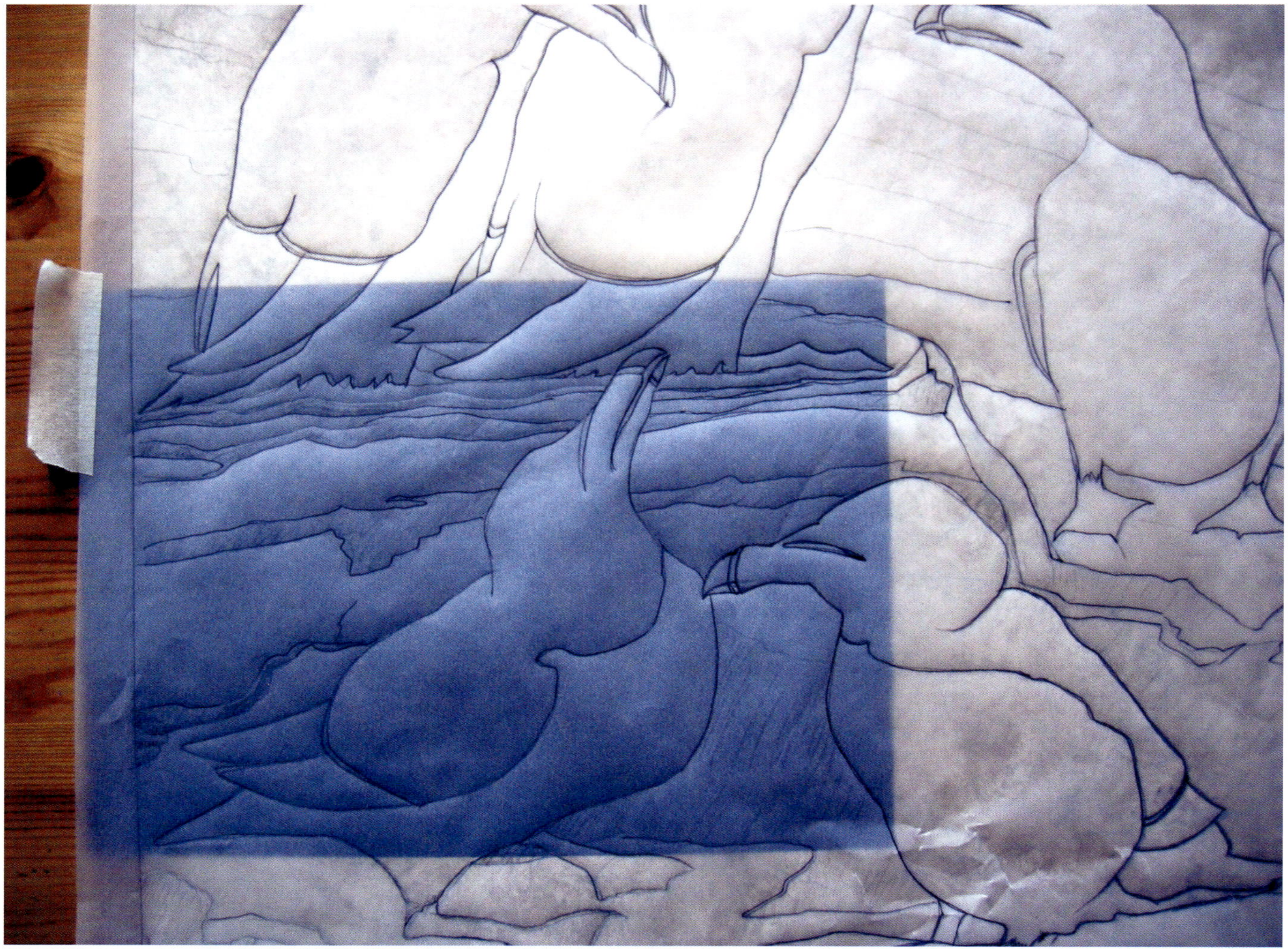

The tracing is stuck down and the lines transferred to the block using carbon paper.

Once the drawing is transferred to the block, the process of cutting begins. Cutting a relief print is sometimes described as "drawing with light", because whereas when you draw with a pen the lines are black on white, when you cut a line into a block, it will print as a white line on black.

The ink sits on the top surface of the block and not in the grooves. So, from the first cut, you need to consider which areas must be black and which white and how you are going to handle areas of half tone and areas of similar tone which are adjacent to one another. Basically you have quite a limited range of marks available so there are some tough decisions. I usually start by thinking about the absolute "must" tonal areas. For instance if it's a snow scene the snow has to be white, and if the bird has a white marking there is no getting around that, it has to have the white marking.

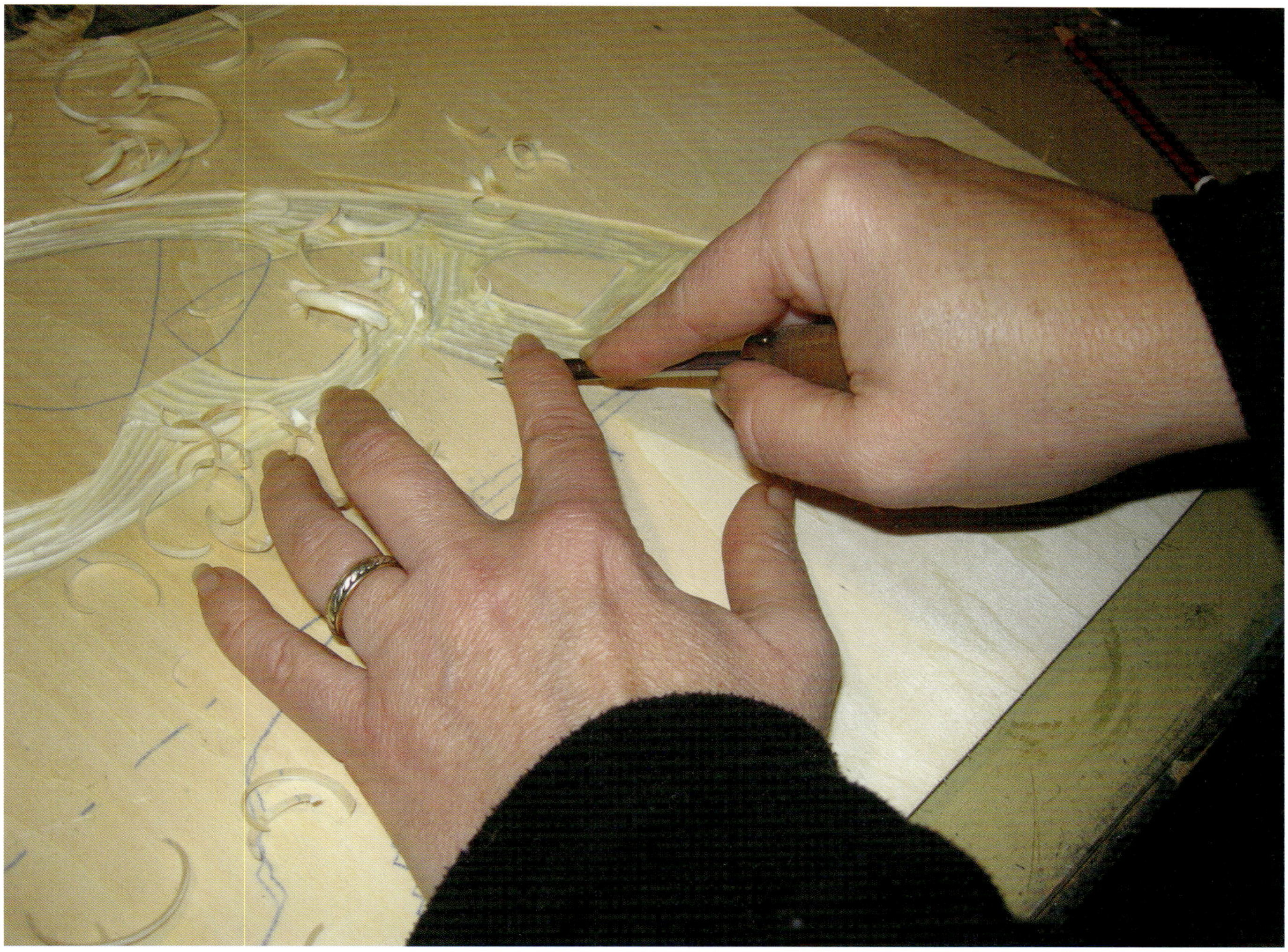

This shows how the tool is held and braced with the left hand to increase control.

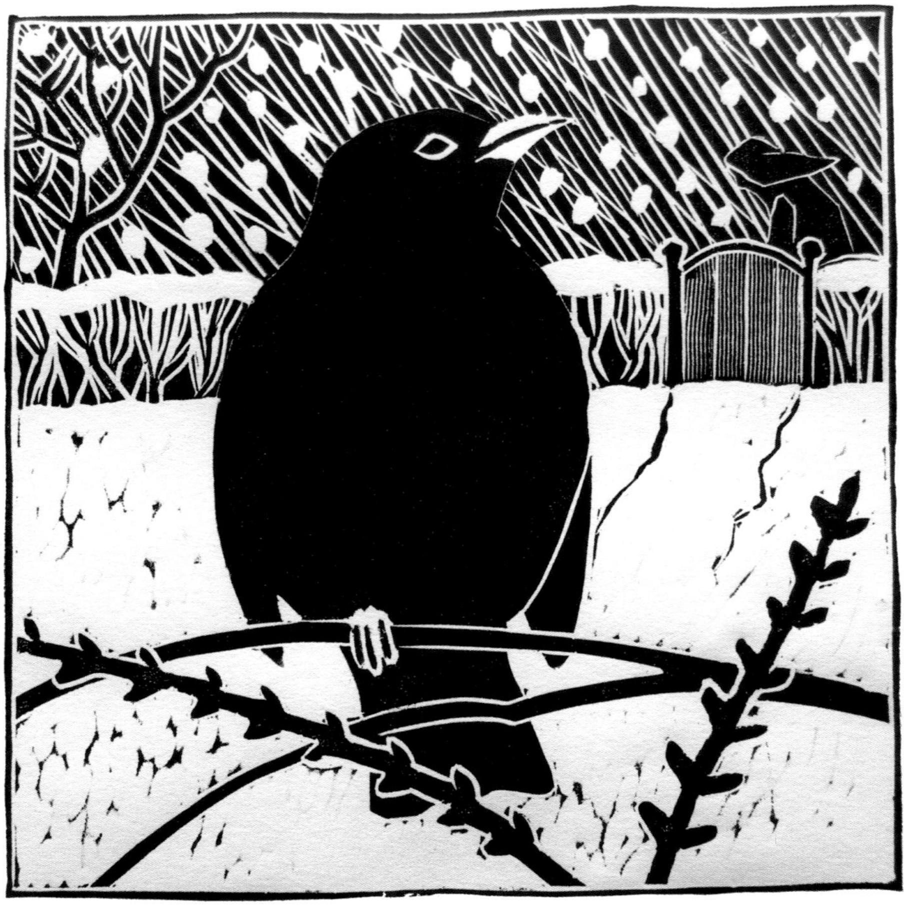

Winter blackbird,
13 cm x 13 cm, 2012

Used by the RSPB as a Christmas card in 2013.

Sometimes I simply start at that point and start cutting, solving problems as I go. You can of course use a white line to separate areas, although that can look a little crude. You can also use an awl to stipple areas to produce a tone, and you can use tools to cut small marks in a pattern in the way a wood engraver would. I use one engraving tool, called a multiple line engraver, to press multiple lines into wood, which gives a half tone. I have also used an engraving tool to make depressions on wood and I have hammered objects into wood. Small mistakes can be retrieved by using a wood filler and sanding, then re-cutting the area.

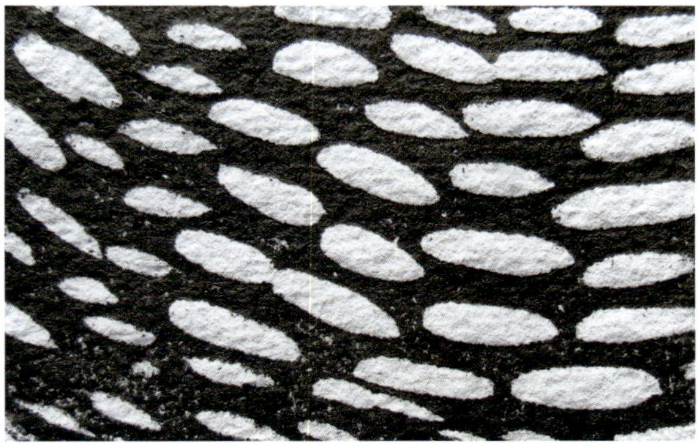

U shaped cuts suggesting feathers

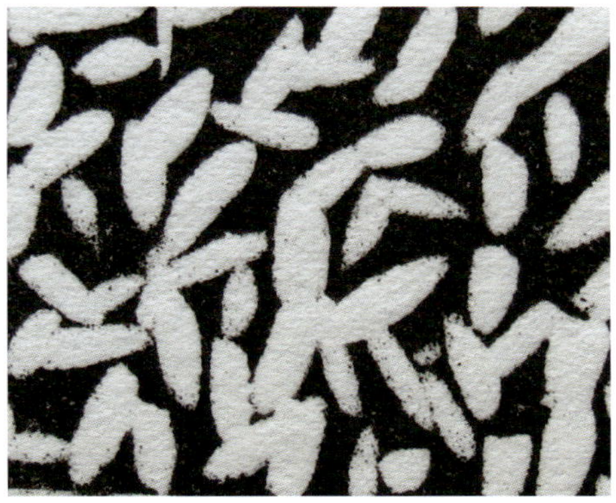

U shaped cuts at random suggest tone

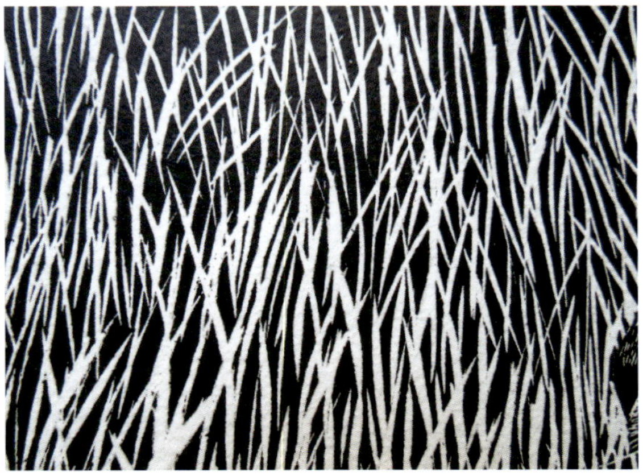

The small V shaped tool is ideal for suggesting grass

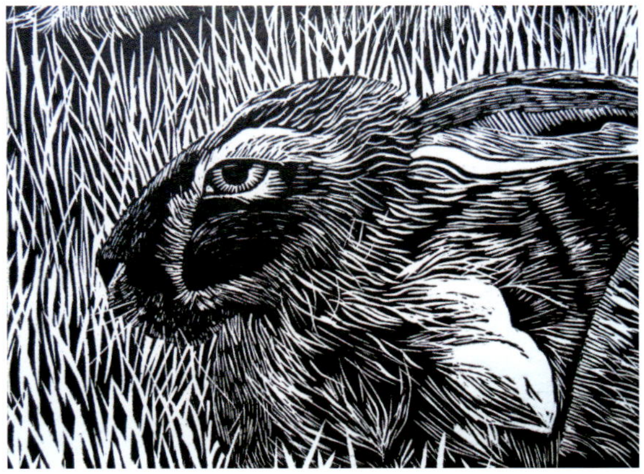

The small V shaped tool is also useful for fine detail

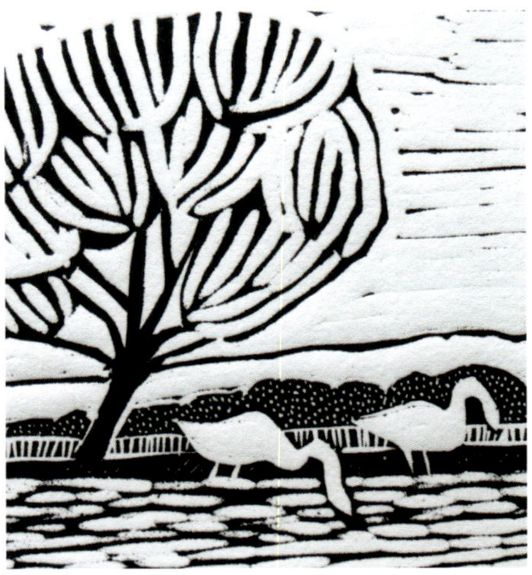

This detail shows the use of a variety of techniques, including stippling, to suggest trees, water and other half tone areas

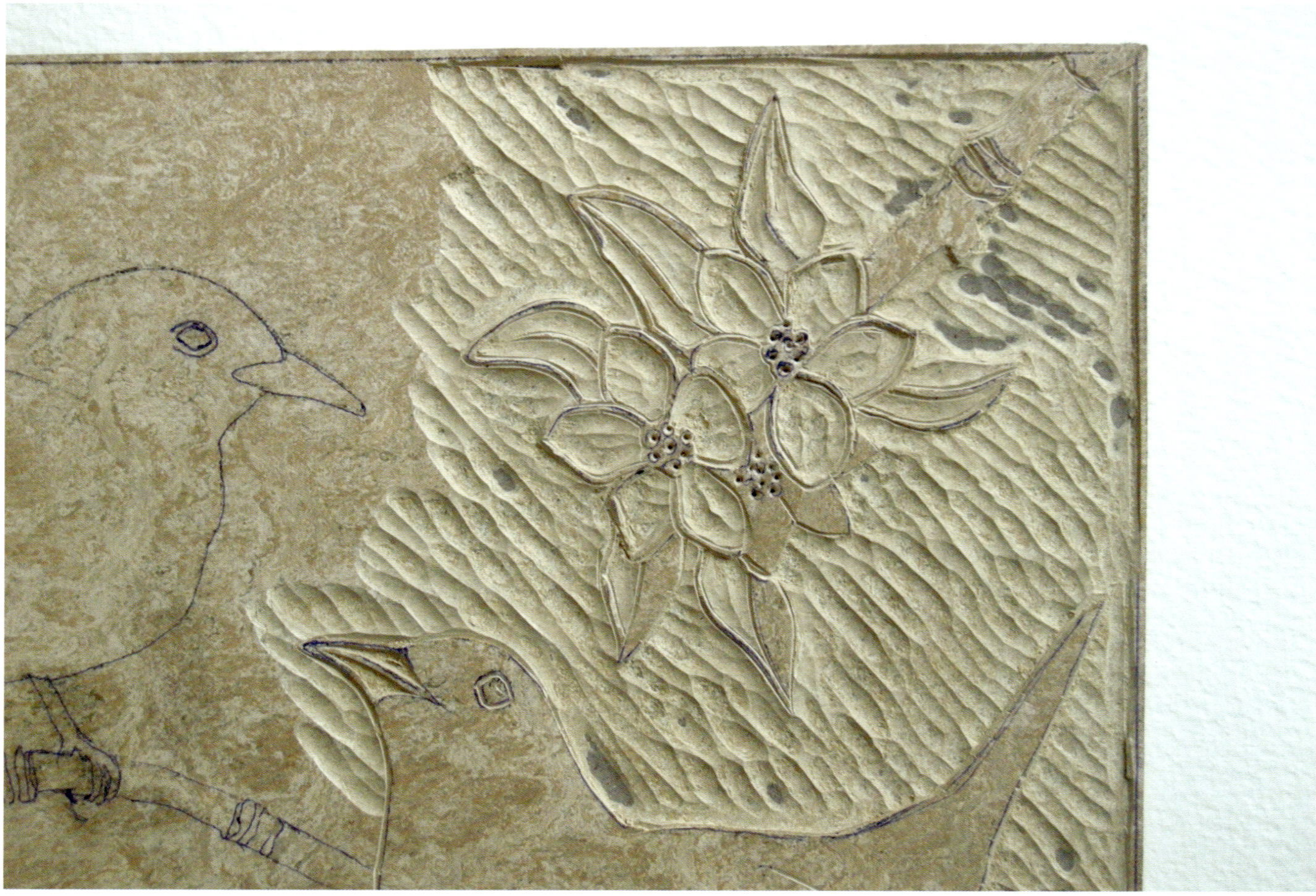

The drawing has been transferred to the block using carbon and the detail is being cut.

Sometimes I include a raised black line around the outside of a print, which gives it a rather "retro" look, but interestingly is also functional. The raised line supports the edge of the roller and prevents it from dipping down and depositing ink onto the cleared areas. In order to use this helpful device you obviously need to choose a roller large enough to span the gap between the outside of the motif and the border.

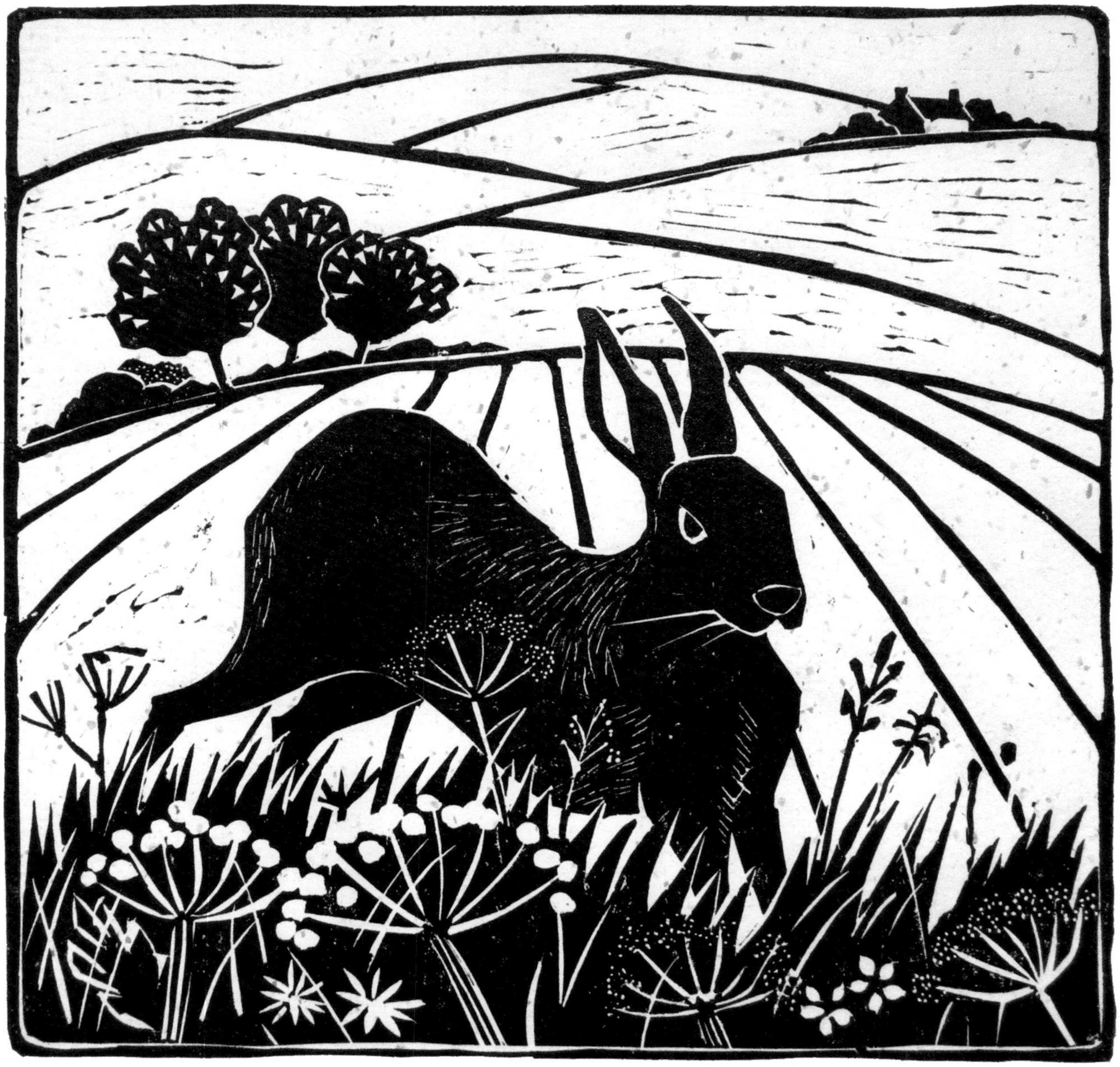

MACHARS HARE,
29 cm x 29 cm, 2006

This print was inspired by hares seen on Arran, superimposed on a local landscape. I intended it to be a hand-coloured print but I printed a handful which weren't coloured. This print shows the use of the raised outline to support the roller and demonstrates how it can reinforce the style of the print.

One interesting technique is to use the cleared areas to reinforce the design. When you clear an area which is going to print white, inevitably there are some marks in the cleared areas which are sufficiently raised to pick up a little bit of ink. It is very important to clear these areas in a consistent direction and, in some cases you can use them to enhance form. For instance, white areas on the breast of a bird, if cleared sensitively, can help to imply the roundness of the bird. So the bits of the picture that are cut away are as important as the bits that are left.

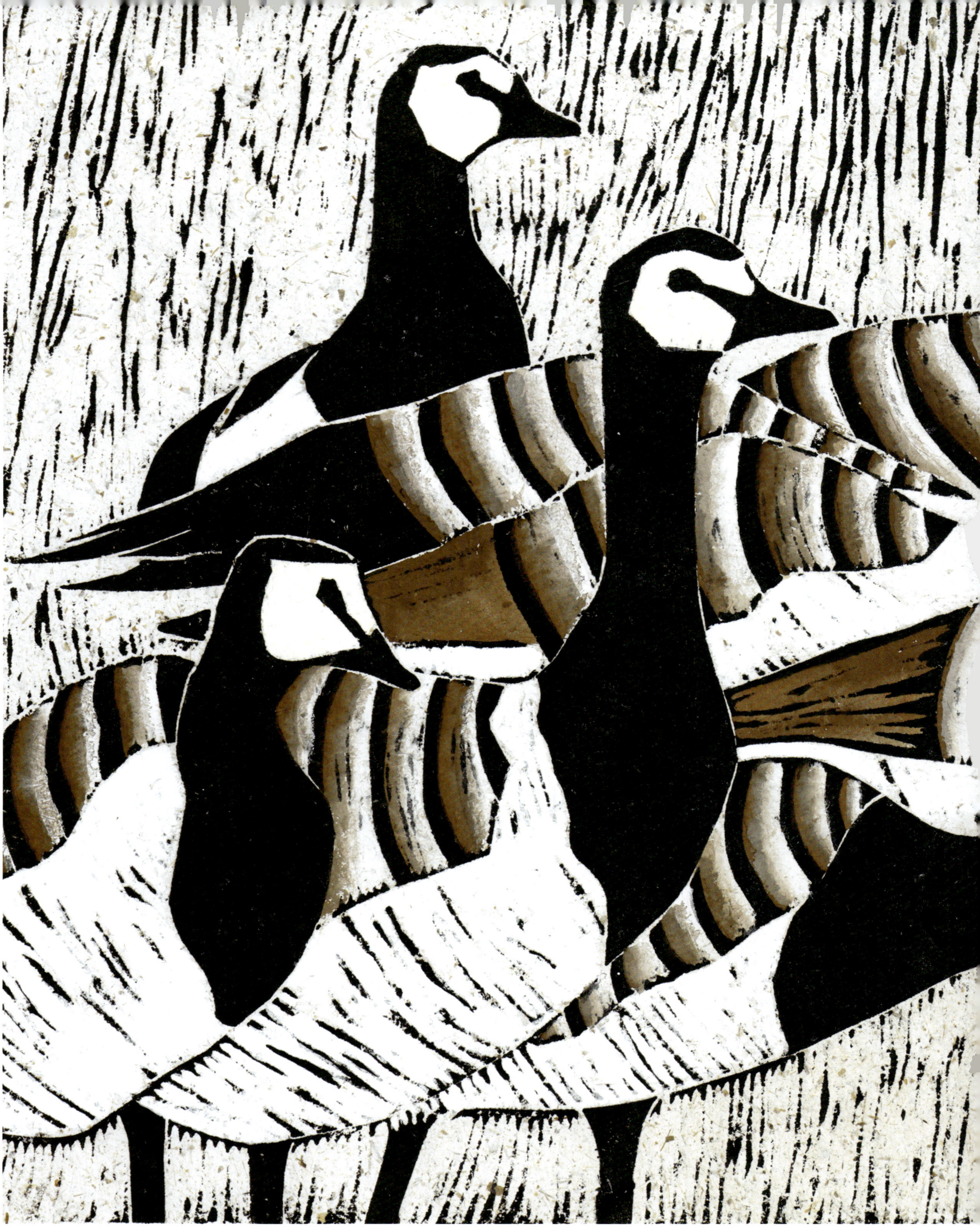

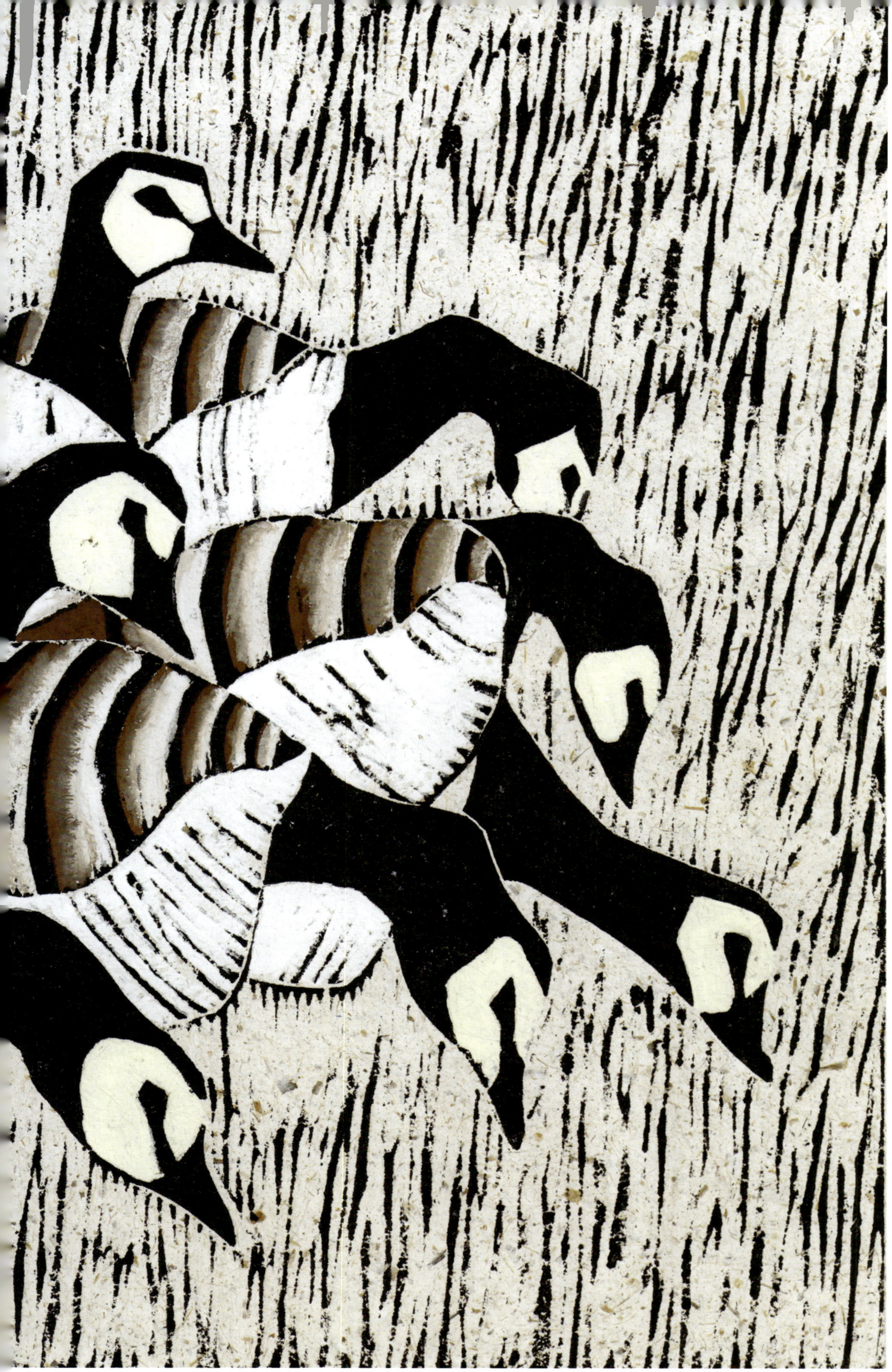

A Gaggle of Geese,
65 cm x 43 cm, 2007

The breasts of the birds have been cleared so as to reinforce their bulk. The background (grass) has been cleared using rough vertical strokes, which suggest vegetation without it needing to be hand coloured.

We seldom get to touch birds. Occasionally, rescuing one from the greenhouse, say, you get a sense of the strange soft/hardness of feathers, the incredible lightness and heat of a bird. But this is all too hurried and rather rare. Once, on Orkney, a recently dead female eider literally washed up at our feet and I just had to plunge my fingers into her soft eider down. When else was I ever going to feel an eider duck's breast? Is there something about carving the form of a bird out of a block that's a bit like feeling the living bird under your fingers I wonder?

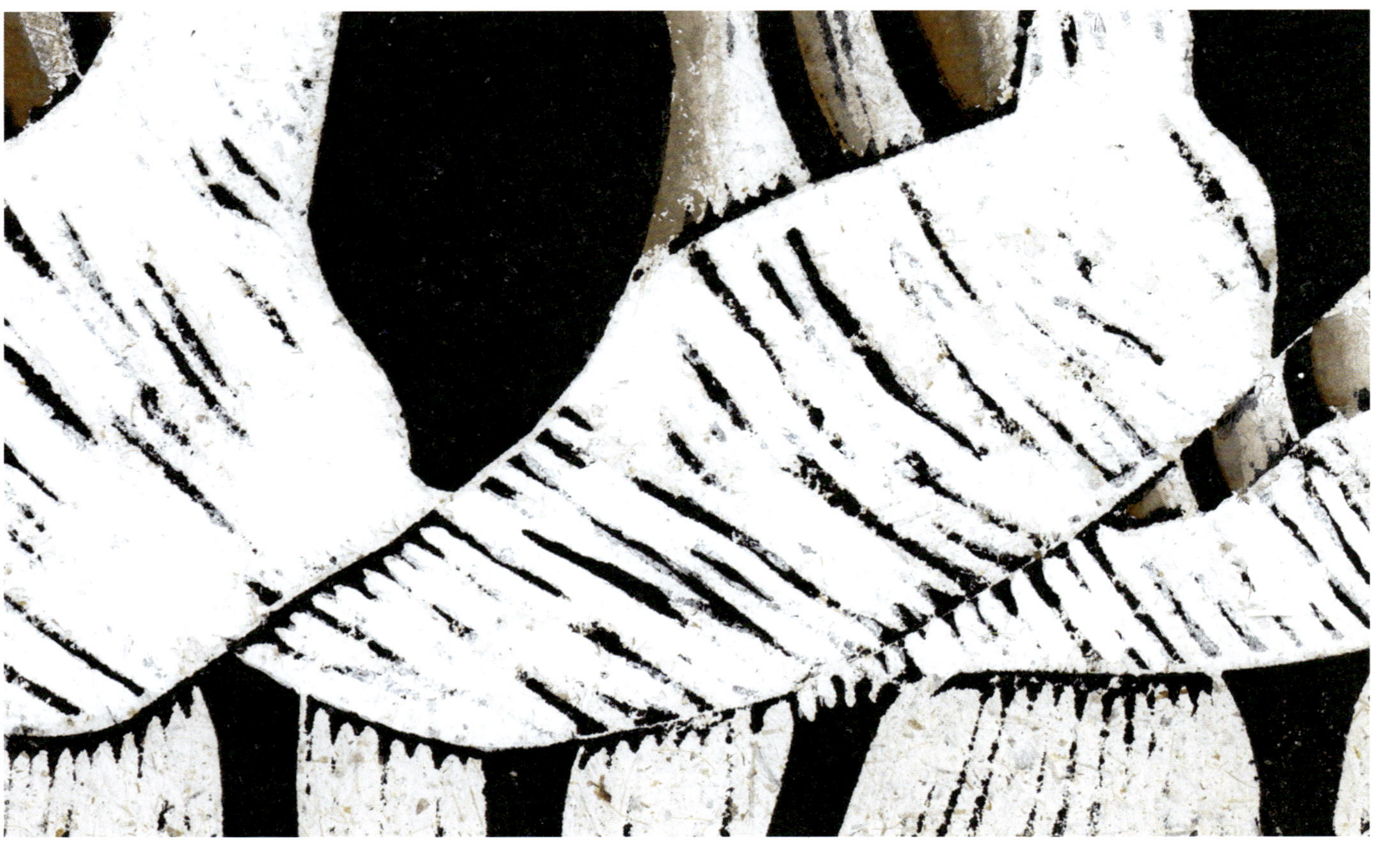

Close up of the breasts of the birds, showing direction of clearing strokes.

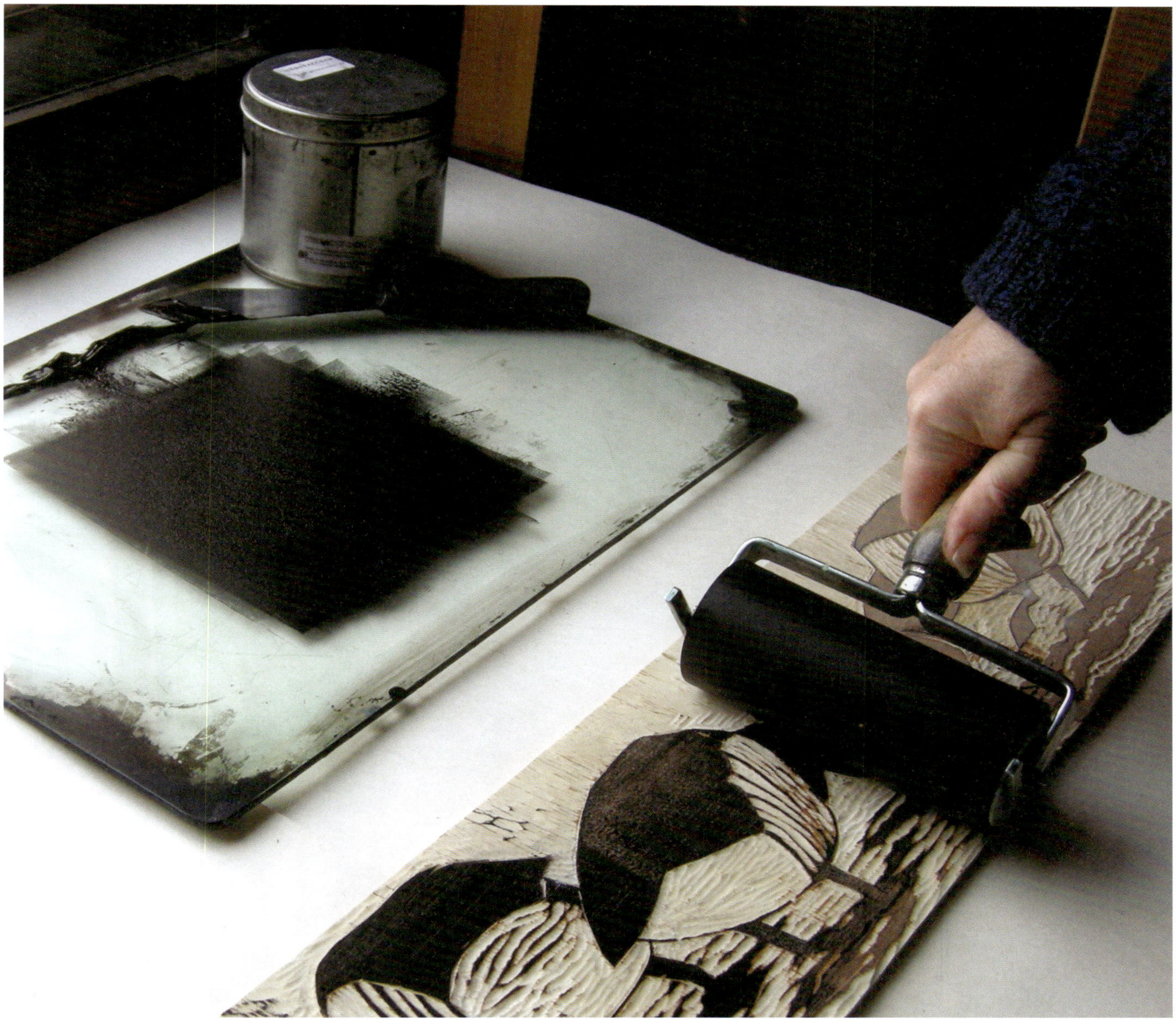

Inking the block. Ink is being transferred from a glass plate to the wood, in even layers, from the roller.

At any stage a proof can be taken. Ink has to be rolled or dabbed onto the block in an even layer. I use oil-based relief printing inks. The ink is rolled out into a rectangle on a sheet of glass and when the consistency is right the roller is used to transfer ink to the surface of the block. The aim is to build up thin layers which do not flood the depressions in the block.

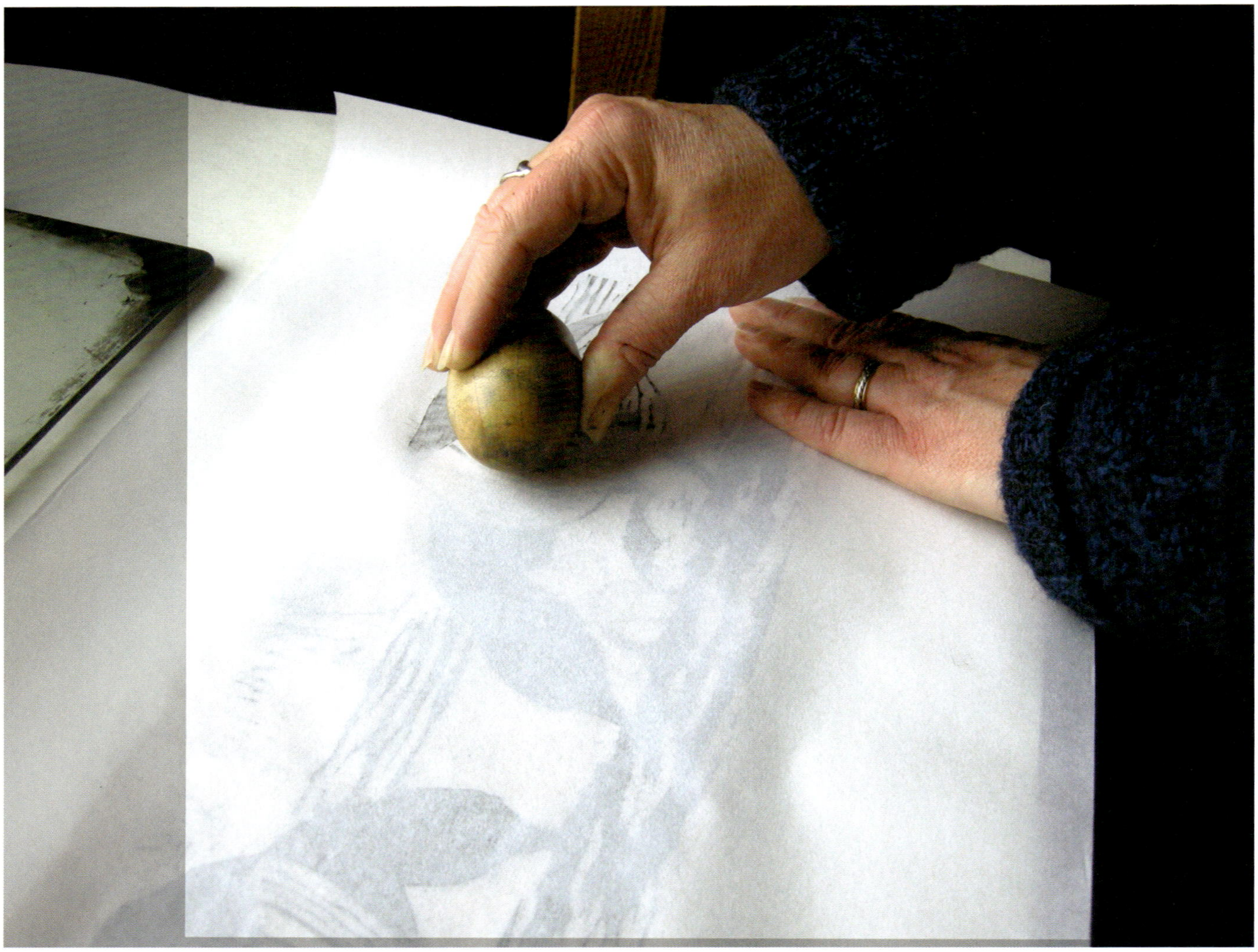

Ink is being transferred onto the surface of the paper by burnishing. The pressure required is surprising and it takes a long time to hand burnish a large plate in this way.

The block cannot be hand printed face down on the paper, as you need to apply a great deal of pressure, so the paper is laid on top of the block and then held in position with a weight. Then the back of the paper is burnished with a burnishing tool. I use wooden ornamental eggs which fit my hand nicely and work well. Some people use the back of a wooden spoon. If the paper is delicate it is a good idea to burnish through a layer of tissue or baking parchment. Thin papers are ideal for proofing and indeed for final prints if no colour is to be added. If you are hand colouring you need to use a paper that will take watercolour without cockling or blotting.

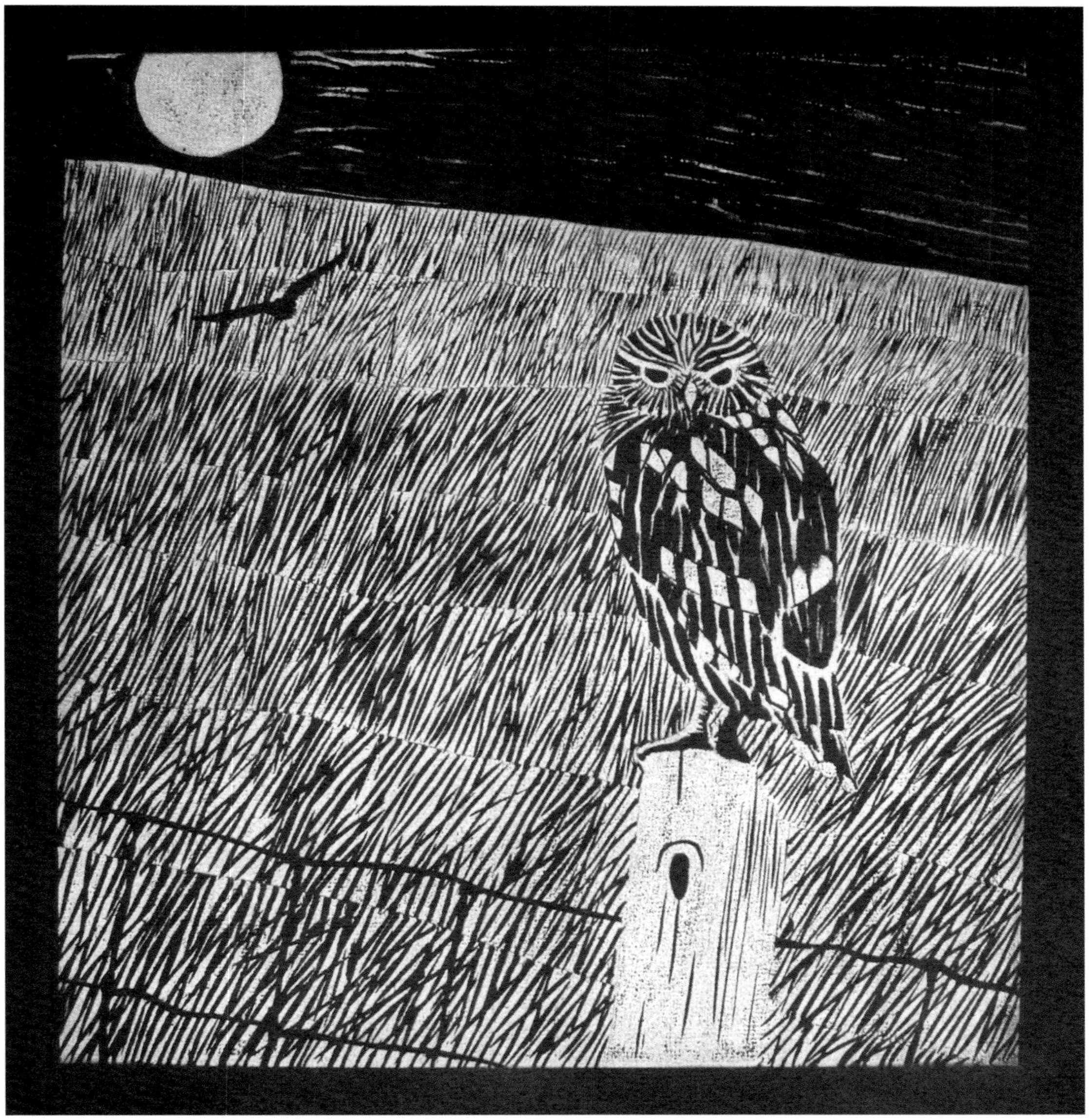

Dusk Encounter,
22 cm x 24 cm, 2010

By printing with white ink black lines are much easier to achieve. This can be helpful if spontaneous thin lines are needed as in figure drawing. Little owls are not present in Dumfries and Galloway – this one was seen in the Yorkshire Dales.

One interesting technique is to print with white ink on black paper. This technique, which was used by Picasso, means that the lines you cut appear as dark lines on the paper, and the uncut areas remain lighter.

The final print is taken in exactly the same way, being careful to avoid marks from the edge of the plate.

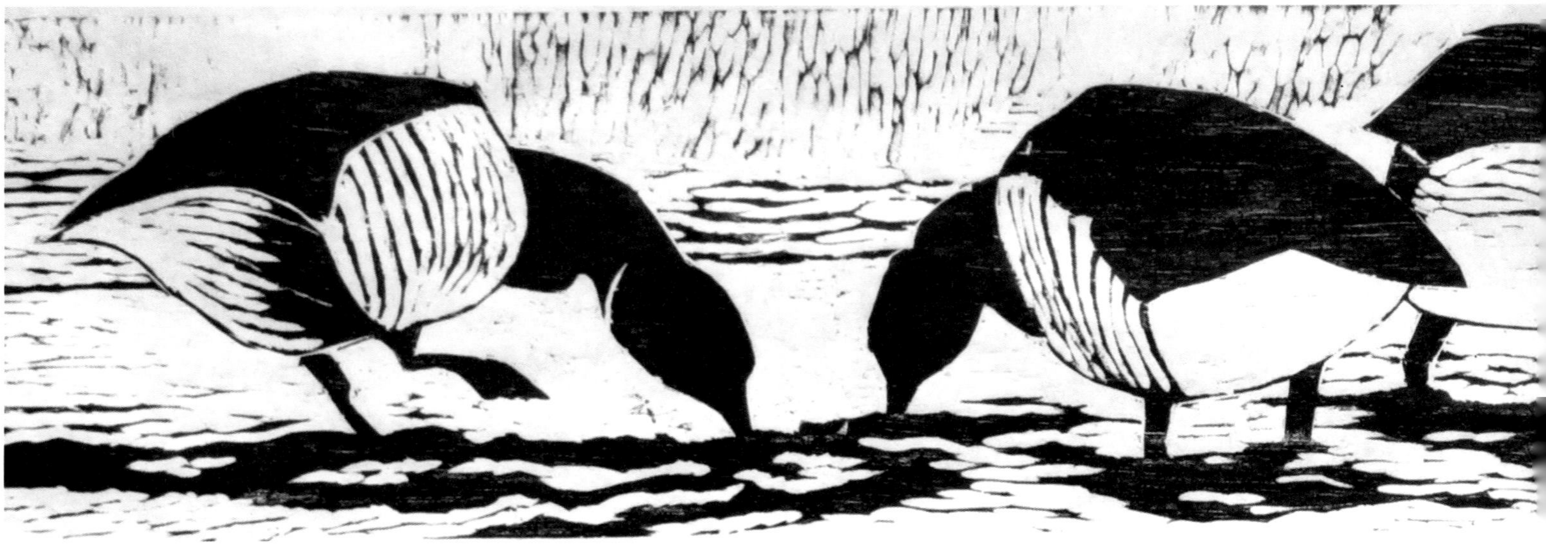

BRENT GEESE,
87 cm x 16 cm, 2012

This woodcut was made out of flooring hardwood and the grain is quite coarse. It was subsequently hand coloured using a wax resist to prevent the inks from spreading in the thin paper.

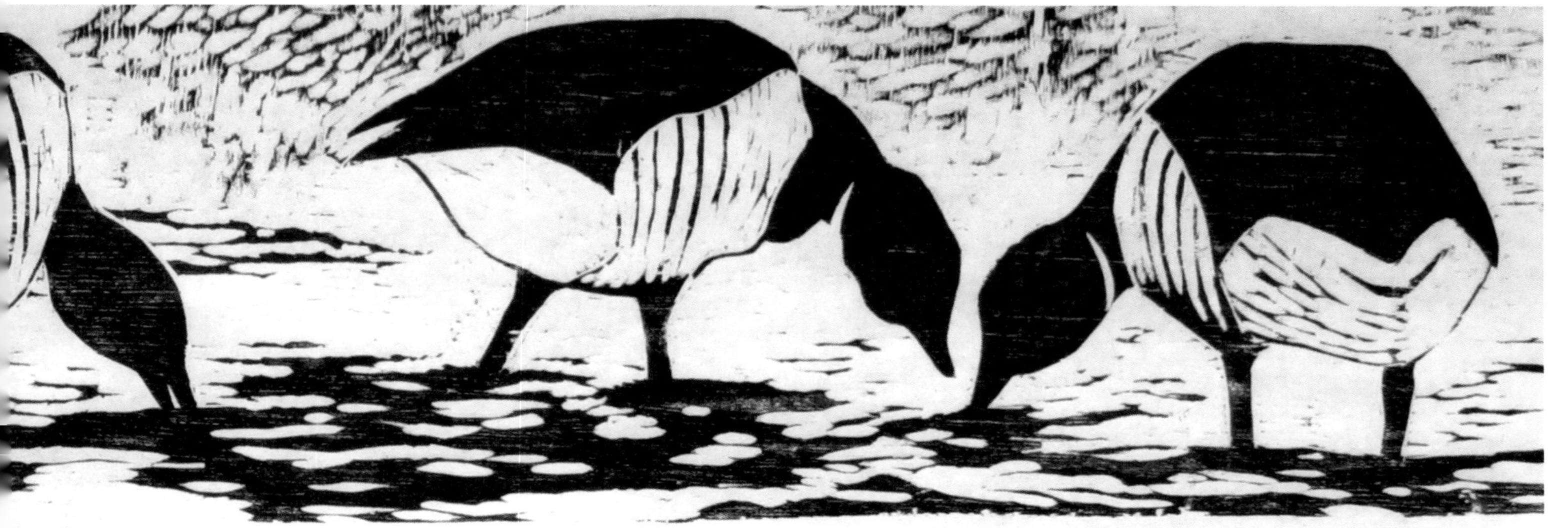

Once I got interested in printmaking, painting more or less died for me. The lure of printmaking is so strong. First there is the surface quality of prints. Almost whatever the print medium, there is something about the finished image which defines it as unmistakably a print. The soft merged tones of an etching, the jaunty specks of uncleared lino on a relief print, the incredible translucency of a Japanese woodblock. Then there is the process. The reversal of the image, the business of creating a white line instead of a black line with linocuts, the physicality of preparing and etching a zinc plate, the smell of a woodblock as it is cut. Printmaking is a visual art, but it is also a craft and the craft process is utterly integral. There are so many variables and there is so much to learn. It's something you get better at over years and years, not a thing instantly mastered. Finally there is the joy or heartache of the final act, when you lift the paper and reveal the finished print with its purposeful and sometimes serendipitous marks.

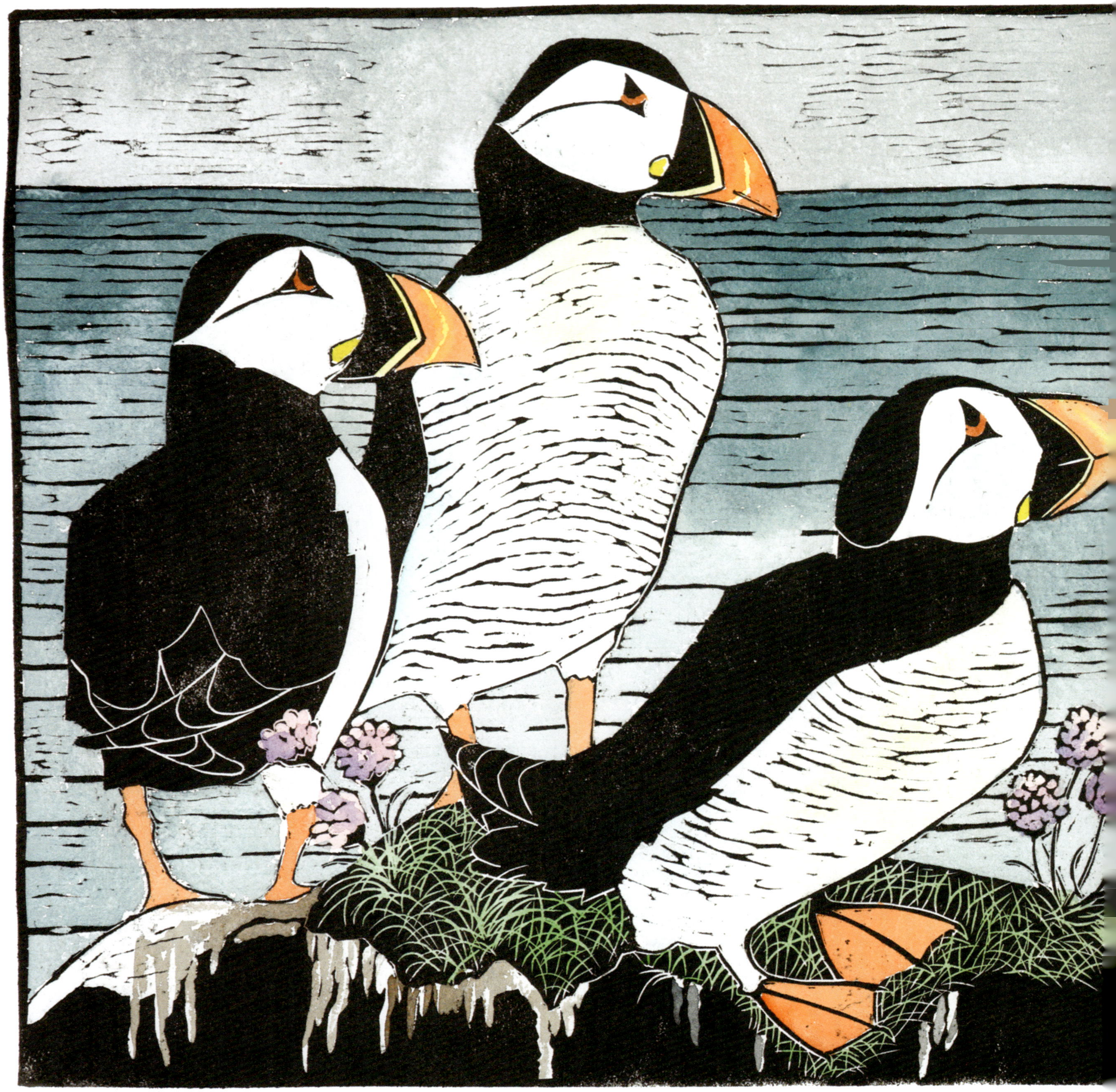

Gathering,
72 cm x 35 cm, 2012

This print has been printed in black and hand coloured. This technique is discussed fully in the next chapter.

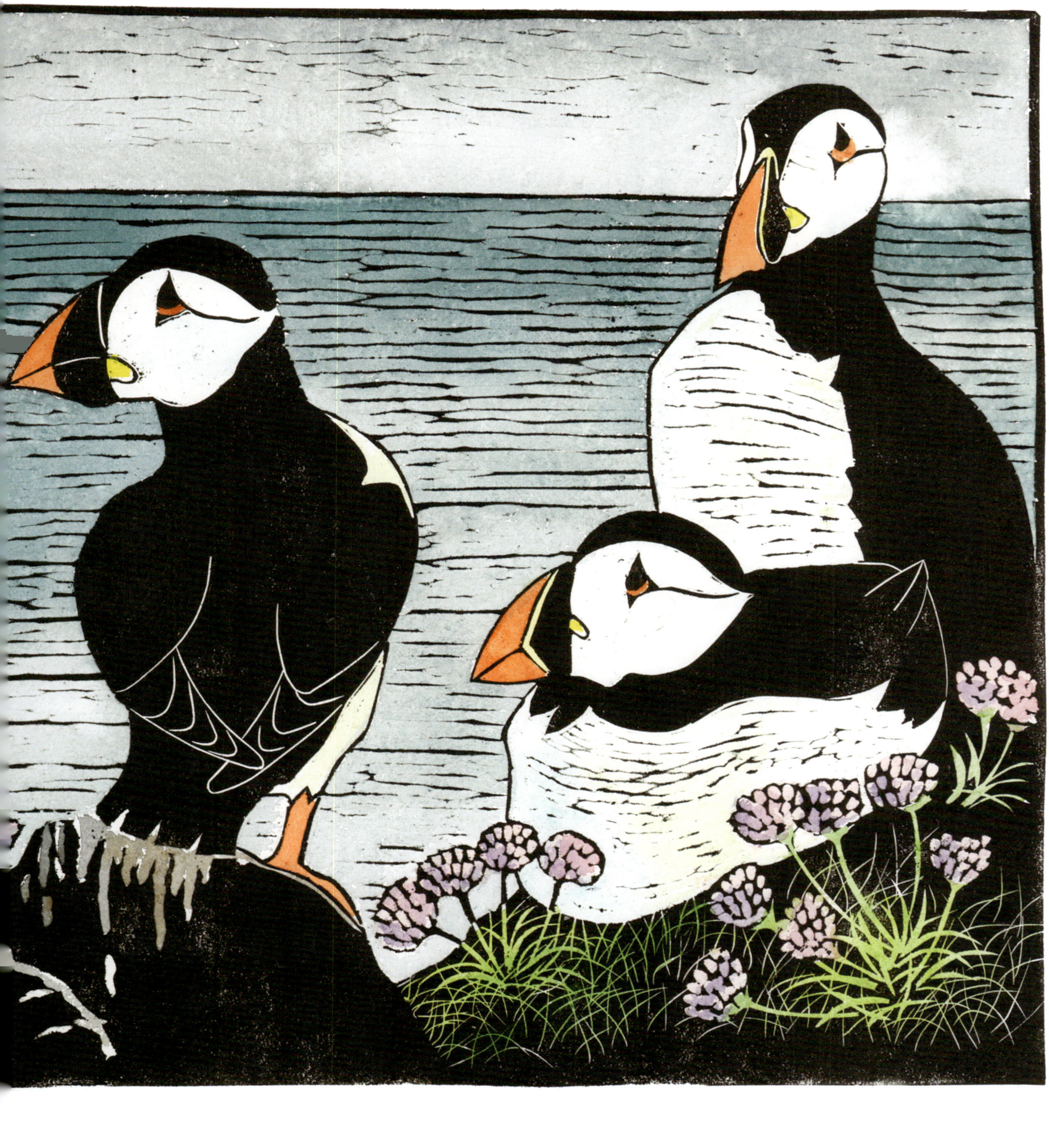

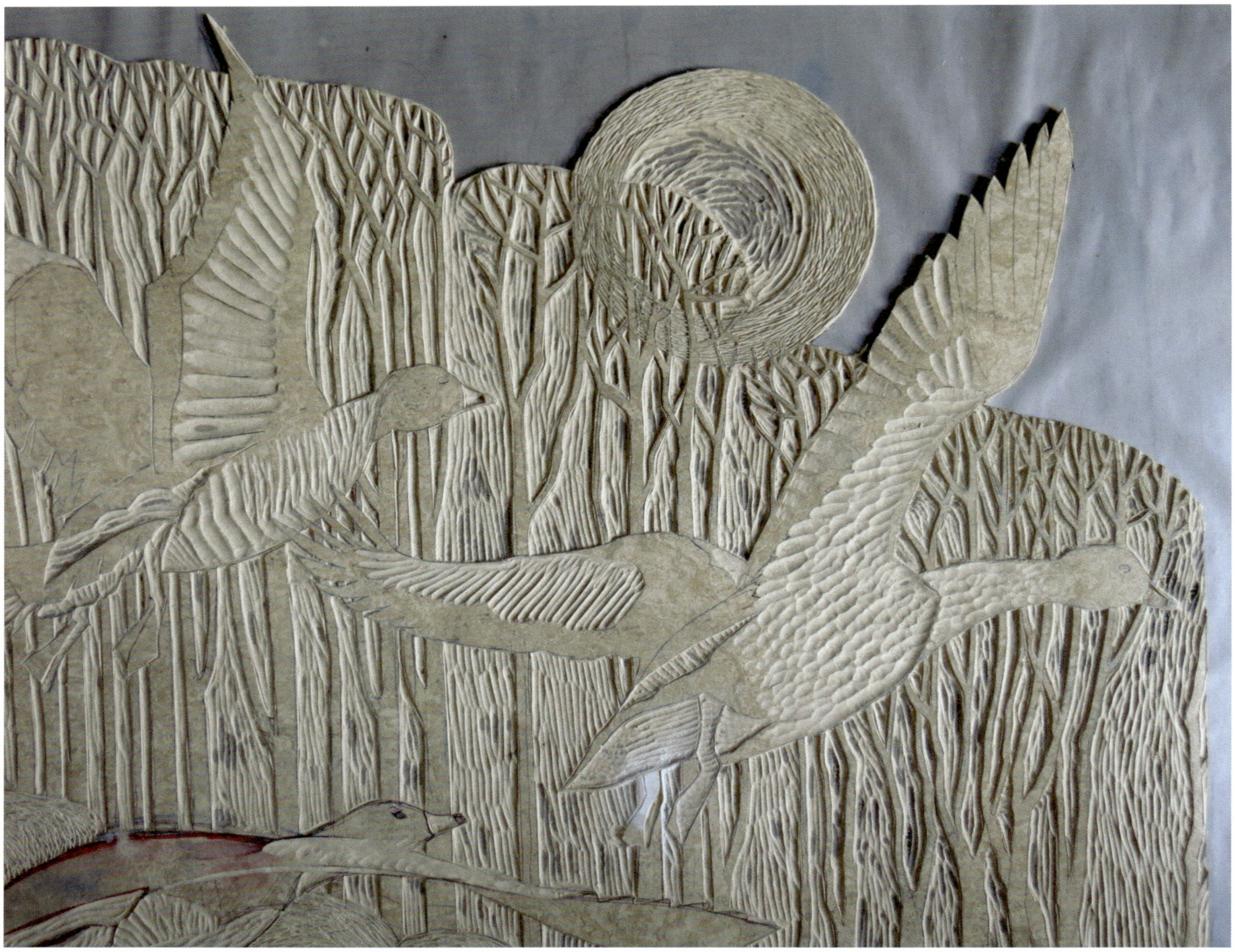

A linocut, just finished, prior to printing. The white area has been filled and re-cut.

The technique described above is almost exactly replicated with linocuts. There are a few differences:

- lino obviously has a very smooth, characterless surface (but so do most woods used for woodcuts)
- lino benefits from brief sanding to help the ink key to its surface
- lino doesn't really take impressions from engraving tools very well
- lino cuts more easily if it is warmed so it is important to have access to some means of warming it at intervals
- lino is easier to cut to size, so complete areas can be cut out or cut off to achieve really white areas and prints can be irregular shapes
- lino is thin enough to print through an etching press, which for large work is quite an advantage and means that it can be used to emboss paper.

Perhaps surprisingly, lino, like wood, can be filled and re-cut. The lino I use is floor lino, which is still made and sold as Marmoleum. It is a bit shallower than the sort of lino you buy from art suppliers, so clearing white areas is a little trickier, (sometimes I simply cut holes into a plate as you can see in some of the illustrations above, if I want clean white areas), but the great advantage is that you can easily cut pieces which are large unconventional shapes. This is explored further in the next chapter, on colour.

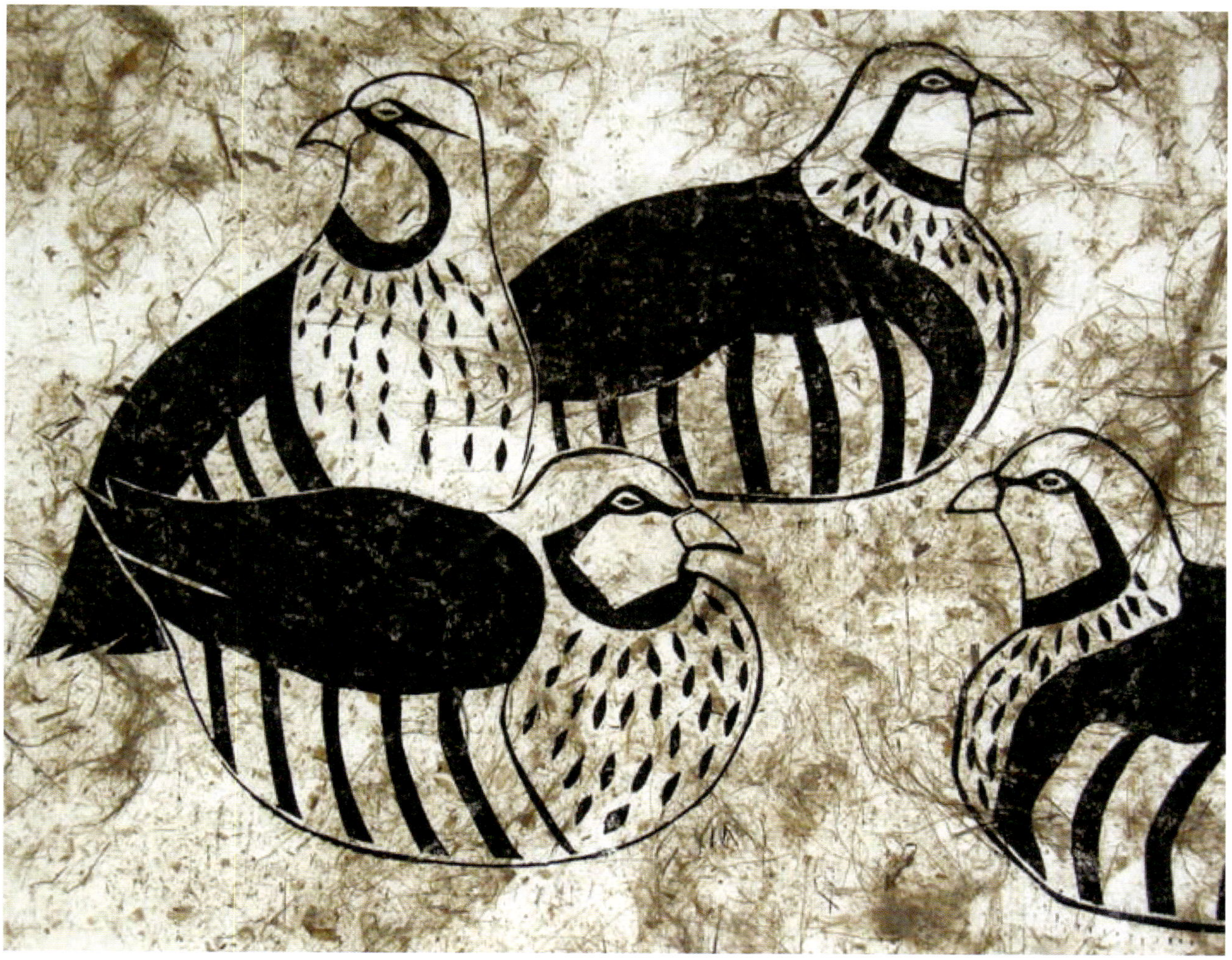

Covey,
39 cm x 32 cm, 2007

Printed in black only onto a fibrous paper, this simple linocut has a primitive feel to it.

Etching lino

One other technique possible with lino is to etch the surface chemically, using caustic soda. Floor lino has a protective coating which must be sanded off, then, like an etching plate, it must be de-greased with methylated spirits. A resist of some sort must be applied to protect the areas which are going to print black.

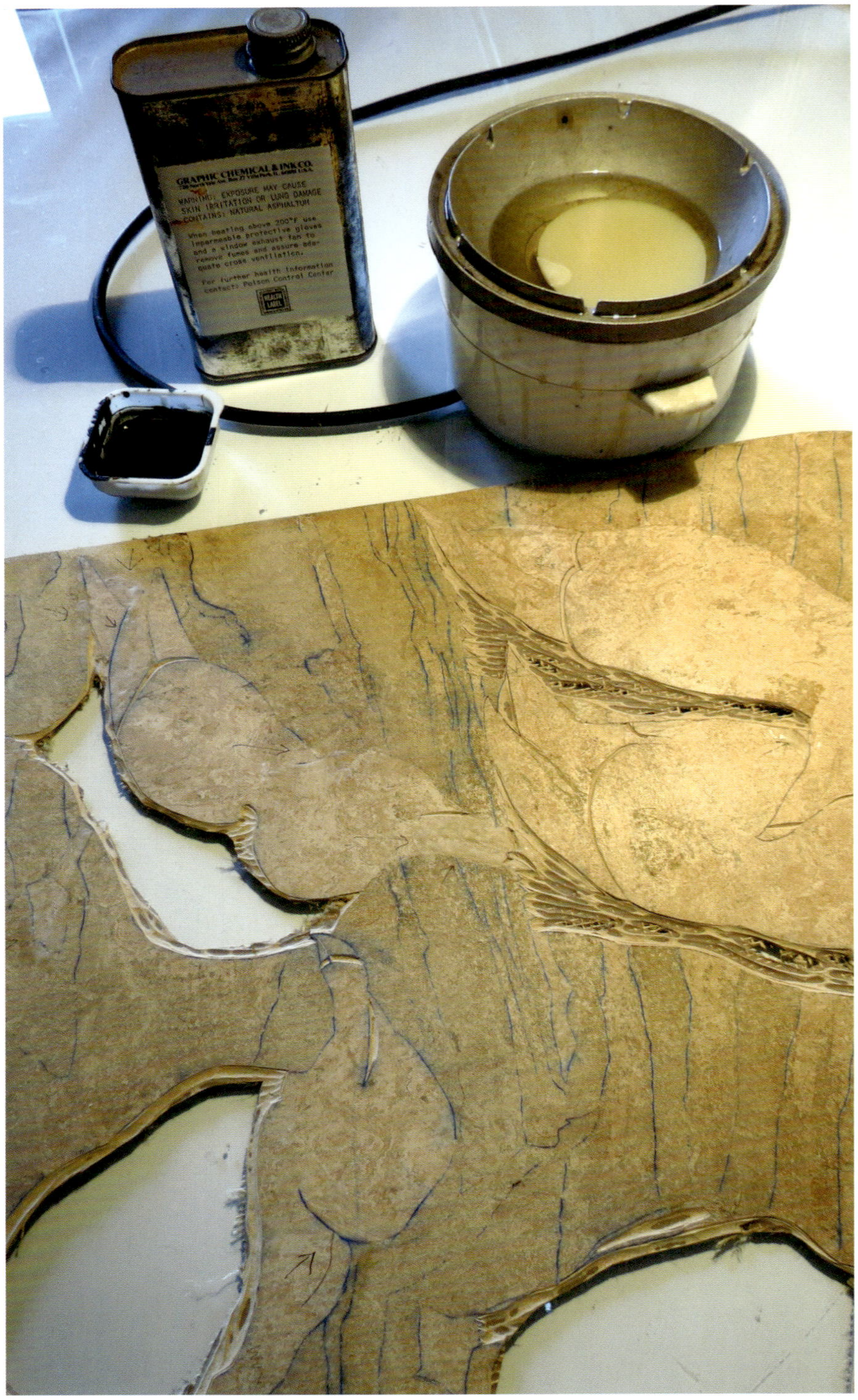

Two types of resist, etcher's liquid hard ground and melted wax, are shown here. The incomplete protection given by the etching ground can be useful – in this print I used the less robust resist on the rocks and the melted wax to protect the birds fully. Some areas, which I want to print a clean white, are completely cut out of the lino.

Melted wax makes an excellent resist. Etching grounds are more fragile and give incomplete resistance. The concentrated caustic soda, which I mix up in a jar, is very unpleasant and can cause burns: it should be used with extreme care. I use a nylon brush to paint it onto the lino (it can run off the edges so it is important to protect the surface underneath with several layers of newspaper). After several hours the caustic soda will have turned the lino into a sort of pulp, which can be scrubbed off under running water (with gloves!), to leave a pock-marked surface, which prints in a half tone.

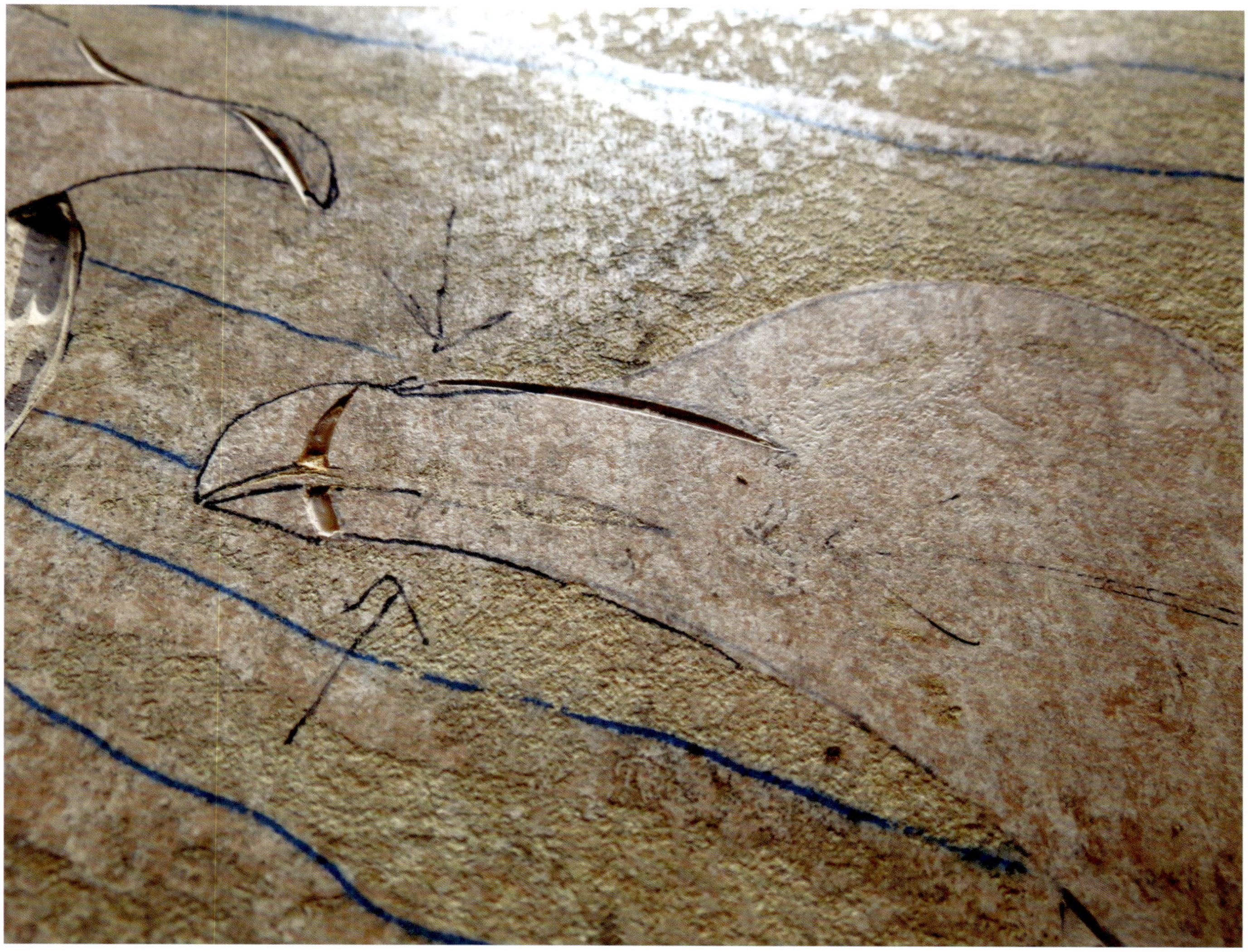

The surface of the lino shows shallow indentations caused by the etching process. The arrows are to remind me to re-etch areas which are printing too heavily, as identified on the first proof.

It is very difficult to control the depth of tone as it depends on the ambient temperature and is also inherently variable, perhaps due to grease or variations in the composition of the lino itself. Limited alterations can be achieved by re-biting, but complex tonal designs are probably over ambitious. Sometimes it is necessary to stick the lino to a flat piece of wood, because the bites are so shallow that any curve in the plate spoils the inking process. In fact the plate often curls under attack from the caustic soda as the hemp backing tends to shrink. It is, in short, a frustrating technique, which can nevertheless yield results of great subtlety, unachievable by cutting with hand tools, or even by machine engraving.

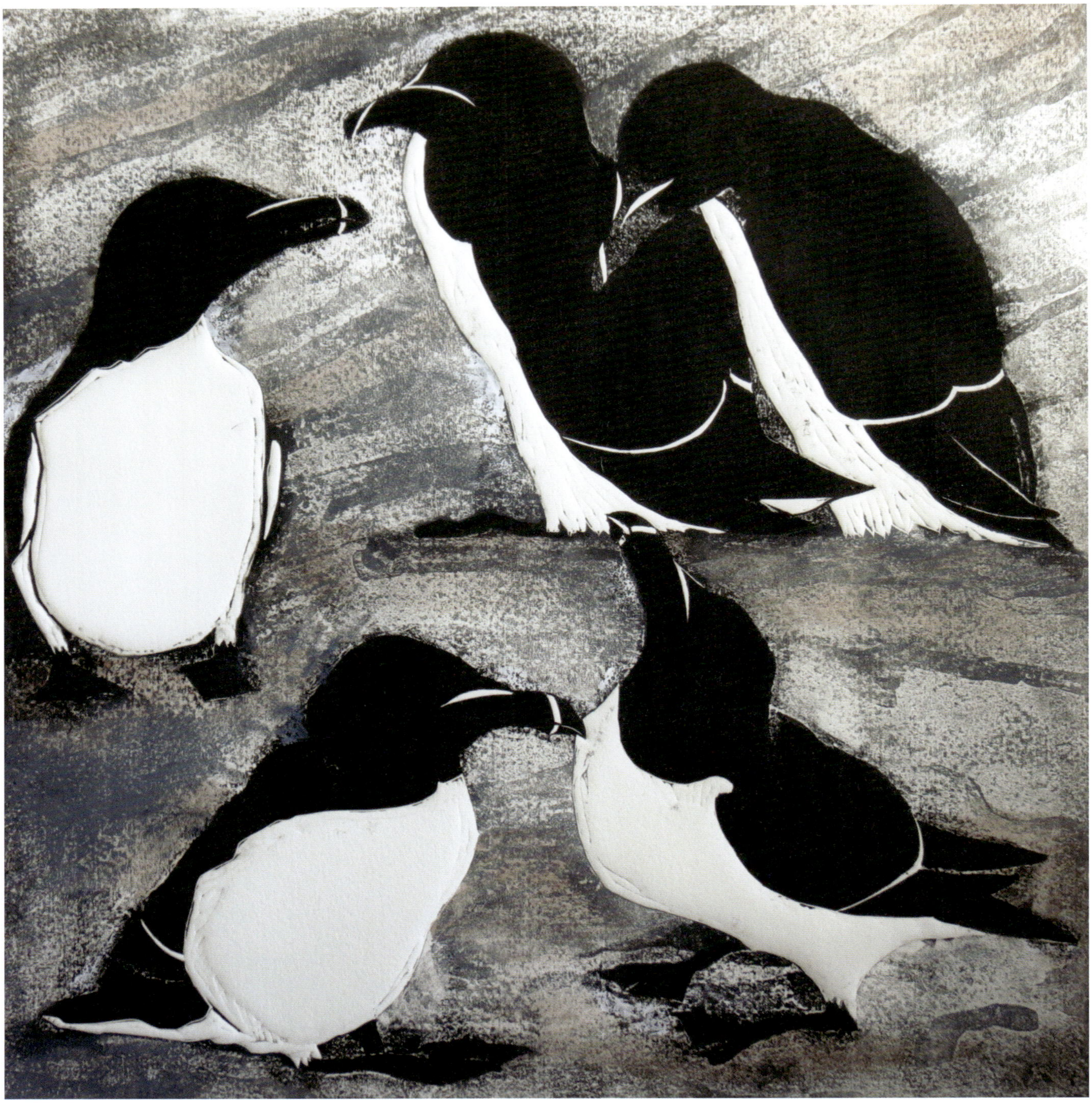

Razorbills,
43 cm x 48 cm, 2013

Printed and hand coloured, the final version of the razorbills. These birds were observed on Orkney at the Brough of Birsay in 2012.

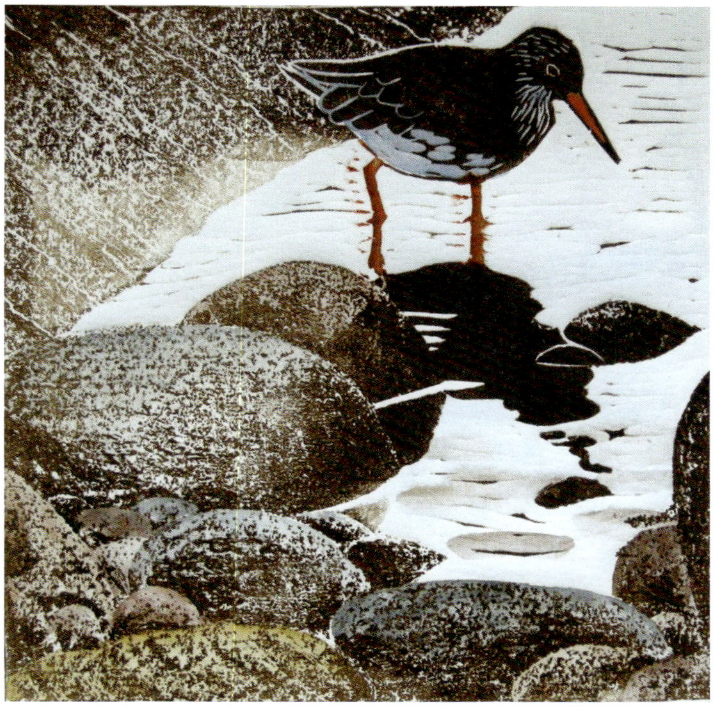

Redshank, stromness,
20 cm x 22 cm, 2014

Another Orkney bird. The rocks have been etched, whilst the bird itself is cut.

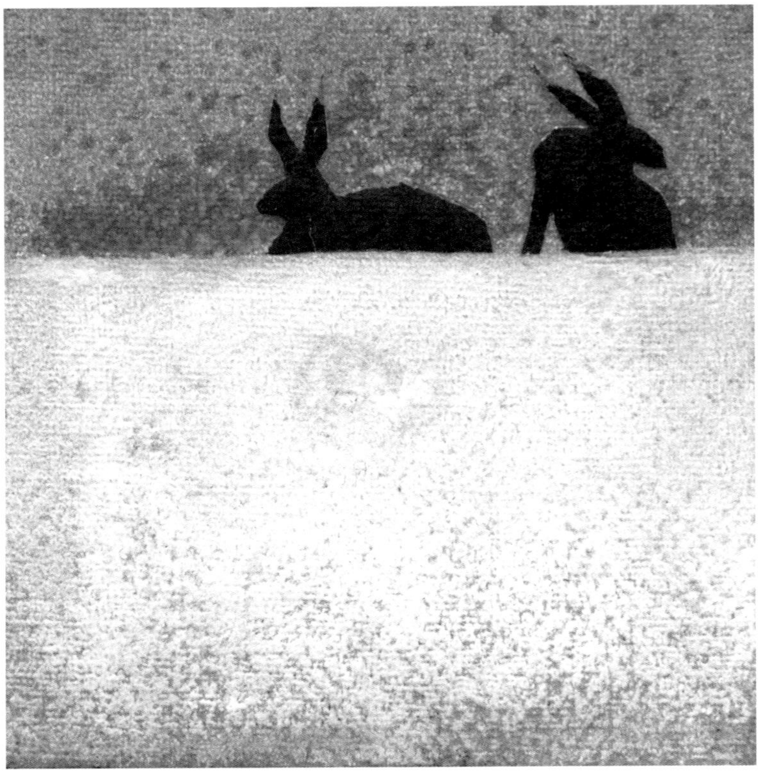

SNOW HARES,
10 cm x 10 cm, 2010

This little picture is a lino etching, with cut areas, printed in white ink on black paper.

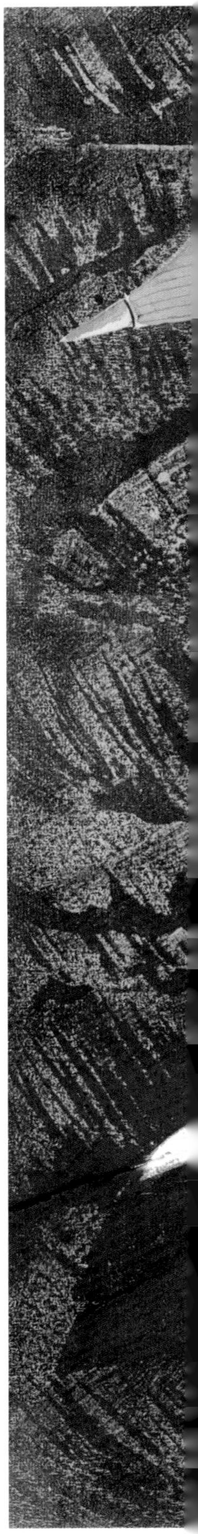

Birds are our link to the rest of the living world. Other than plant and insect life, we don't get to see many of our planetary travelling companions: not the ones with backbones anyway. Birds are the great exception. They are everywhere. They might make a desultory effort to hide (some more than others) but no trip to the corner shop or to the end of the garden is birdless. Most people most days see a bird or two, whereas many people never see say a badger or an otter. They people our lives with their song and their amazing and enviable ability to fly. Their antics amuse us and their lifestyles amaze us. Where would we be without them?

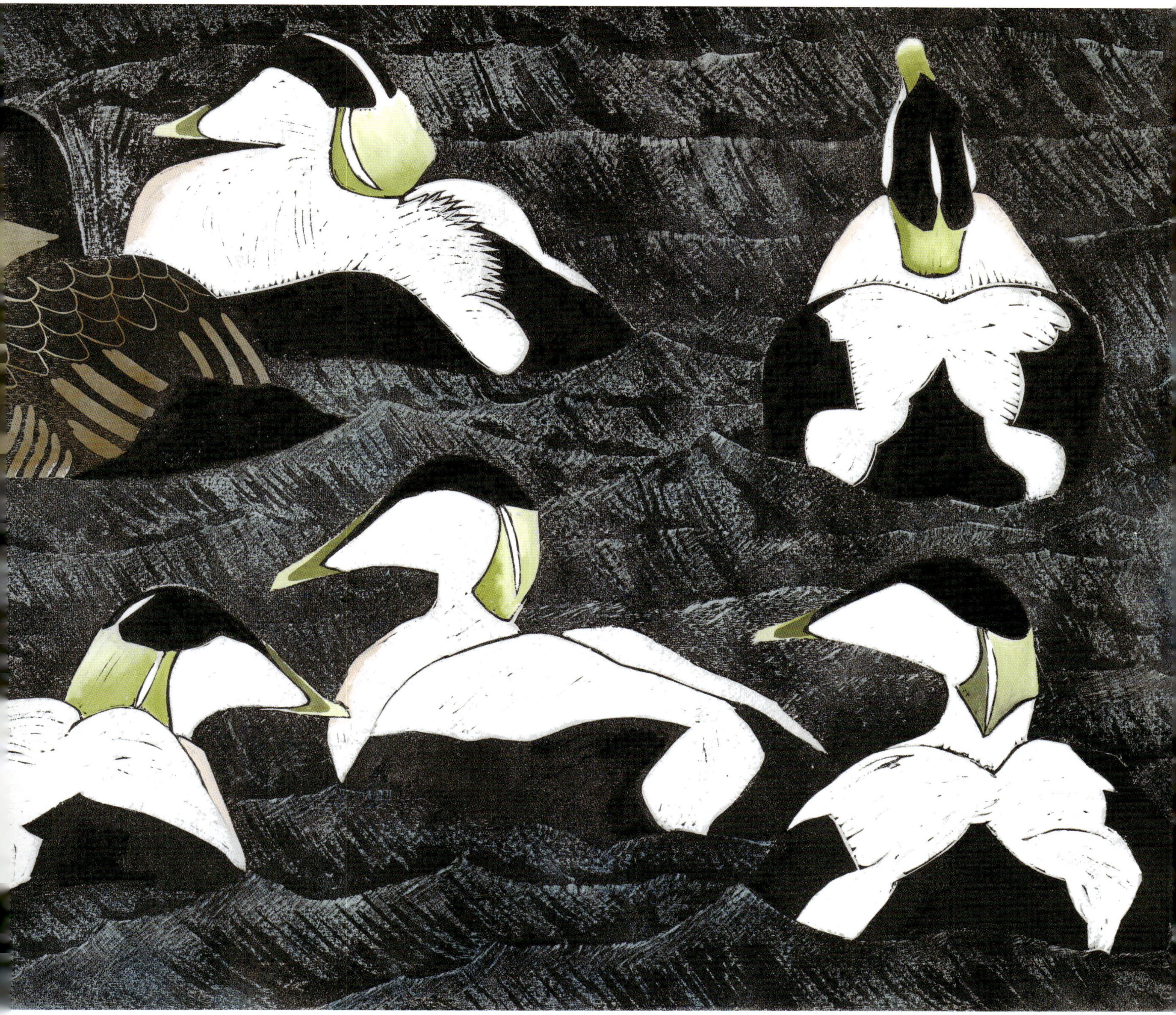

A RAFT OF EIDERS,
73 cm x 53 cm, 2010

The water and the female bird have been etched and the male birds cut. I used an engraver to increase the depth of the etch in some areas. The print is made onto a dampened coloured cotton rag paper through the press and then hand coloured. These birds were very close to the shore at South Queensferry.

Embossing

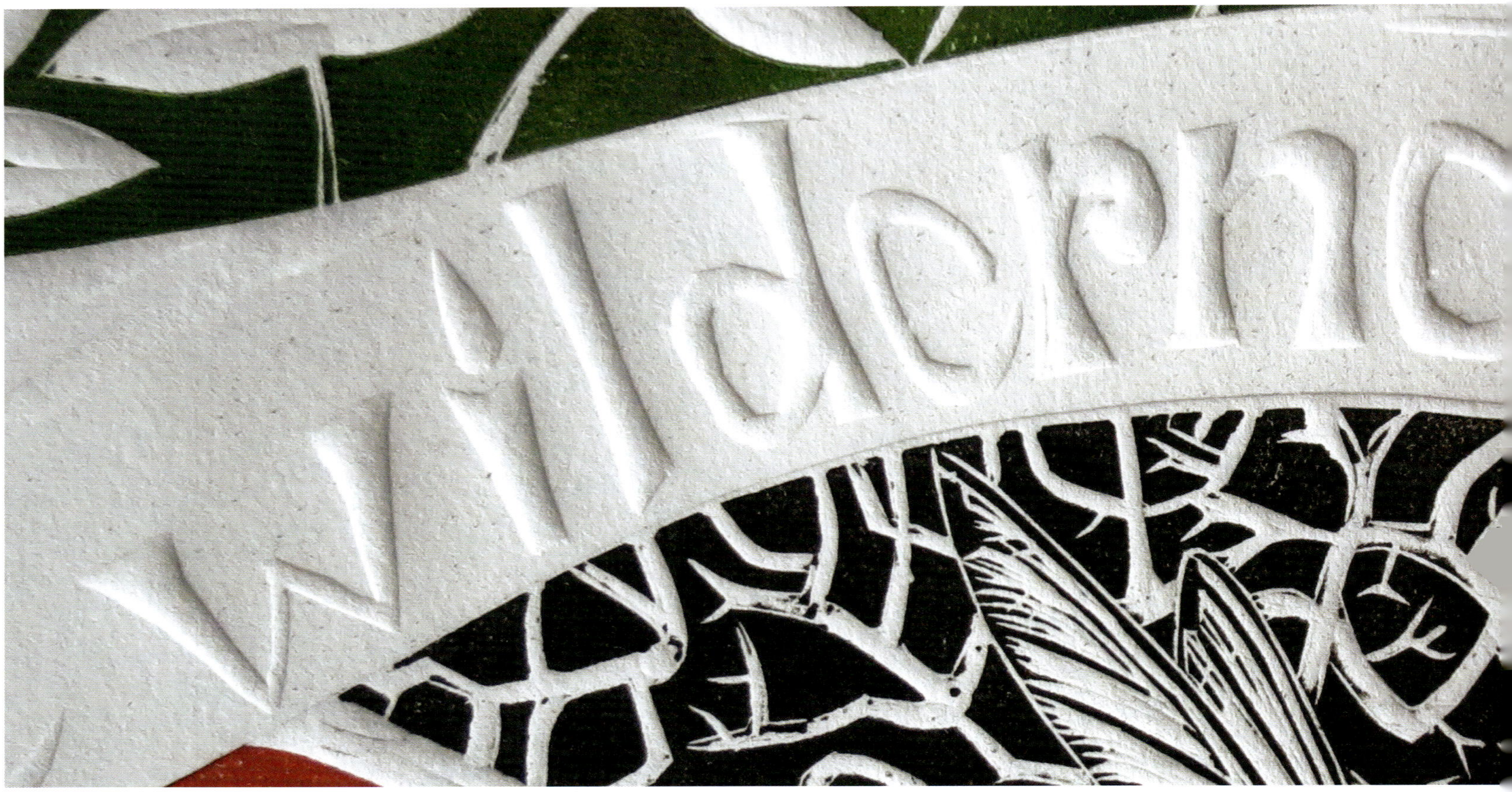

Because lino is thin enough to pass through an etching press, it is possible to use a clean, freshly cut, linocut to emboss a dampened sheet of paper. The paper has to be a reasonably thick rag paper, but needn't be smooth (in fact a rough paper will be more interesting as the surface texture will flatten against the lino, but not elsewhere). I use three etching blankets and substantial pressure. It is seldom possible to print a clean embossing once the plate has been inked, no matter how carefully it is cleaned, so it is a good idea to take off a small edition before inking the plate and printing it conventionally.

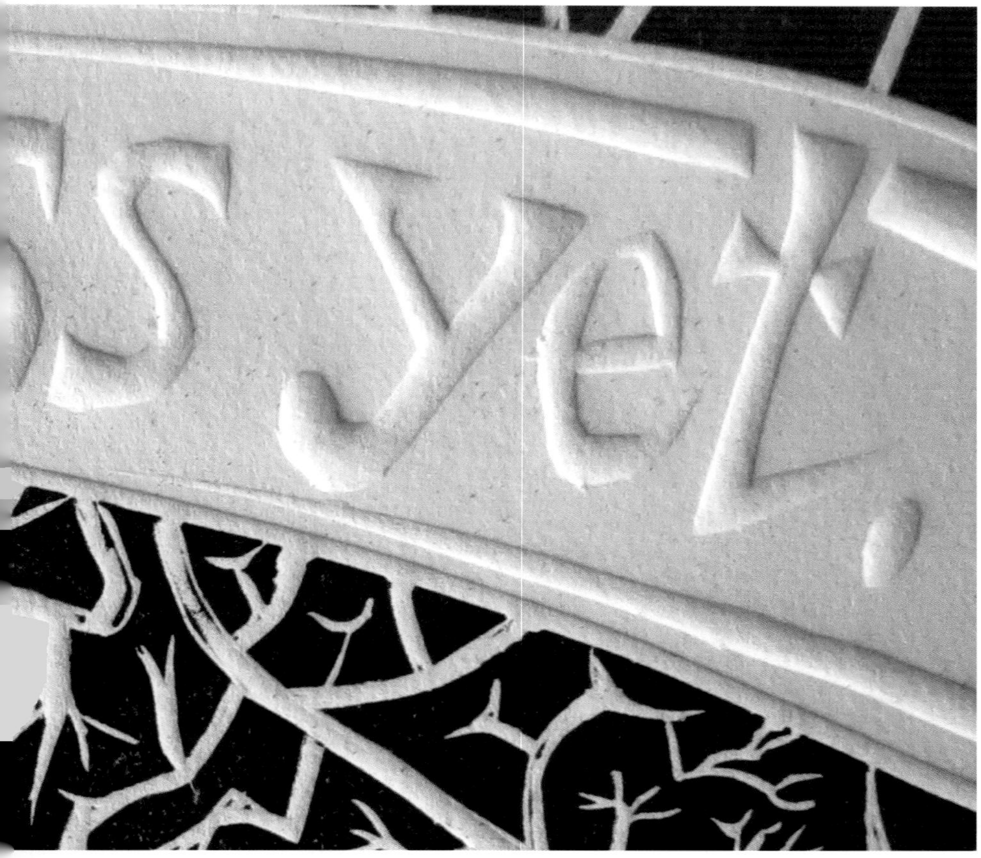

EMBOSSED LETTERING FROM FORSINARD (DETAIL),
70 cm x 31 cm, 2011

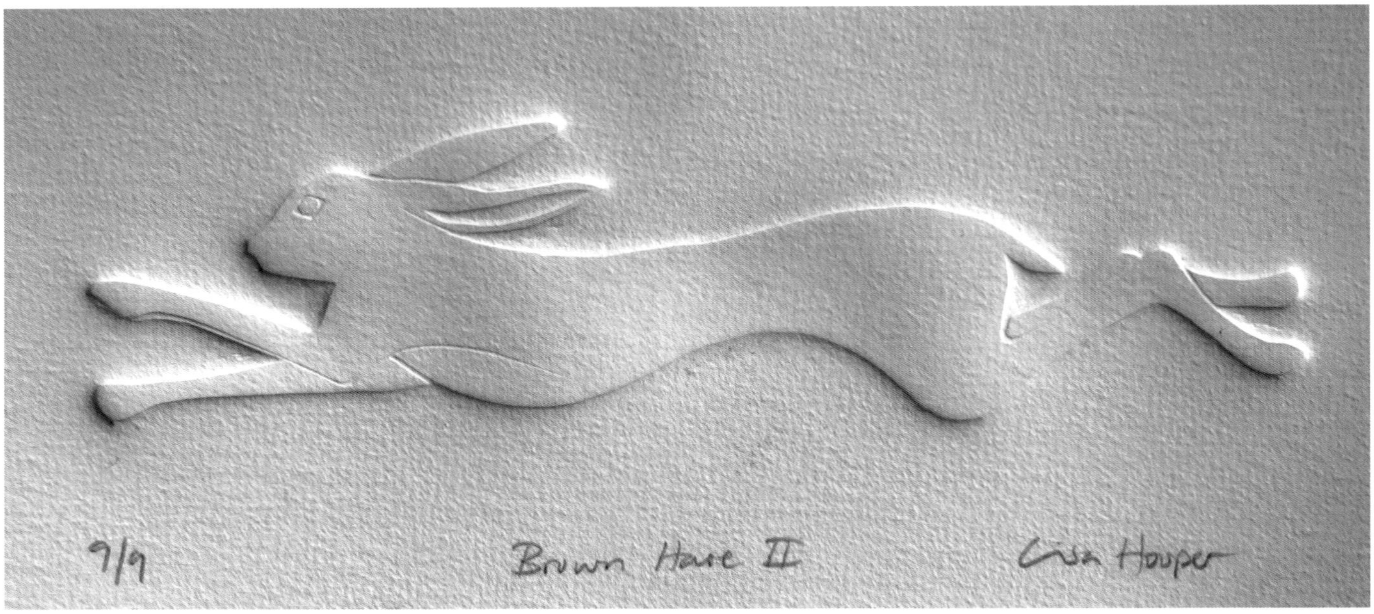

Brown hare embossing,
48 cm x 22 cm, 2008

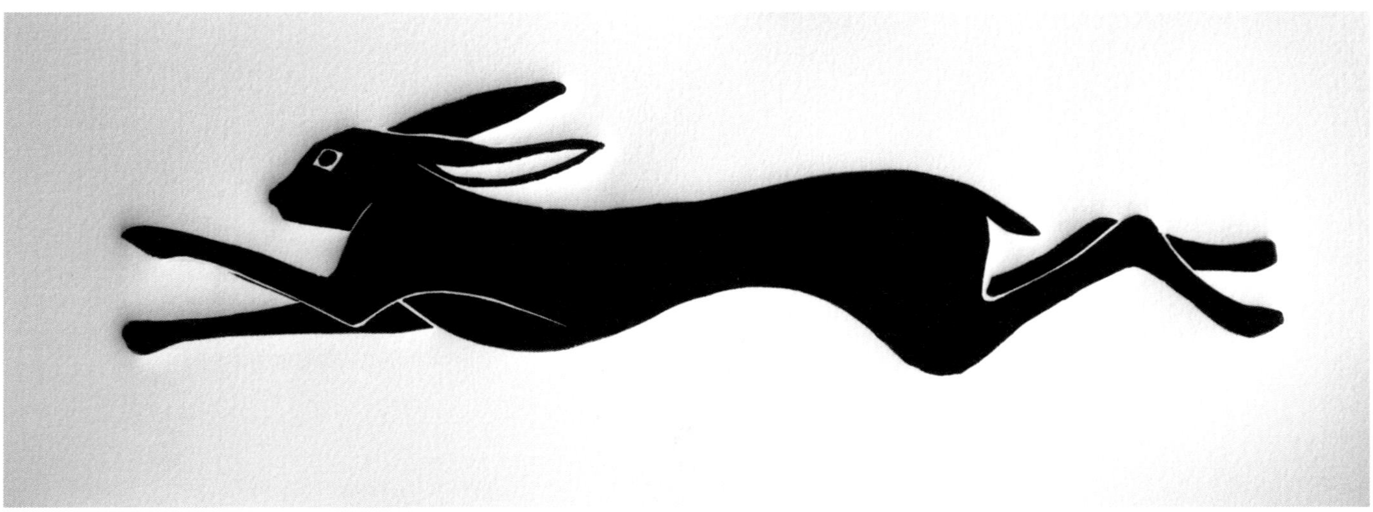

Brown hare,
48 cm x 22 cm, 2008

Linocut, printed in brown.

People often ask "How long did it take you to do that?". It's an odd question. In a way the answer is "My whole life". Given this reply, the child of some friends came up with a variant, which is perhaps a better question: "How long would it take someone who didn't know how to do it?"
An artist friend once told me people who ask how long something took really want to know what inspired you, but I'm not so sure. People still want to see some industry, some craft, in this age of instant gratification.

As for inspiration, that can come from all over the place: an interesting piece of paper, some driftwood, some birds spotted on a walk, a photograph reconsidered. Sometimes a picture pops into my head, fully formed, just before sleep. One thing is certain, new experiences and places inspire and so do new media. And the more you are working creatively, the more ideas you have.

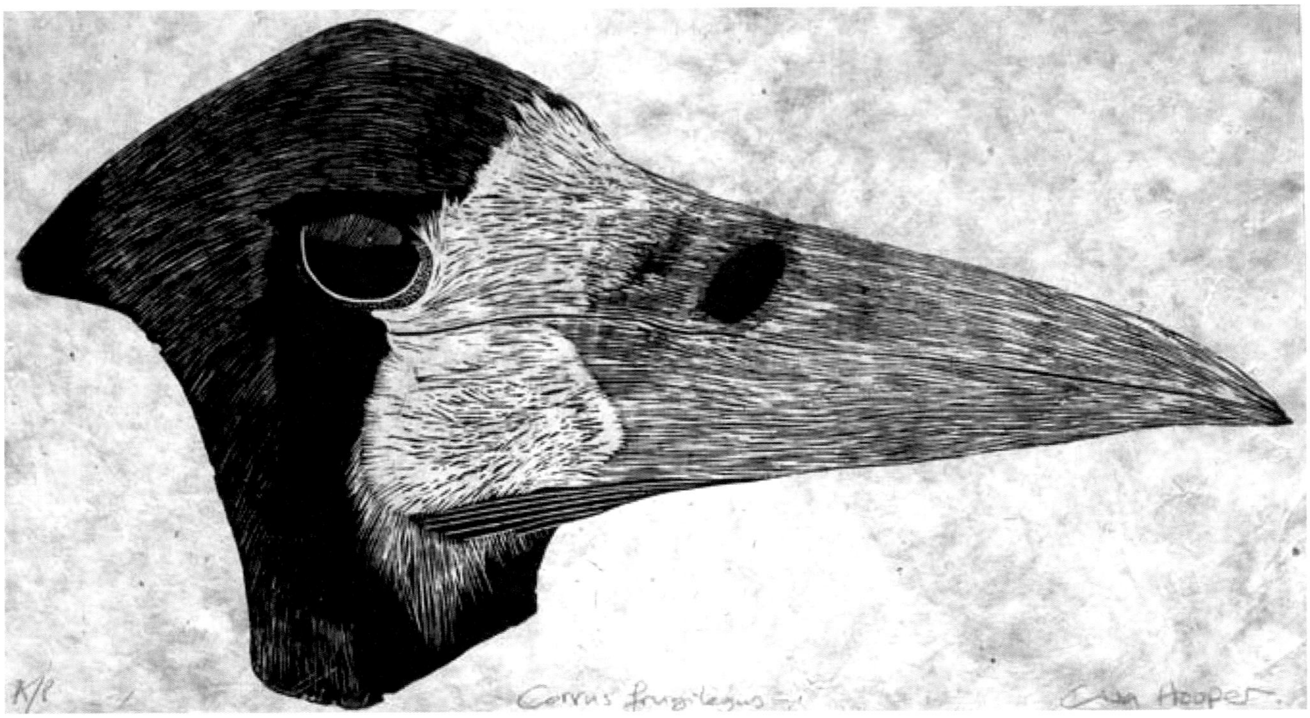

Corvus frugilegus,
56 cm x 31 cm, 2010

Although the intricate style is not very typical of my work, it is quite challenging to use a found object in this way. I have experimented by printing this onto batik backgrounds and different papers to try to make less illustrative pieces.

Driftwood prints

Living close to the sea, there is always temptation to be found on the strandline. And not just from driftwood. I once found a piece of internal display board which had broken into the shape of a rook's head. I hardly trimmed anything off, but obviously carved out the detail to produce the print above.

But on the beach, driftwood is the main attraction. The grain is very often enhanced by the wear and tear of being in the sea, although equally printing from driftwood can be disappointing. Unseen damage to the surface becomes obvious and surface grain proves either too deep or too shallow to print successfully. Just occasionally it works.

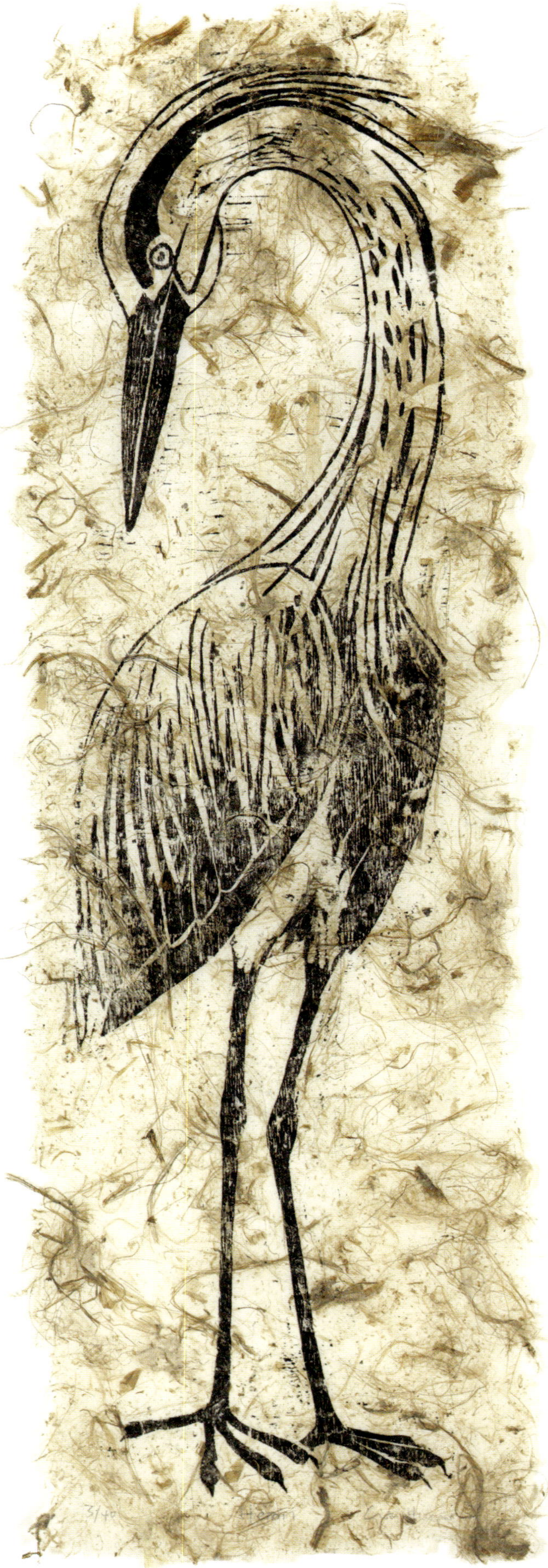

Heron,
21 cm x 70 cm, 2011

This was an example of the piece of wood suggesting the image. It was somehow heron shaped. This piece also illustrates the power of a good choice of paper. The fibrous banana paper complements the primitive simplicity of the image.

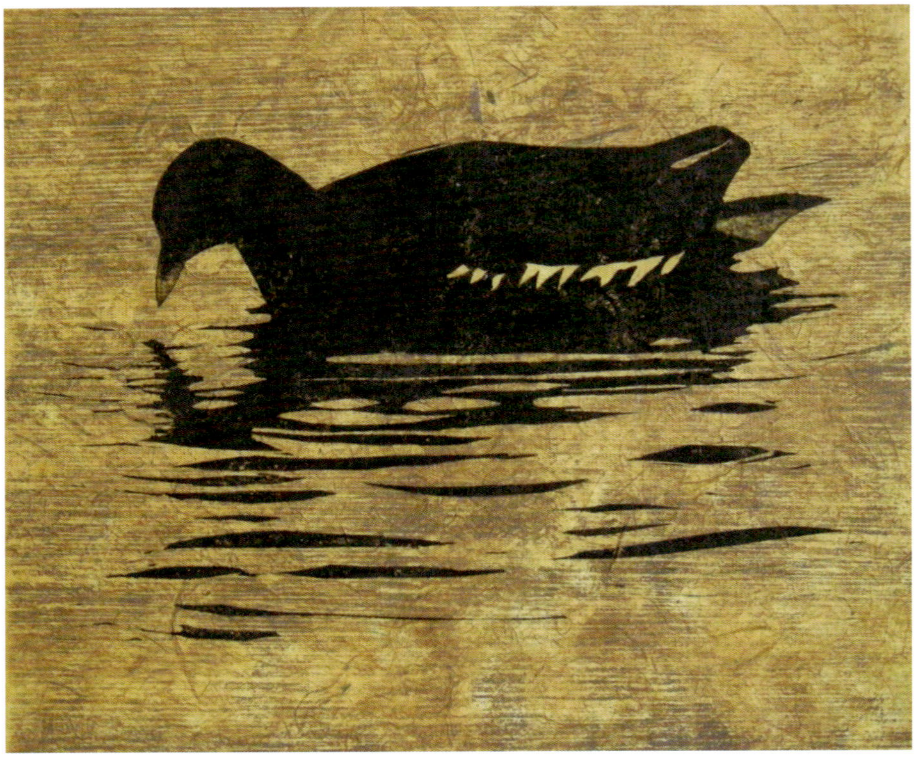

Moorhen,
26 cm x 23 cm, 2009

This was printed onto gold paper to enhance the atmosphere of morning or evening light and to complement the simple colour scheme.

Combinations of driftwood and linocut can also be successful. The moorhen was made by printing the water from a piece of driftwood, in a sort of taupe colour, carefully masking the white parts of the bird. Then the bird linocut was overprinted in black, and I wiped the areas of the bird where there was a slight highlight. These techniques owe much to Thelma Sykes, who masterfully combines wood and linocuts in her prints, using the wood-grain to represent water.

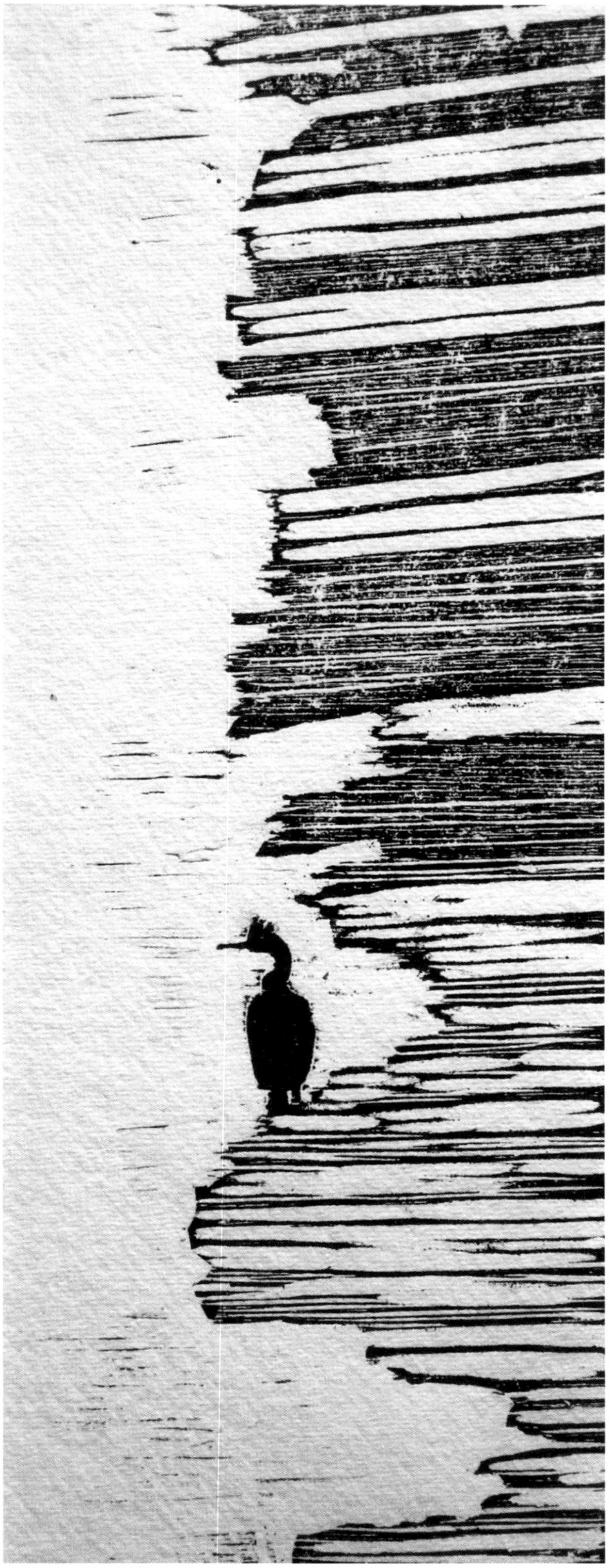

A proof from the piece of wood found in Orkney with the cliffs and bird cut.

Careful registration and the selective use of grain can also be effective. The print of a shag at Yesnaby was suggested by the similarity between the grain of driftwood and the structure of the cliffs on Orkney. The piece of driftwood from which the cliffs are printed was actually found on South Ronaldsay. I had to fill and sand the grain of the area where the bird silhouette appears, as I wanted it to print solid black. I cut the profile of the cliff carefully, having trimmed the wood so that the orientation of the strata was just right.

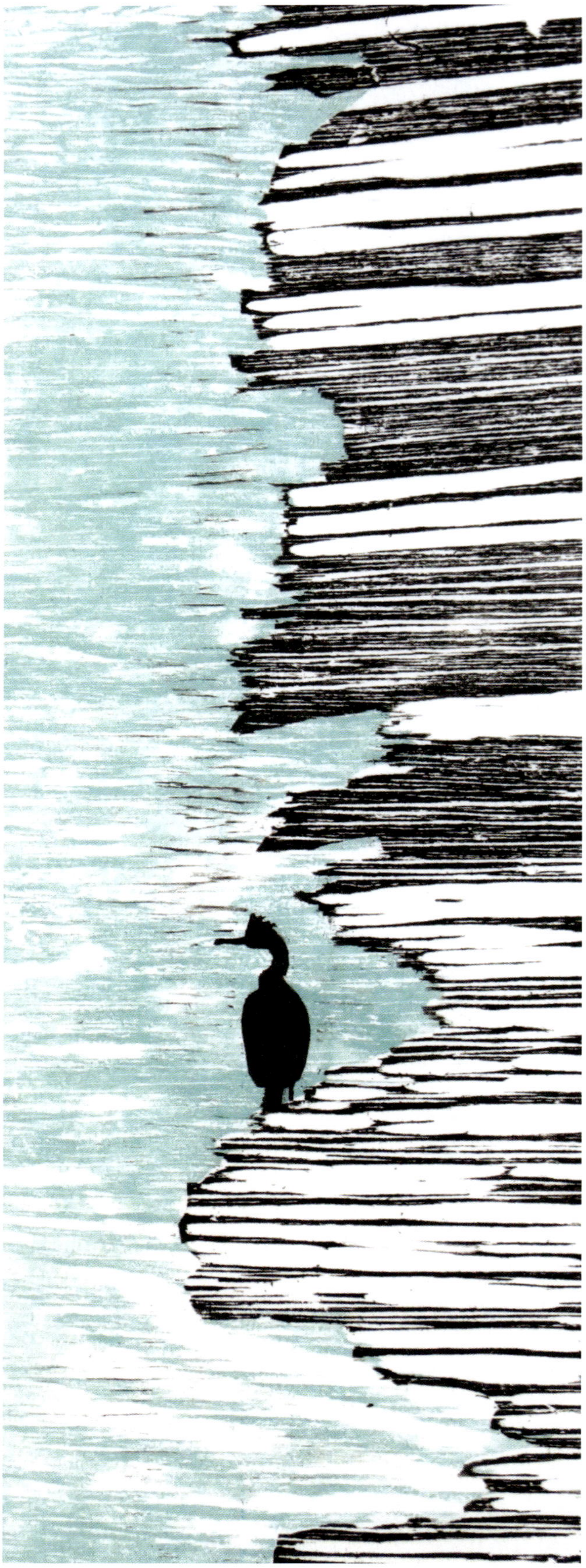

Shag, Yesnaby,
25 cm x 45 cm, 2012

The second piece of wood printed alongside, in blue. The two plates come together showing how wood grain can suggest water and rock strata. The piece was later finished by hand colouring the cliffs only.

Then I found a piece of driftwood locally with a good "sea" grain on it, selected an area which had a good set of marks in the foreground and cut a complementary block to the cliff. I then printed the blocks in separate colours, registering them so that they met.

Introducing colour to relief prints

'My heart in hiding
Stirred for a bird, - the achieve of, the mastery of the thing!'

From *The Windhover*, Gerard Manley Hopkins

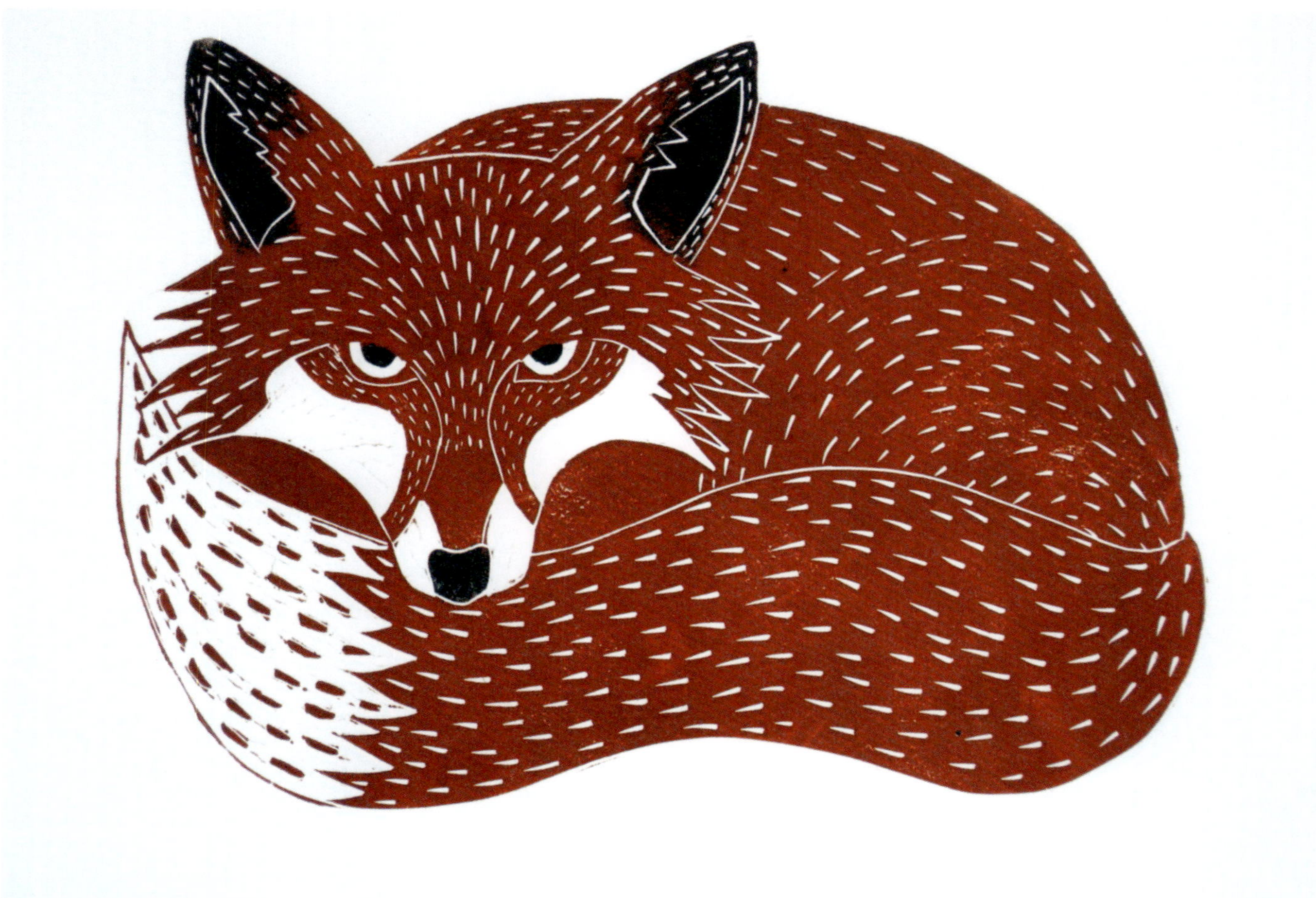

Fox,
24 cm x 20 cm, 2014

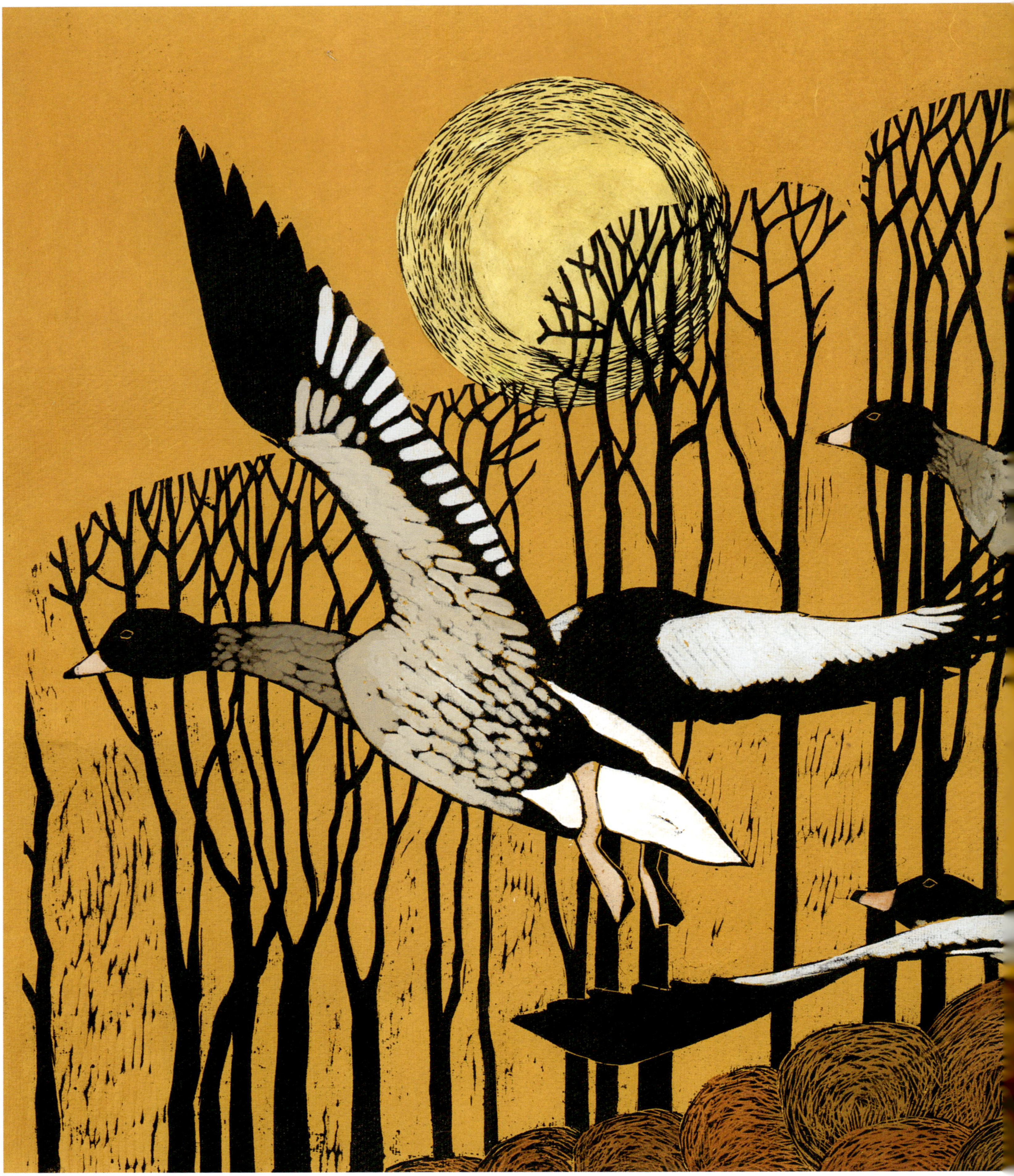

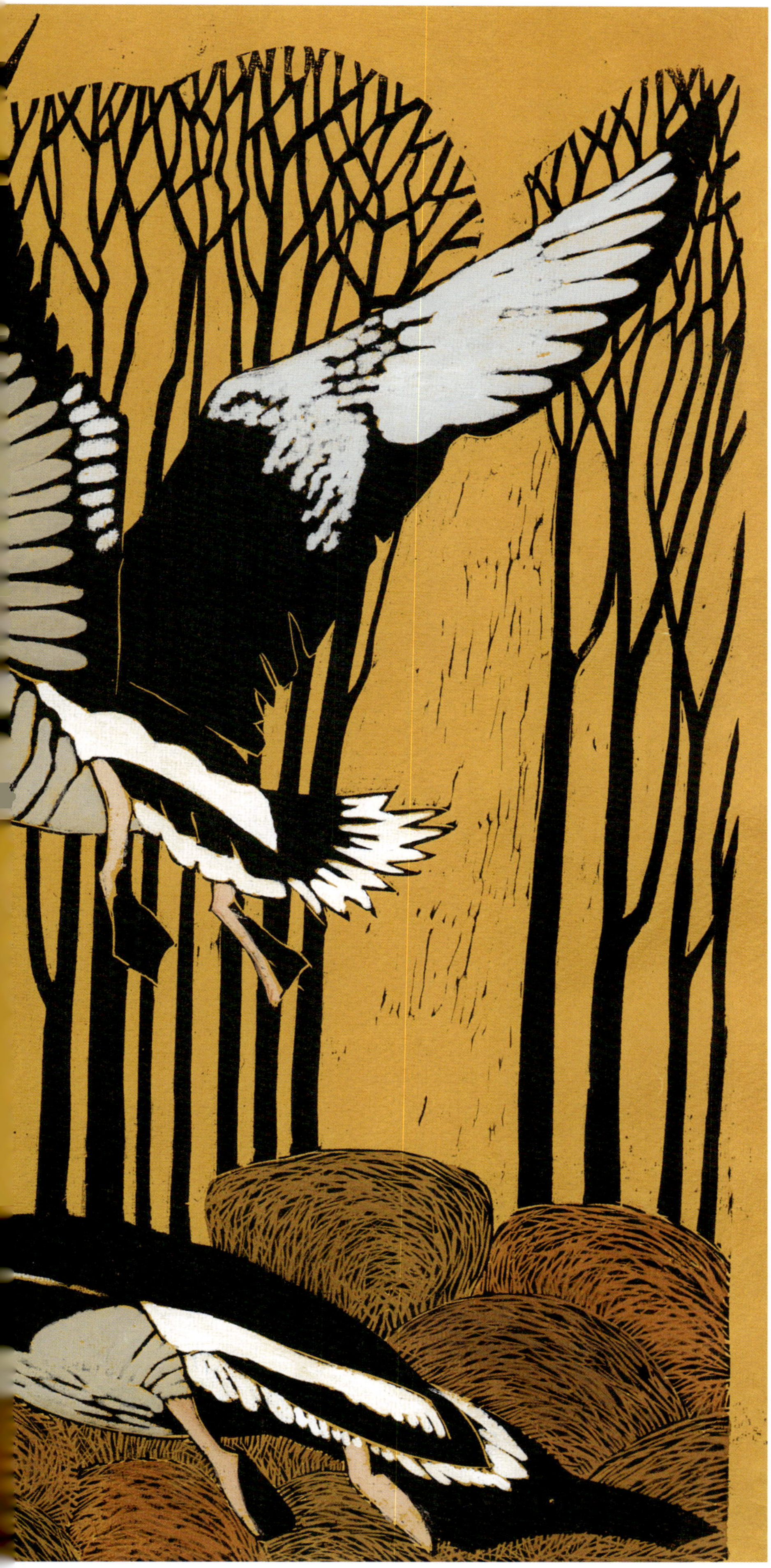

Pinkfeet rising,
72 cm x 54 cm, 2013

This print was inspired by the flocks of wintering geese on the Rhins at the extreme western tip of Dumfries and Galloway. The rows of beech trees are a particular feature of the landscape.

Adding colour to a single plate print.

Designing and printing a single plate in one block is an interesting discipline but it has its limitations. Colour is such an important part of our visual world. As I worked on relief printing I quickly started to explore ways of introducing colour to my work.

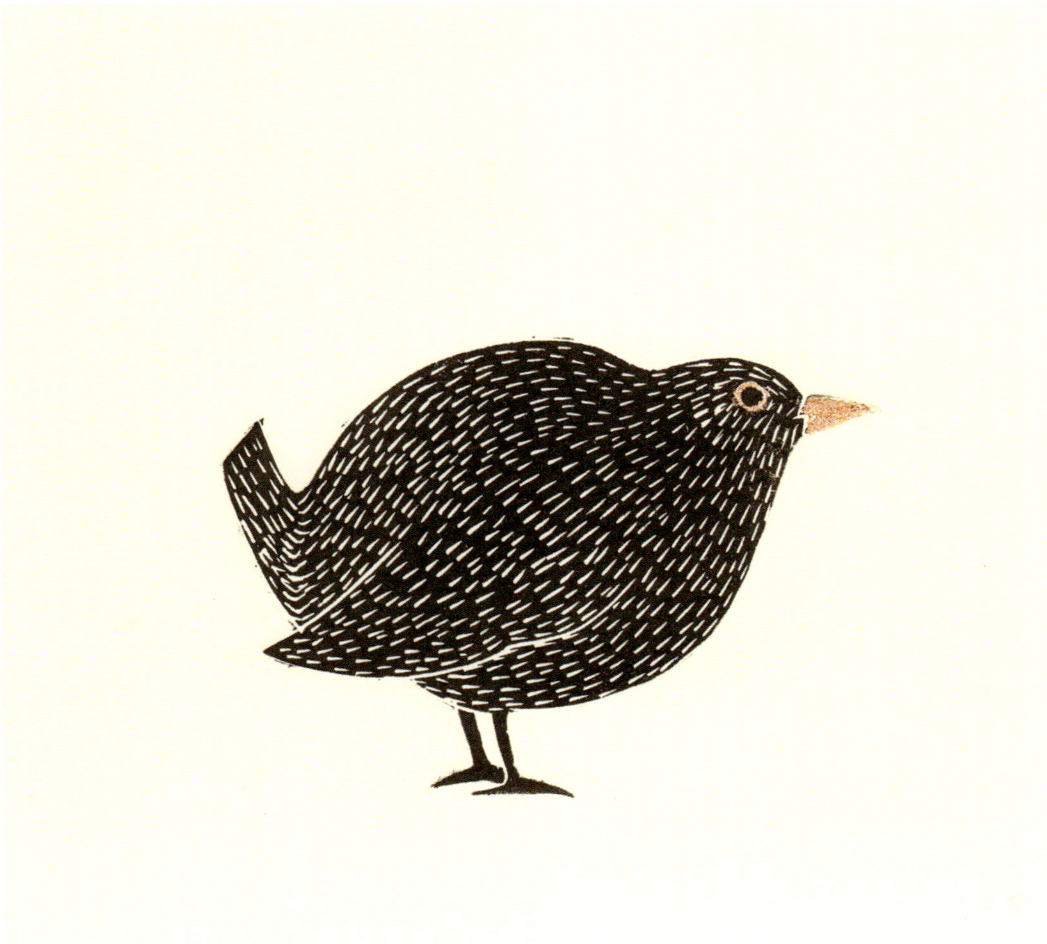

Fat Bird,
18 cm x 14 cm, 2013

Inspired by Inuit art, this simple one colour image has been lifted by the hand application of copper leaf around the eye and on the bill of the bird.

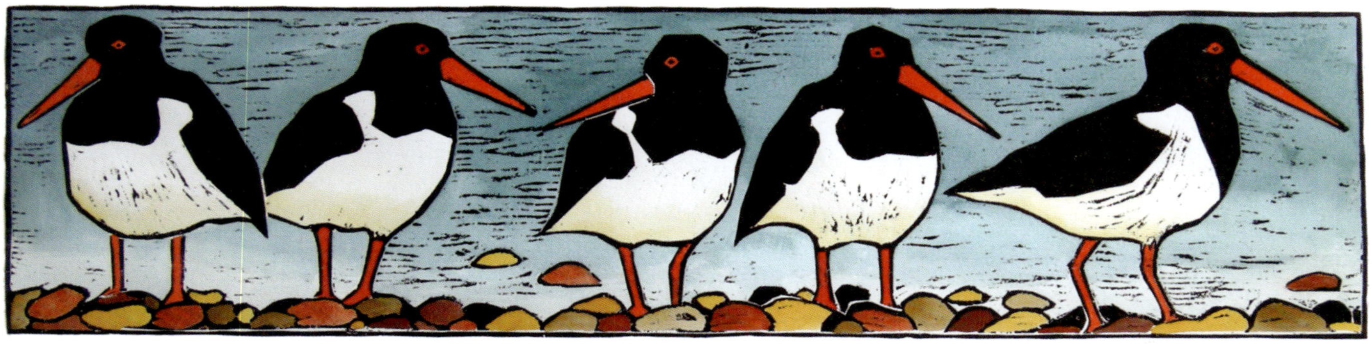

Oystercatchers,
75 cm x 21 cm, 2006

This print was completed relatively soon after moving to Dumfries and Galloway where oystercatchers are ubiquitous.

It's hard to make bird art. First of all it's not just about the bird, it's about the setting, the landscape, the place it lives in, the element it lives in. Birds on white backgrounds won't do (usually!). Then there is the whole issue of accuracy. There doesn't seem to be much point in painting every feather when we have cameras, so I don't want to represent the bird too strictly. On the other hand it has to be a plausible representation of a species – serious proportional or colour errors are unacceptable. So the room for manoeuvre is quite small. For me there is always something about the character of a bird or a group of birds which grabs me. Sometimes this will be about pattern (for instance feather patterns repeating in a group of birds), and sometimes it will be something less easy to describe. Perhaps it is the skulking pose of a blackbird who thinks he is unobserved, perhaps it is the masked gangster in a waxwing or the swagger of rooks. Or maybe it's just their beautiful reflections in water or the strange bold markings on birds such as razorbills.

Whatever this quality is, without it a print will founder and with it, if executed ably, it will fly.

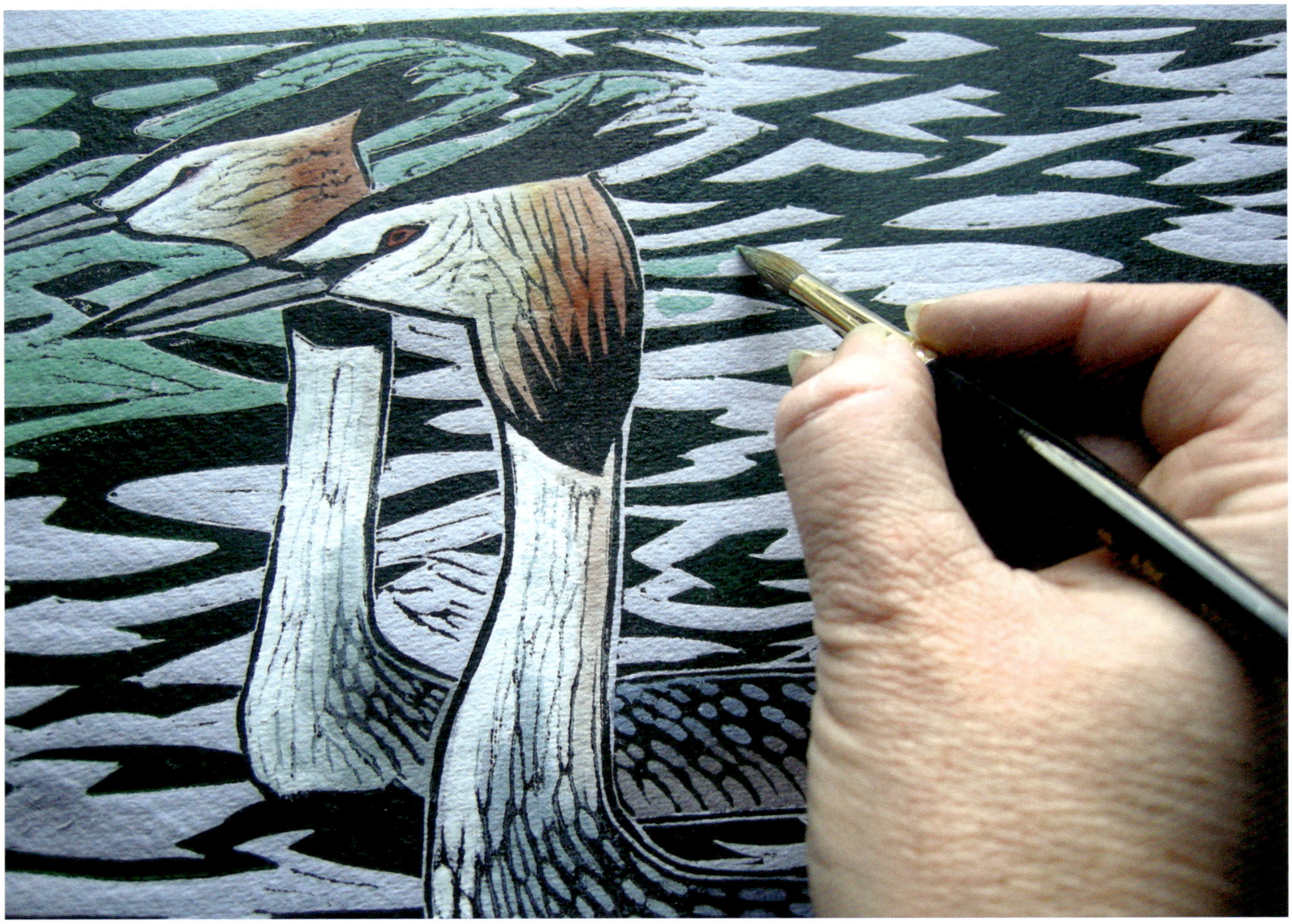

Hand colouring *Let"s dance*.

The simplest method is to print in black with an oil based ink and hand colour the print in water-colour when the print is dry.

Opposite is an example of a print before and after hand colouring. It is also possible to use opaque water-based paints over coloured paper.

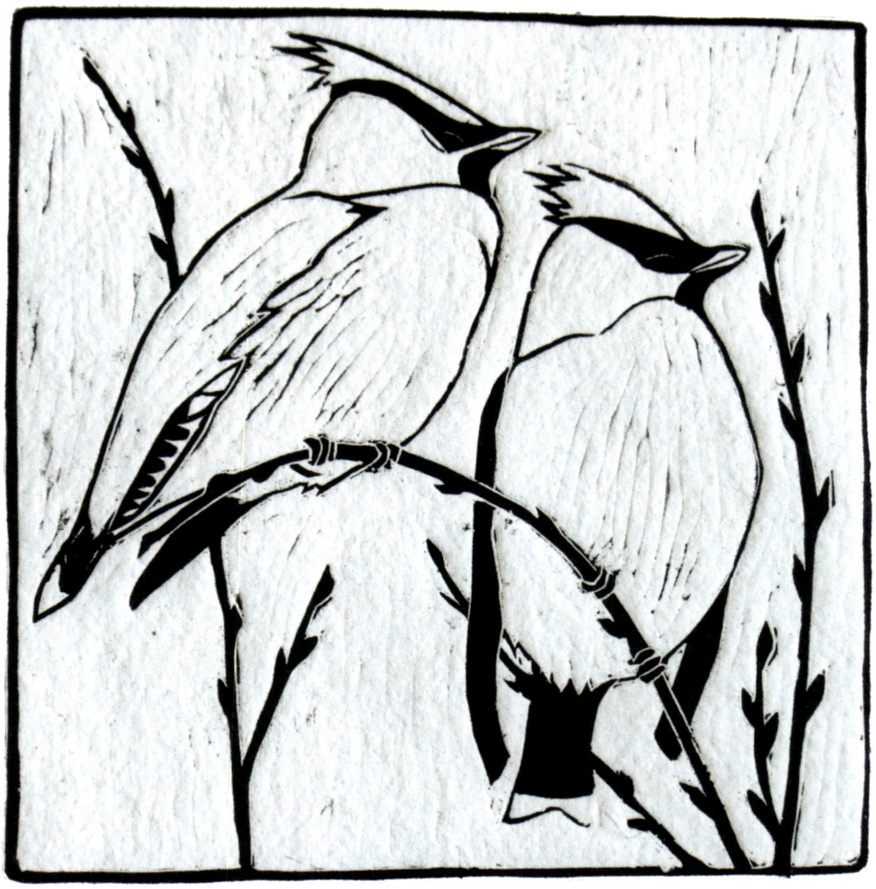

A linocut of Waxwings, printed in black.

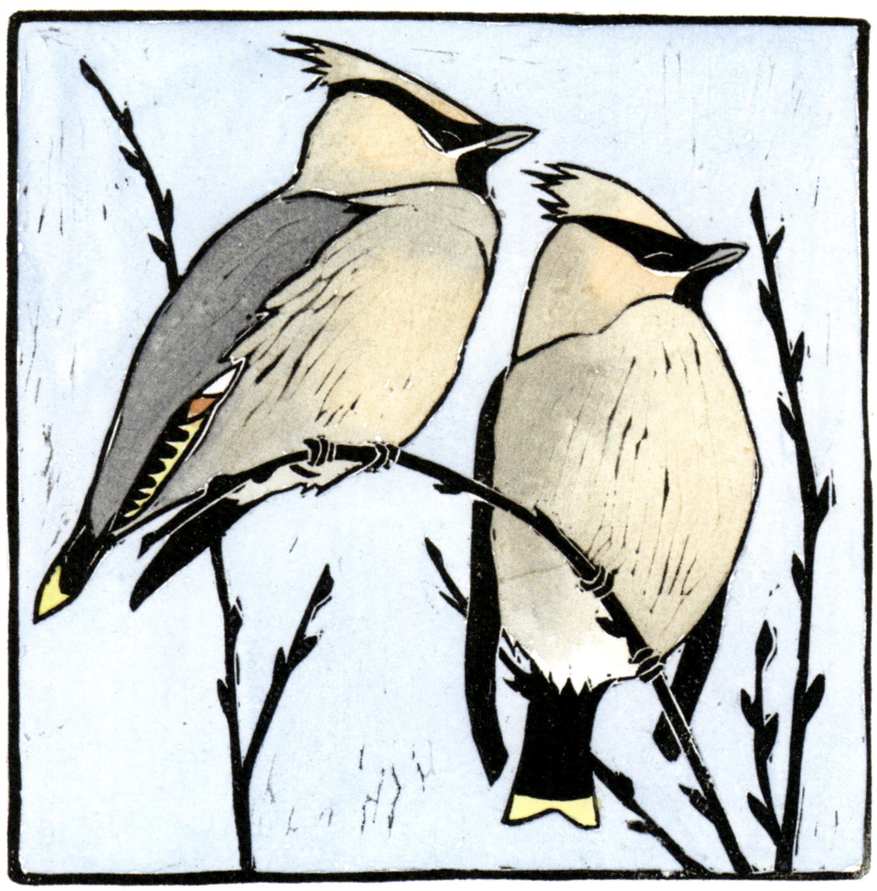

WAXWINGS,
18 cm x 18 cm, 2012

The same print hand coloured.

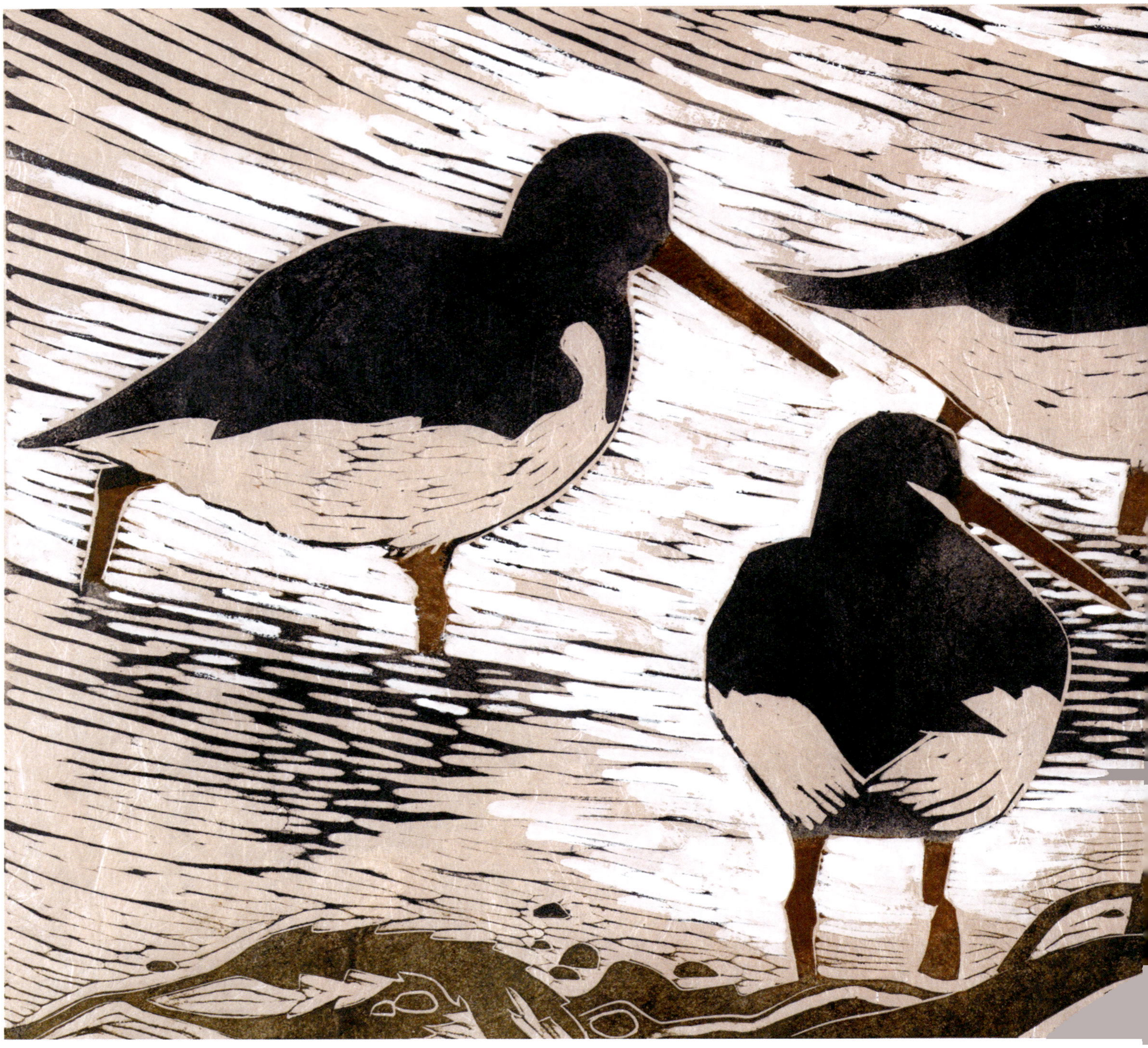

Ebb and Flow,
72 cm x 30 cm, 2010, linocut

This print, on silk paper, is hand coloured. In addition the seaweed has been inked in brown, using a dabber so that it blends into the black.

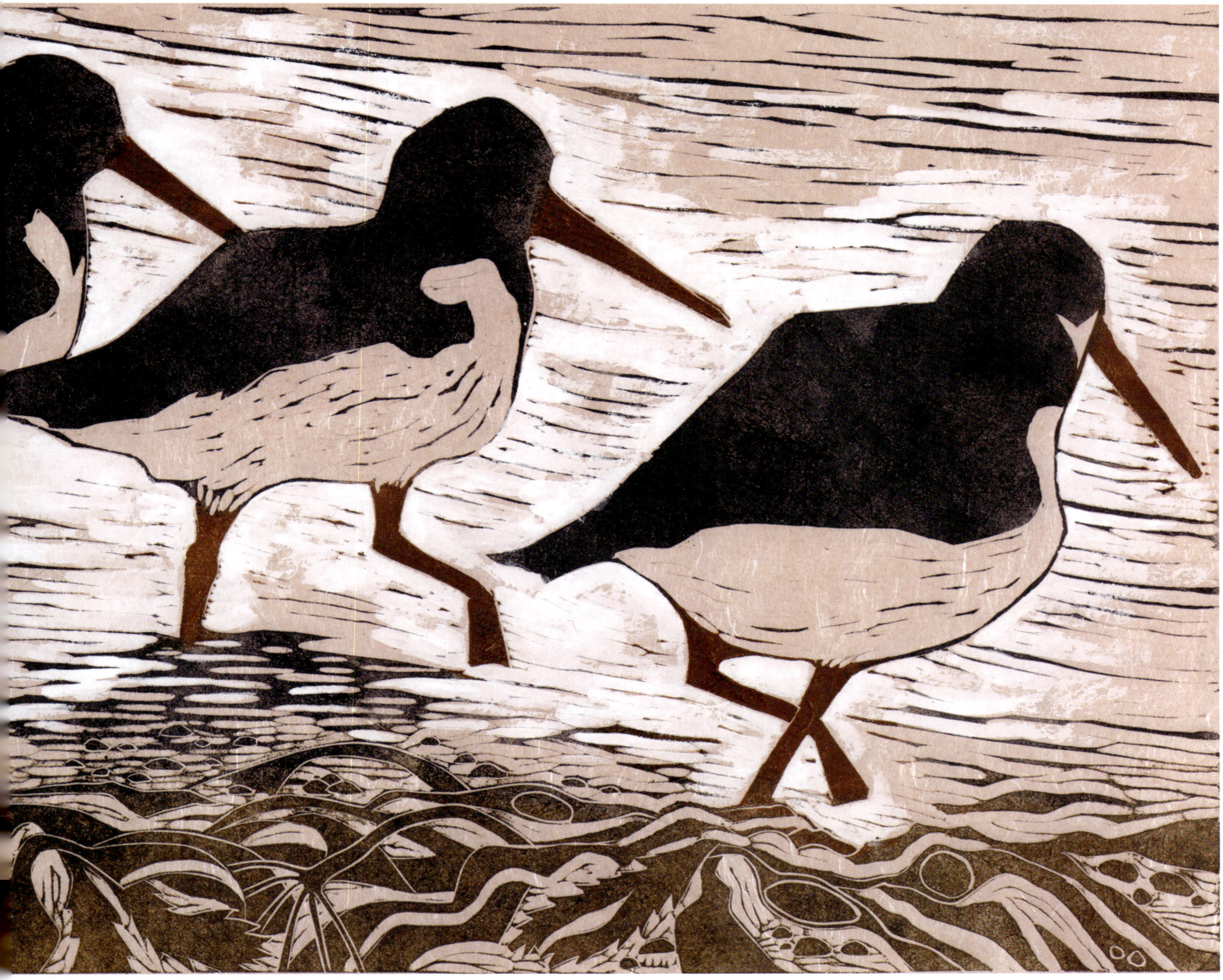

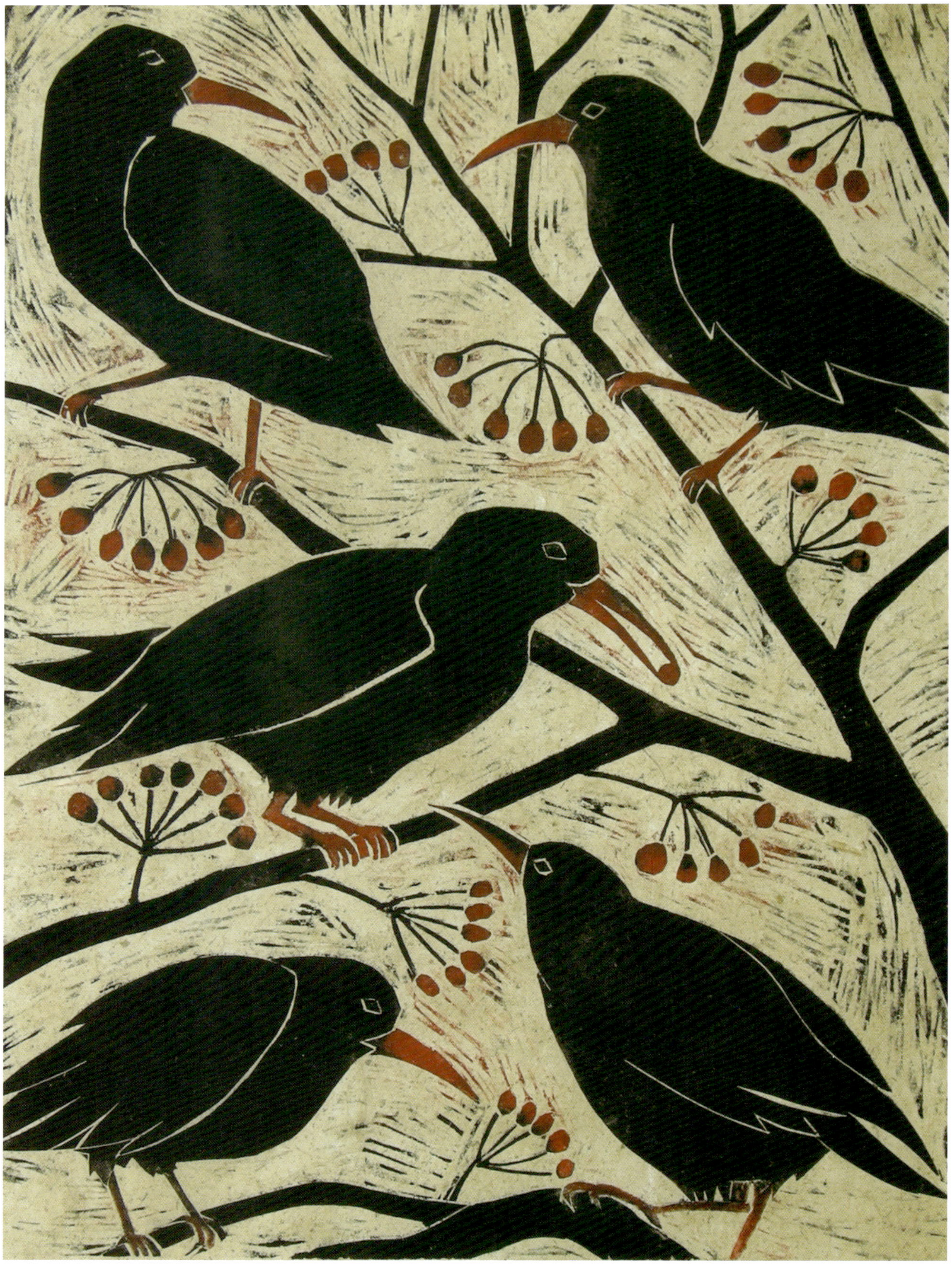

A Chattering of Choughs,
48 cm x 66 cm, 2010

Although this is a simple, single plate print, by printing it onto brownish paper and using a dabber to introduce the red on the bills, feet and berries, the whole print is lifted.

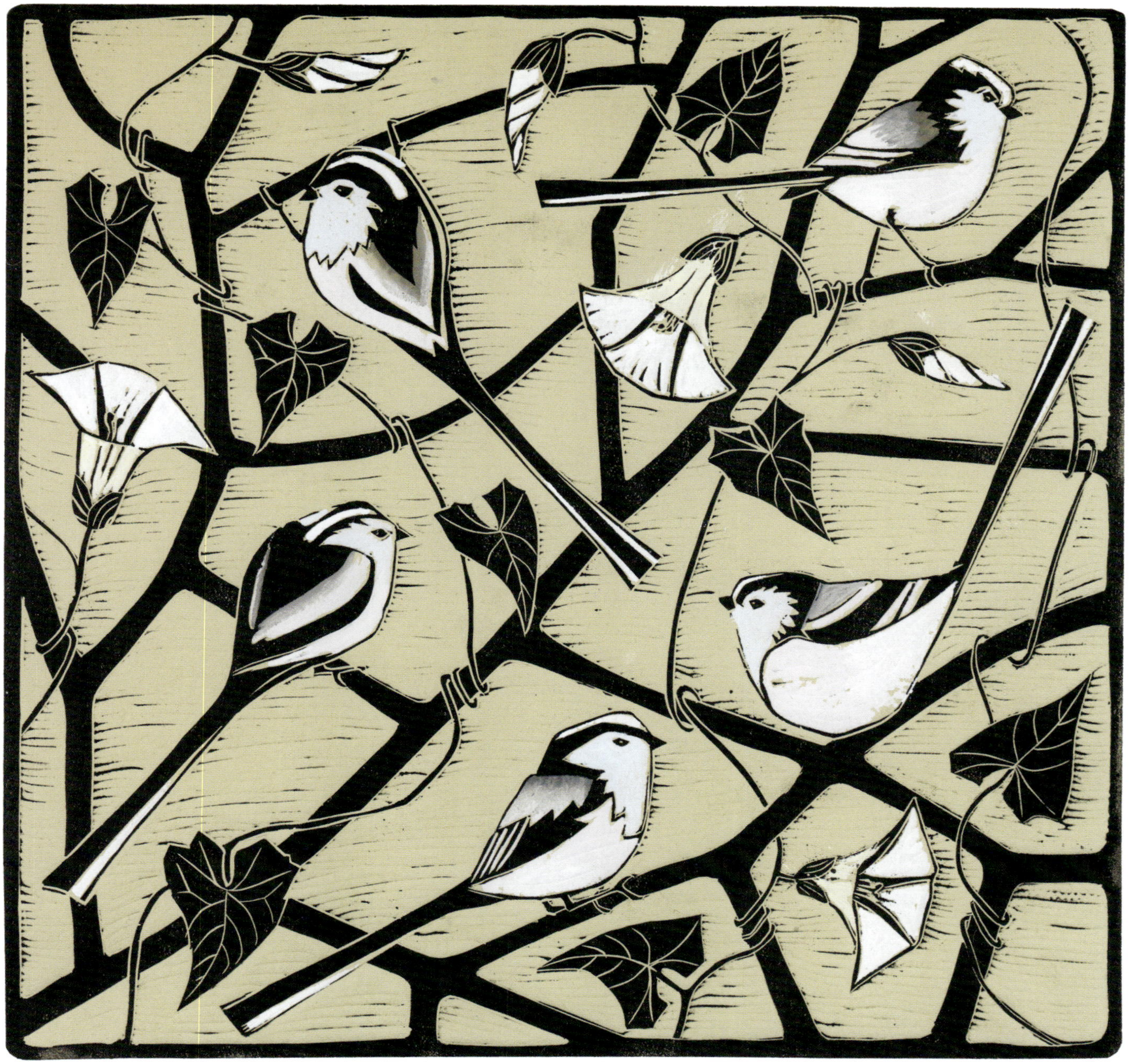

Flying Visit,
37 cm x 35 cm, 2010

This print, which attempts to capture that moment when a flock of long-tailed tits arrives and departs, was printed onto buff paper and hand coloured. I printed about half of the edition on an orange paper which worked just as well.

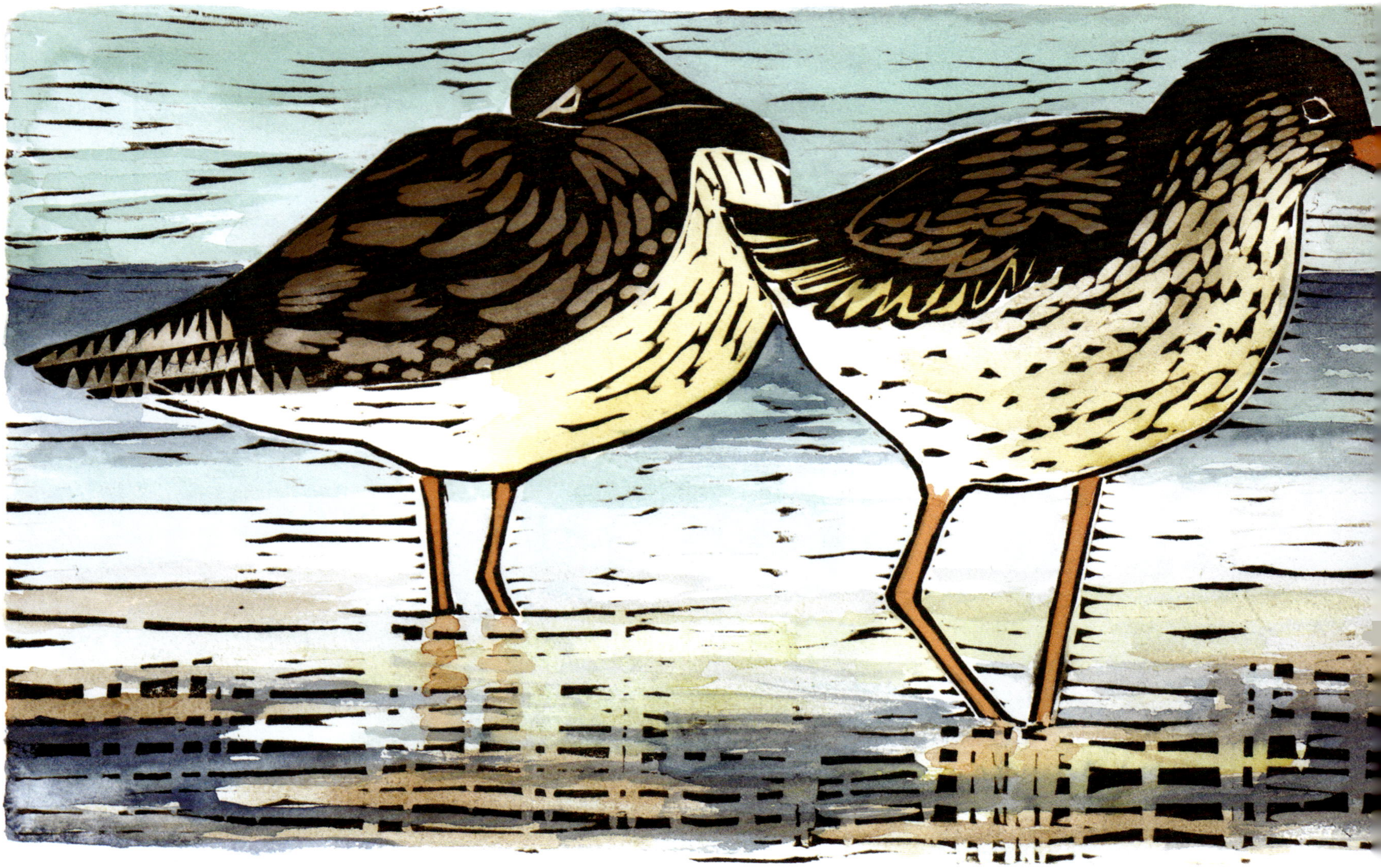

Redshanks,
62 cm x 22 cm, 2009

Quite a complicated plate to hand colour, this woodcut was based on a group of redshanks in the local harbour.

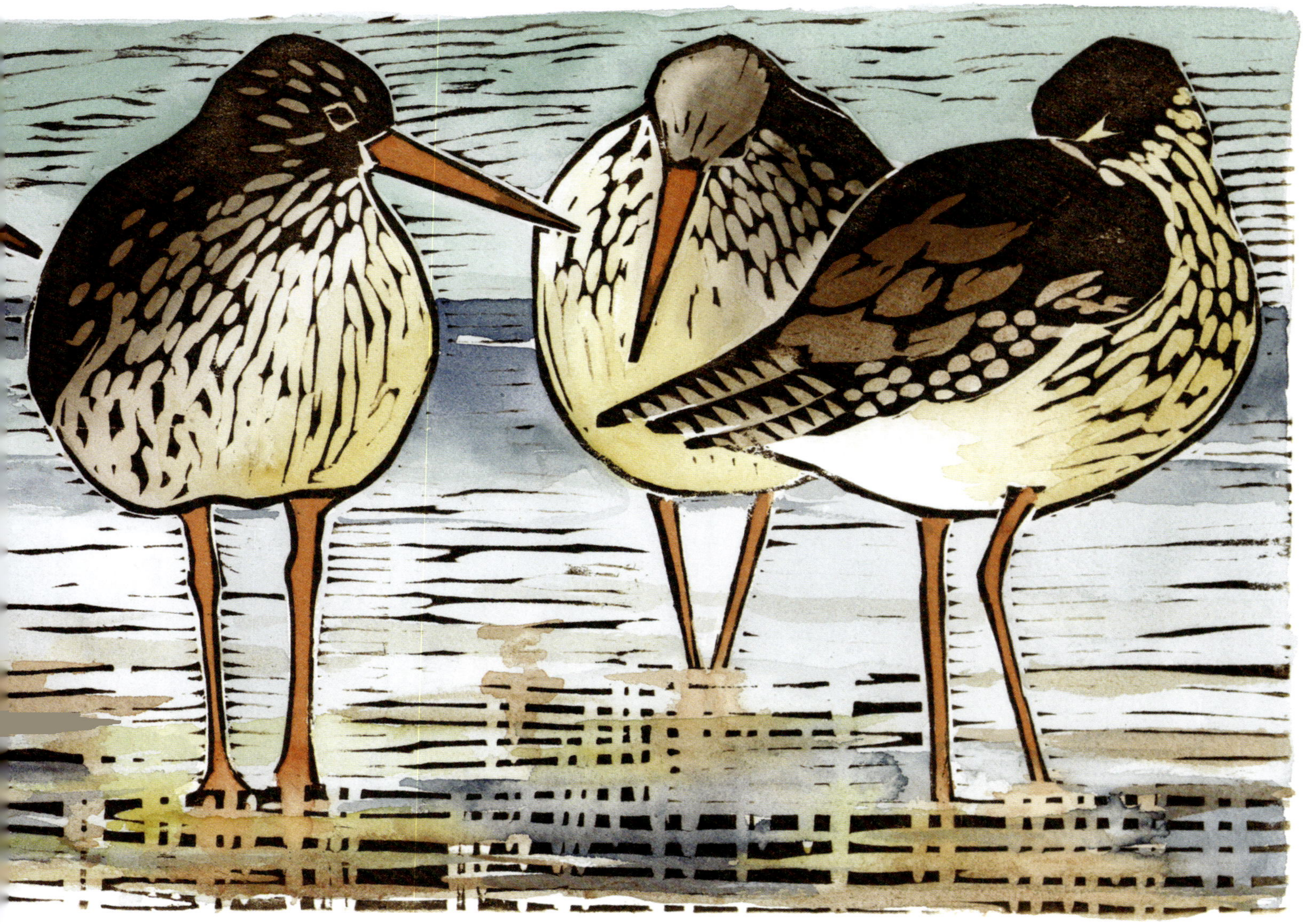

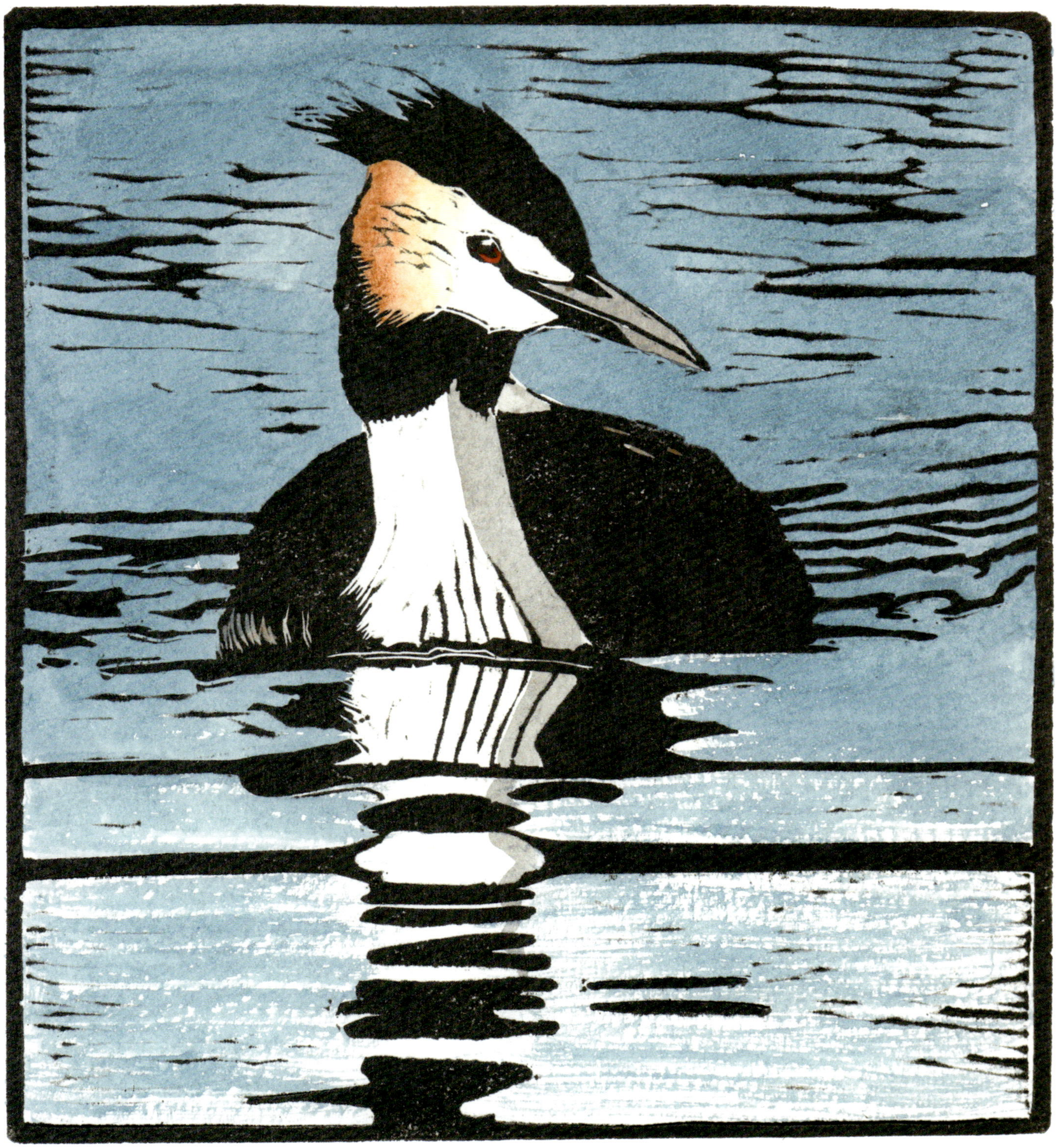

GREAT CRESTED GREBE,
18 cm x 20 cm, 2012

The watercolour brushwork in the foreground on the water, using a dryish brush, suggests light dancing on water.

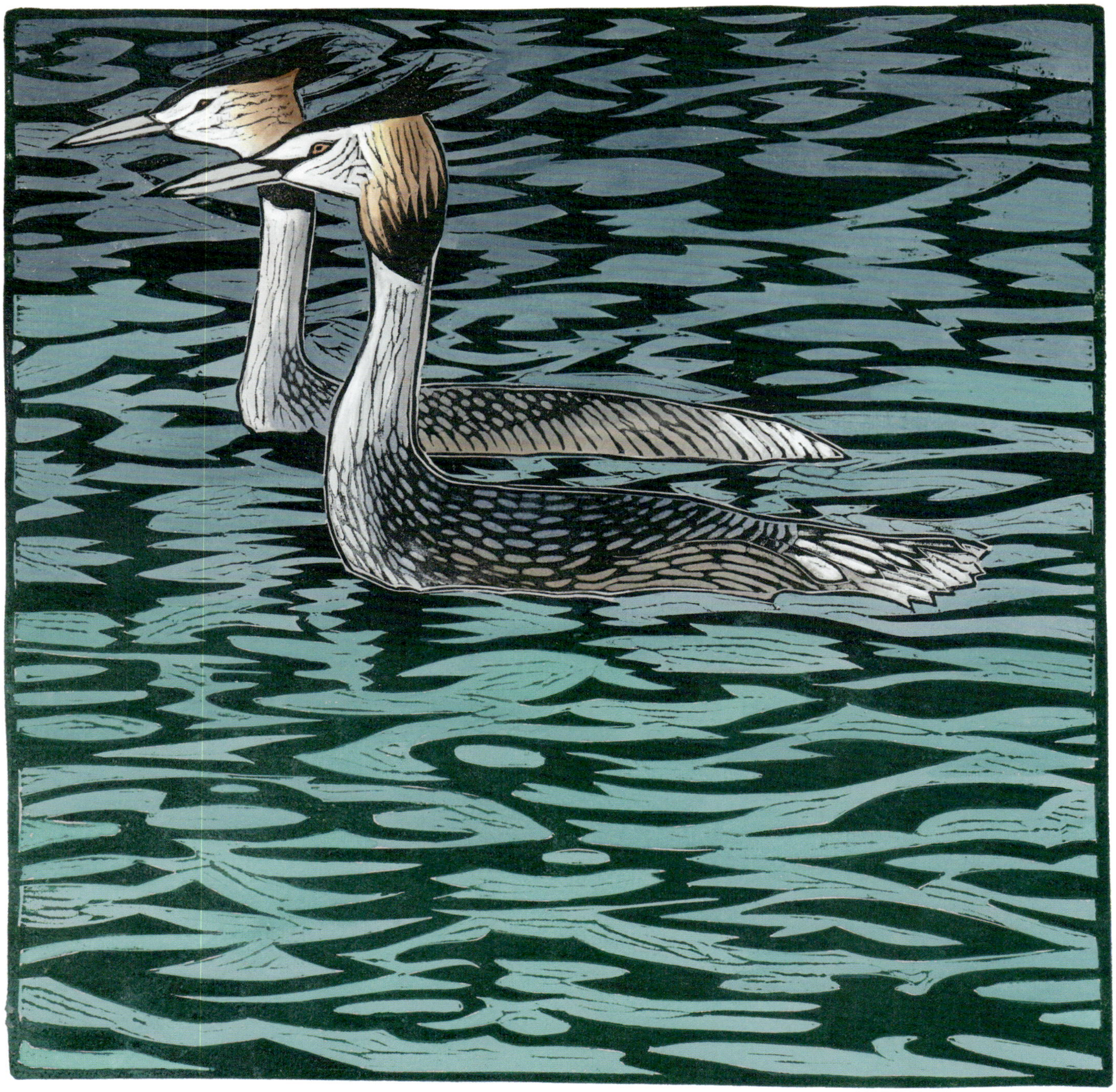

Let's dance,
48 cm x 48 cm, 2011

This pair of courting great crested grebes was printed onto dampened, coloured cotton rag paper, through the press (causing slight embossing) and then hand coloured. I enjoy working with square images and the offbeat composition and bold patterns in the water help to make this a success.

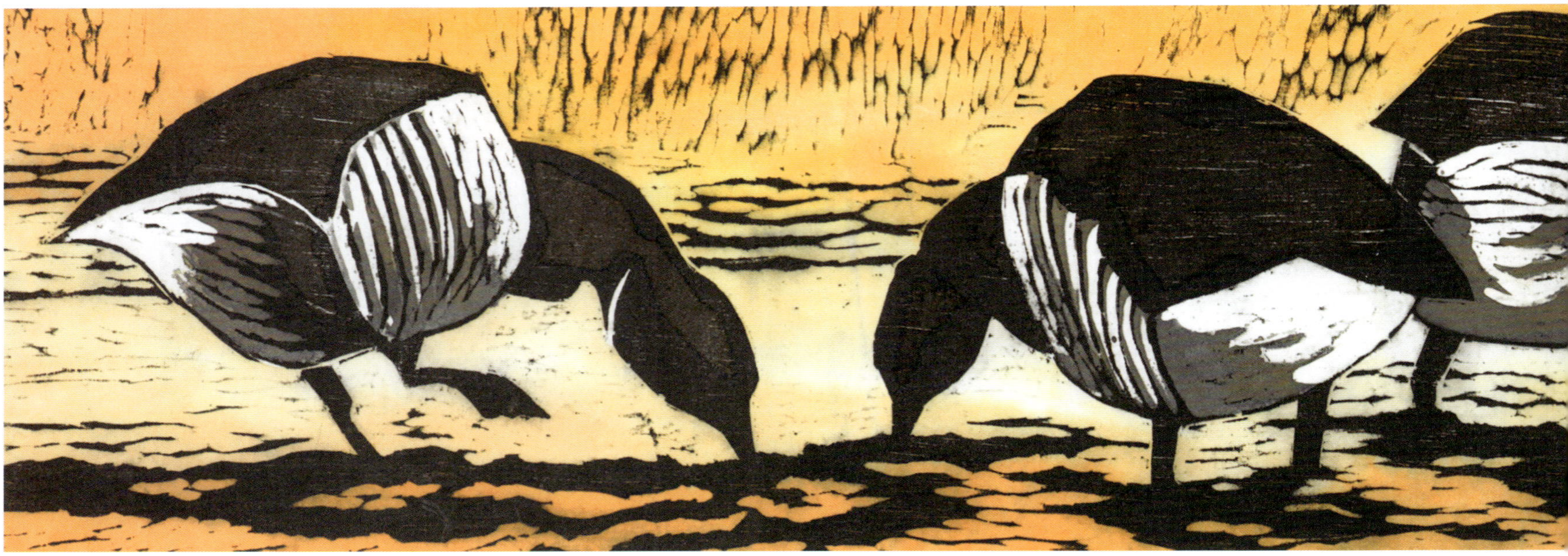

Brent geese, Loch Ryan,
87 cm x 16 cm, 2012

This print, which is very long, had to be made onto Chinese calligraphy paper from a roll. Hand colouring this paper is tricky because paints tend to bleed. I therefore used melted wax as a resist to build up the colours, and ironed the wax off afterwards. The birds were picking over the seaweed at low tide on Loch Ryan, near Stranraer.

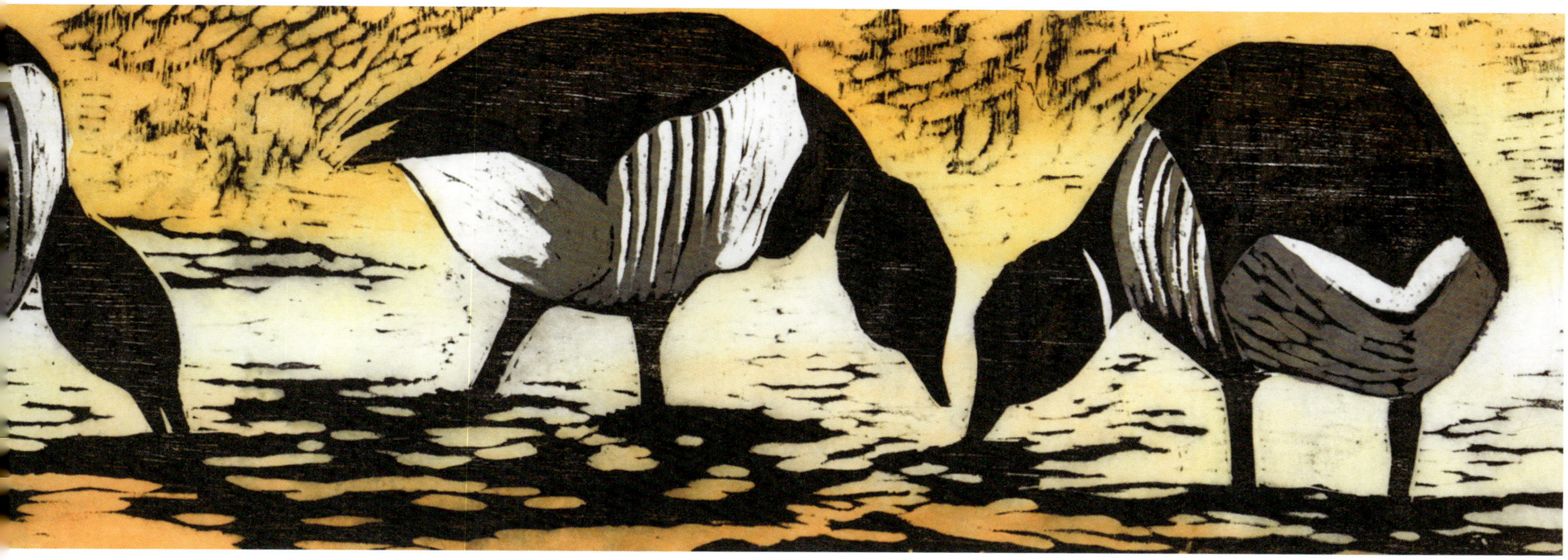

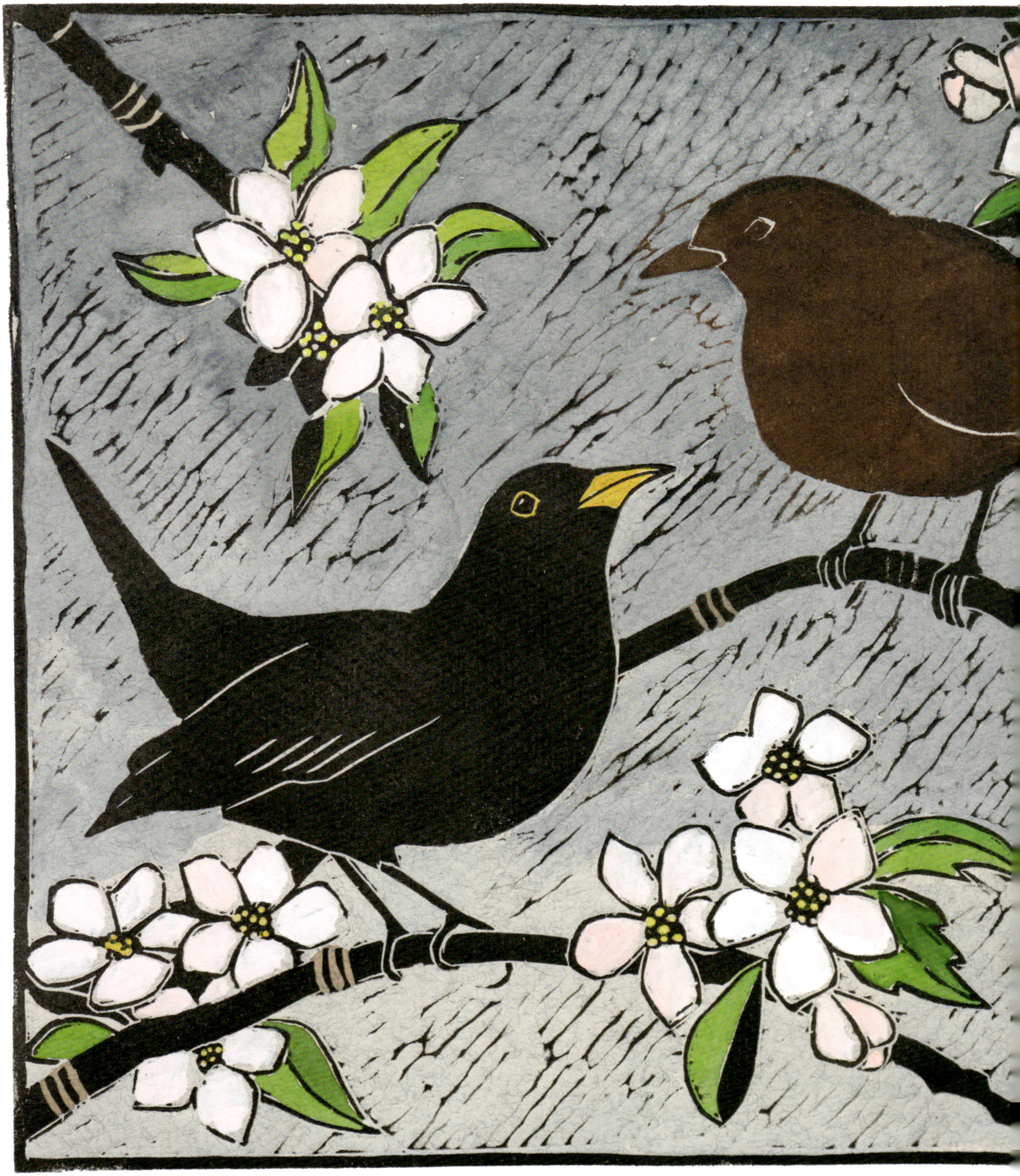

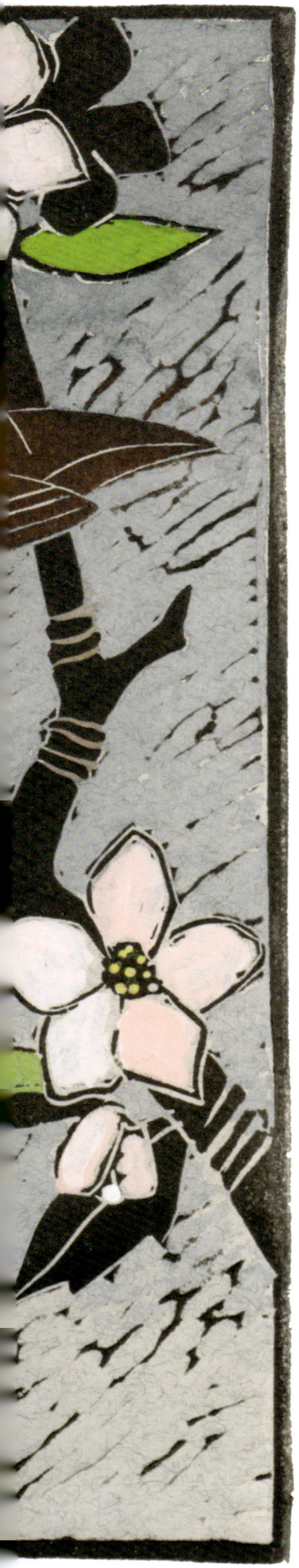

Spring rain,
25 cm x 24 cm, 2012

Blackbirds in apple blossom. By using a dabber I was able to colour the female blackbird with brown ink and the rest of the plate in black. The other colours were added by hand afterwards. The directional and incomplete clearing of the plate in the background is deliberate and suggests rain.

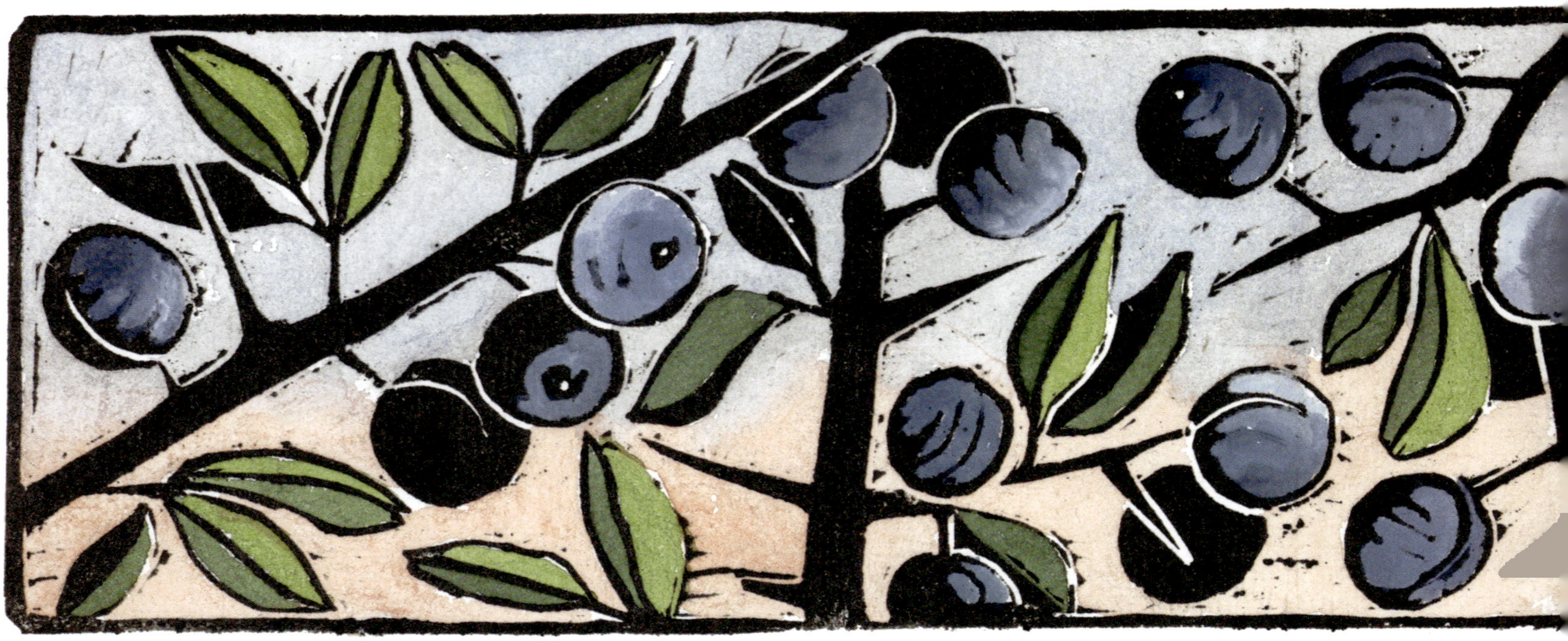

Sloe Jen,
39 cm x 9 cm, 2010

Hand coloured linocut. Initially I printed this onto a deckle-edged concertina folded piece of paper. The folds represent the complexity and density of the blackthorn bush, but the flat version is equally pleasing.

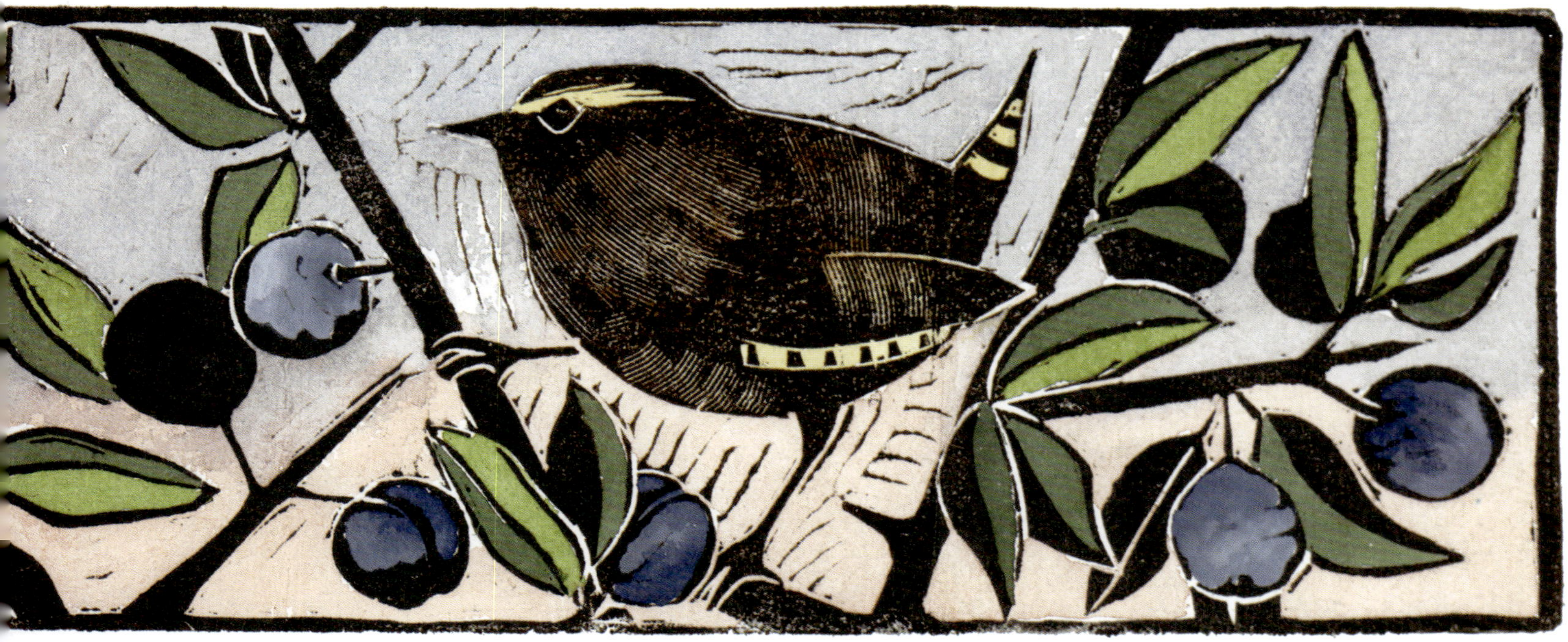

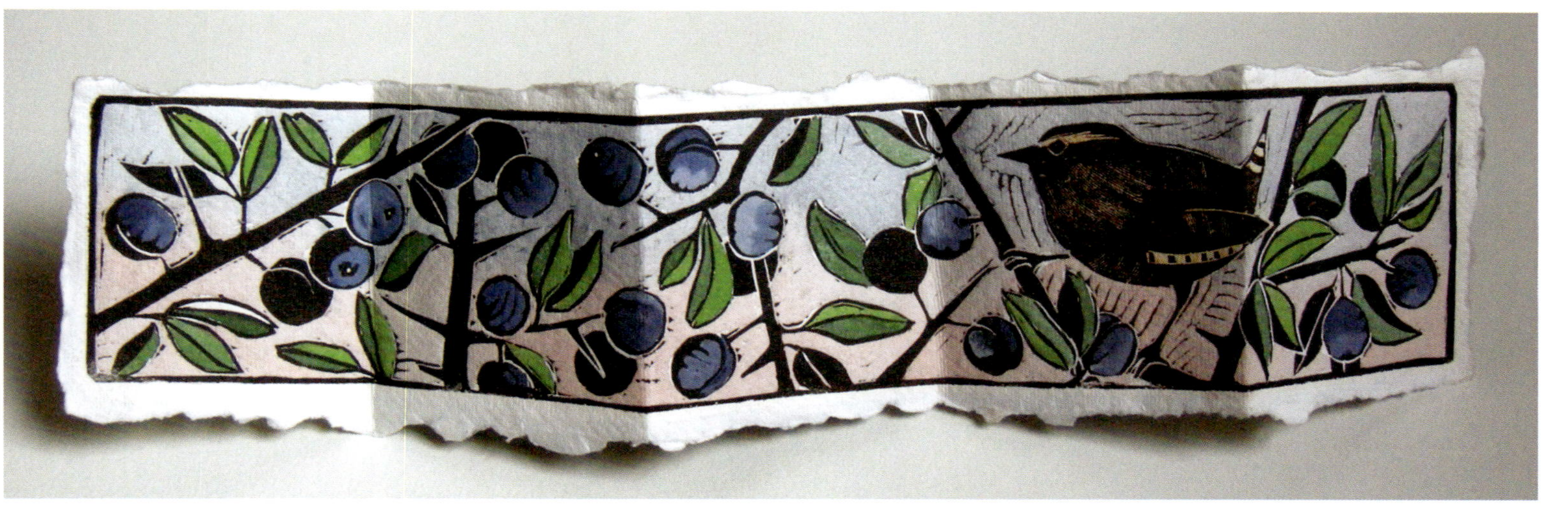

Folded version.

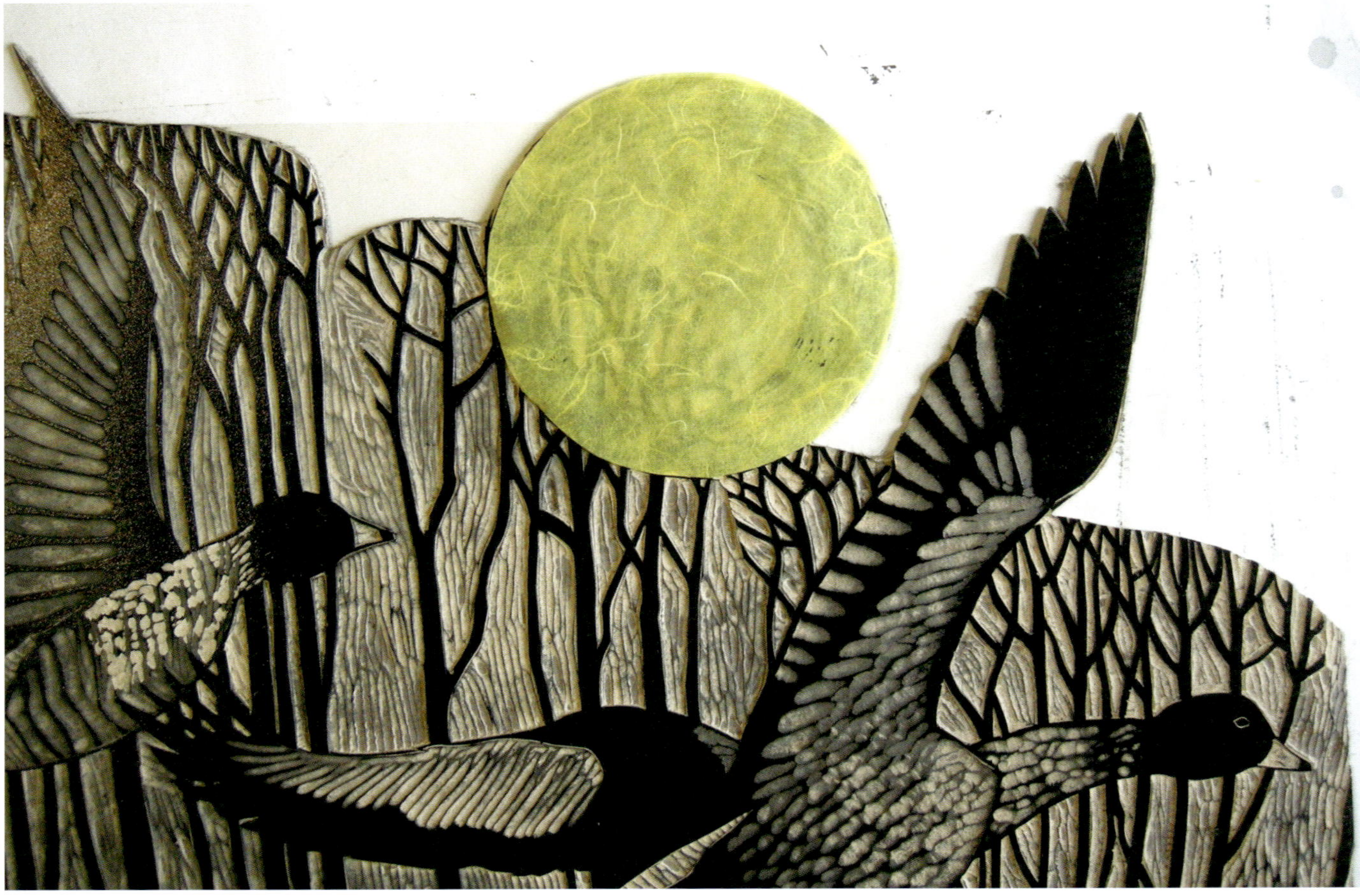

Here, the yellow circle, which is to represent the sun, has been coated with glue and positioned over the exact spot on the plate where the sun has been cut, glue side up.

As I print with a press I have also used Chine Collée, which is a technique usually associated with etching. The plate is inked up and then pre-cut coloured tissue can be placed, glue side up, on the surface of the plate prior to laying the printing paper on top.

The press transfers the ink to the paper, but it also sticks the coloured tissue to the surface so that the ink in this area prints onto the face of the tissue.

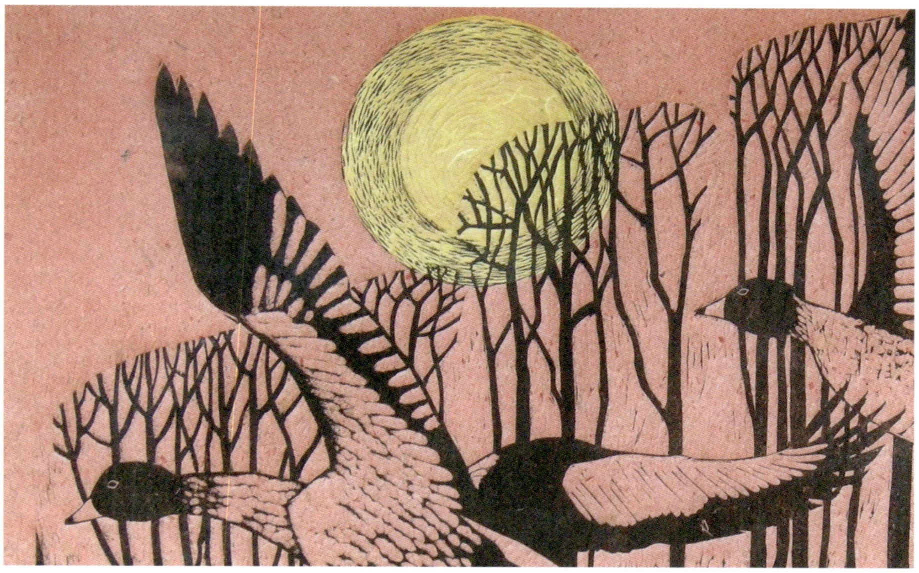

The yellow tissue has been overprinted and stuck down by the pressure of the press. The print requires further hand colouring, but this area is fully resolved, and there is no danger of paint covering the very small black marks which I wanted to retain on the edge of the sun.

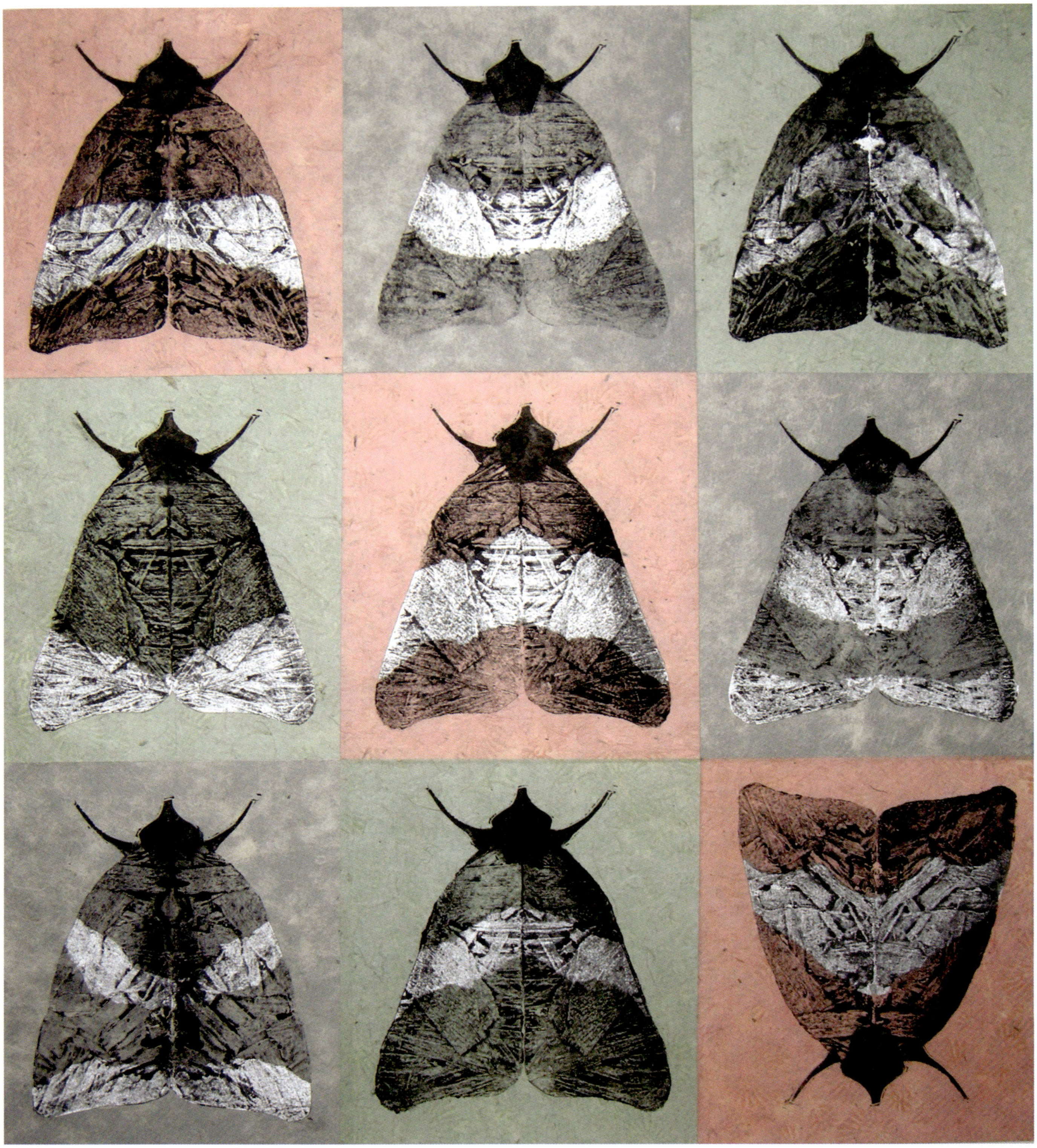

Driftwood Daggers,
50 cm x 56 cm, 2012

This rather playful print also uses Chine collée. In this case a found object, a piece of coarse chipboard from the beach, had some wonderful grain on it, which reminded me of the patterns on moths. By printing from both sides of it, and offsetting, I managed to print several versions of two imaginary moths. The torn silver strips are sandwiched between the ink and the paper.

Reduction and multiplate printing

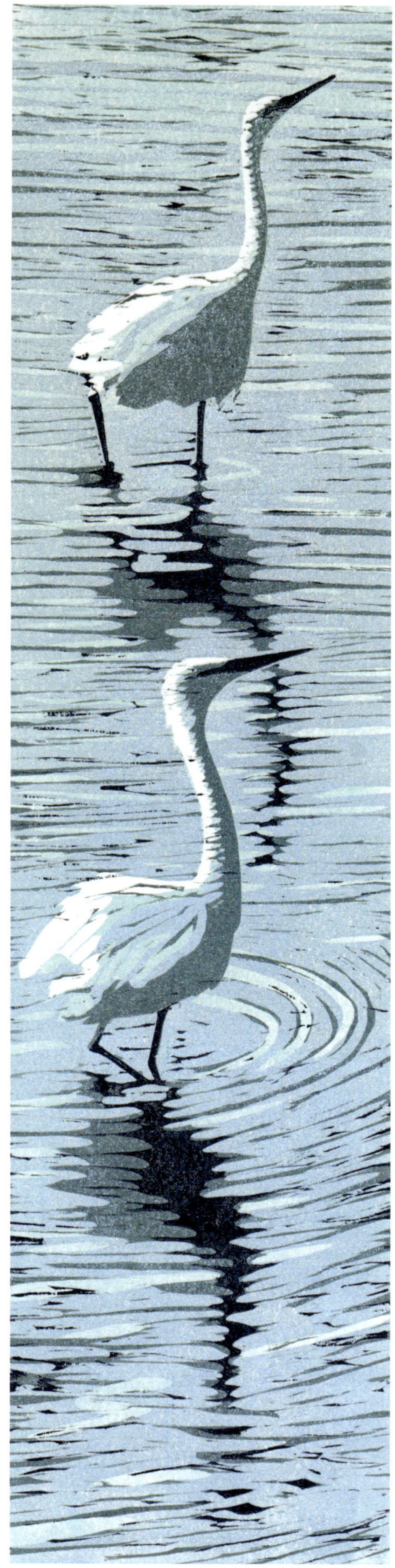

An alternative to hand colouring is to print each colour separately from one or more plates. This gives a more consistent result and a different look and feel to the print. The process is quite exacting because obviously you need to print from blocks that are identical in size and shape and you need to make sure that the blocks are always printed into exactly the same position on each piece of paper, so that the printed areas line up or "register".

By using one plate, at least one set of variables is removed. This method is called reduction or suicide printing. Instead of using one block of wood or lino for each colour, the colours are printed in succession from one plate, cutting away more of the surface each time. This means that the whole edition has to be printed in parallel, that is, you have to print the first colour onto 10 or 20 pieces of paper, before cutting the block for the second colour, as you can't go back and print some more once the block is cut down again.

The prints still have to be registered. There are several ways of doing this: the basic principle is that the plate and the paper must be returned to precisely the same relative positions every time a print is taken. One method is to take a piece of paper bigger than the block and make a fold down the left side, like a flap.

You can lift the flap for a moment and position the plate face up on the paper, about an inch in from the fold, and draw around it. Every time you print, the block sits within this line.

Courtship,
12 cm x 47 cm, 2009

Seen at Pennington Marshes in Hampshire on New Year's day, these little egrets were already thinking about spring. I originally tried to make this print using driftwood, but it proved to be too crude a surface.

Black guillemots,
40 cm x 21 cm, 2010

This linocut is made by reduction: all of the colours are printed in succession from one plate. Known locally as tysties, black guillemots nest in Portpatrick Harbour and appear to be very confiding in that environment.

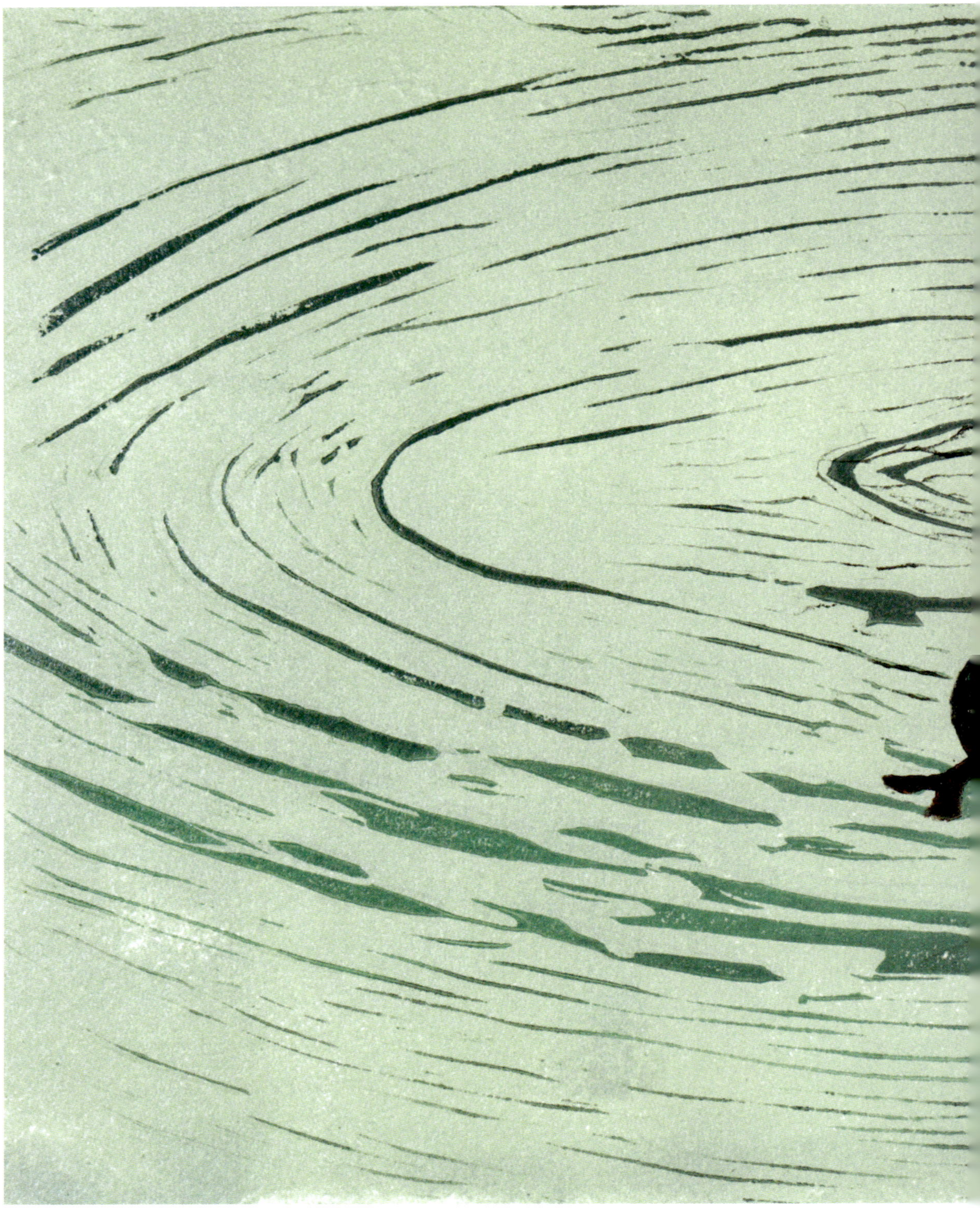

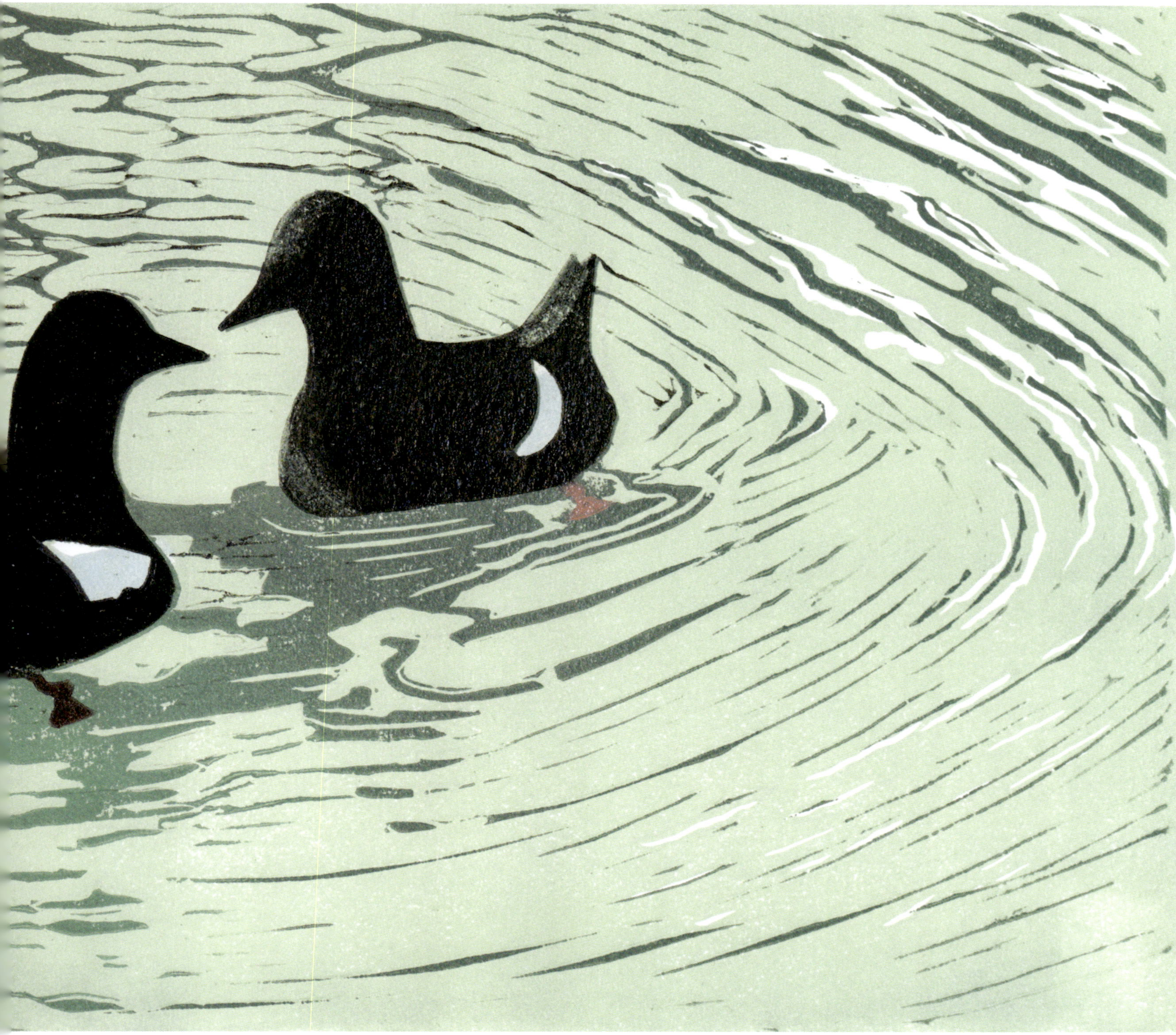

Then you fold the flap over and mark two or three spaced, horizontal lines off the edge. When you are ready to print you place the inked plate within the outline, take your paper and place the left hand edge into the gutter of the fold, lay it on the plate, drop the folded flap down and mark short continuations of the three lines onto the back of the paper.

Then you burnish the print. When you come to print the next colour you follow the same procedure, but line the three lines on the flap up with the marks on the back of the paper before lowering the sheet for printing. One advantage of this method is that the paper does not have to be cut carefully to the same size and need not even be squared off – as long as it has one straight edge.

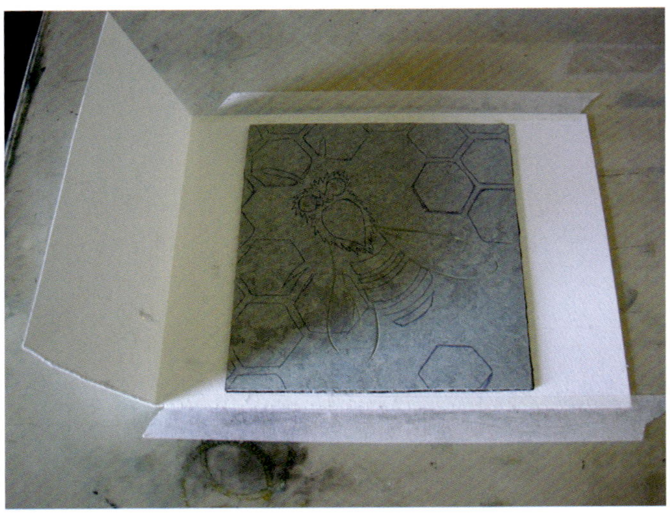

This shows a linocut, positioned within the registration device, with a line drawn around it.

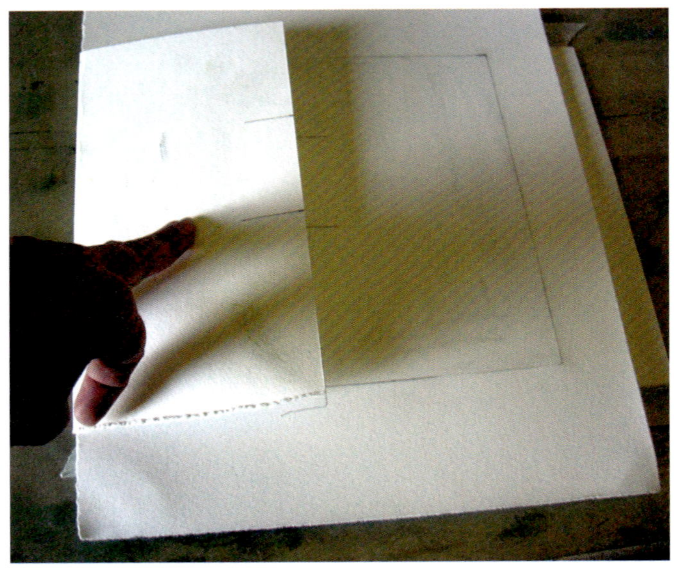

The lines marked onto the flap.

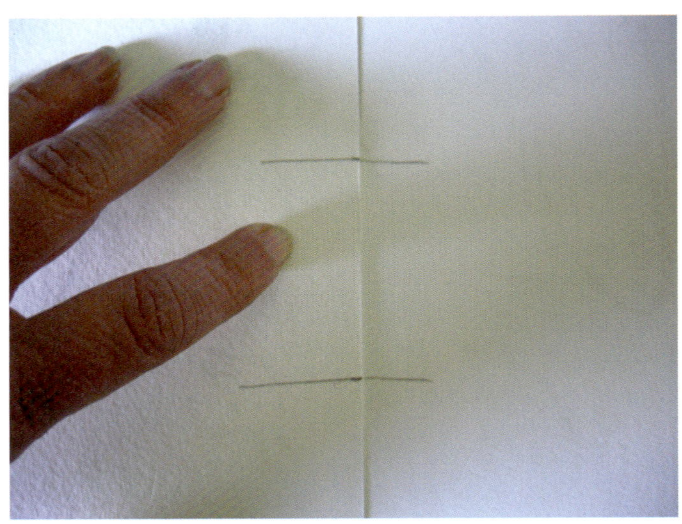

Lining up the marks.

Of course, the colour sequencing and design of the plate are all important. Generally the technique is to print dark colours over light ones, and you need to have a good understanding of the opacity of the inks: will overprinting cover the colour underneath, or modify it? If you choose the wrong colours, or too quickly limit your options by using tones that are too dark, it is impossible to go back. Sometimes I use several colours blended across a plate in one go, as in the second plate in the sequence below.

The first colour printed in the sequence for my bearded tits print. The white areas are cut away and the whole of the rest of the print is pale yellow.

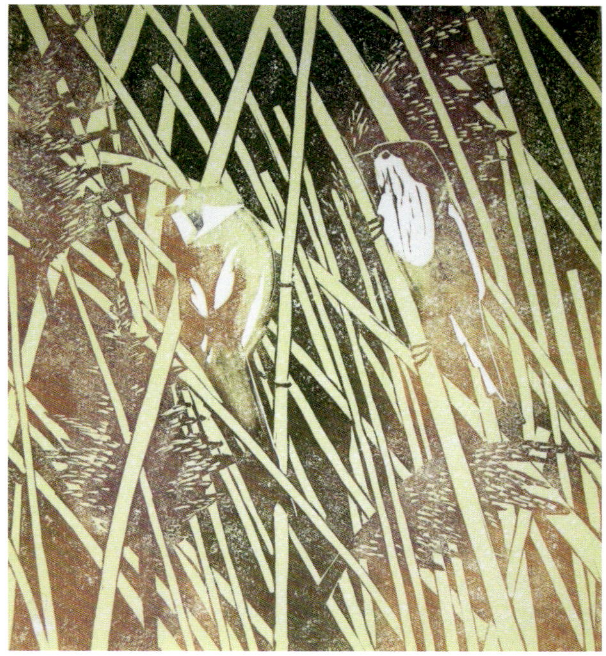

The second stage sees a huge transformation as the plate was inked in three colours at once, using a dabber.

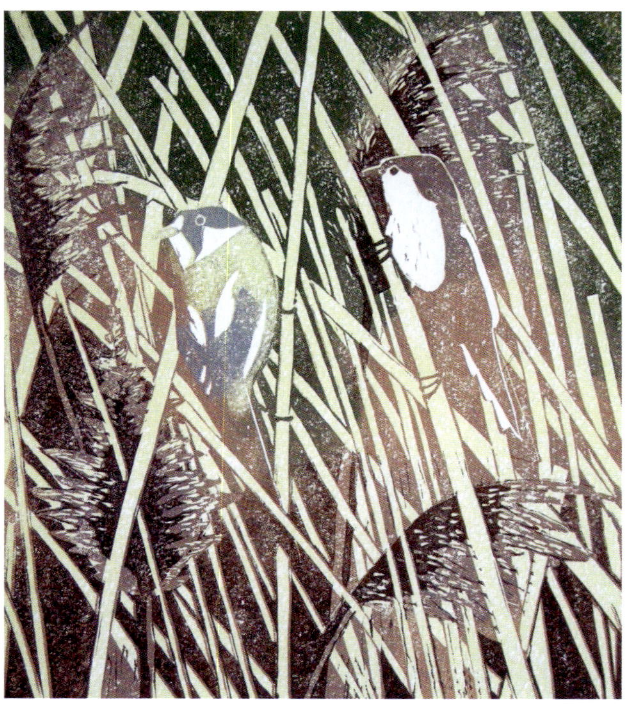

The dark brown plate lends definition to the reeds.

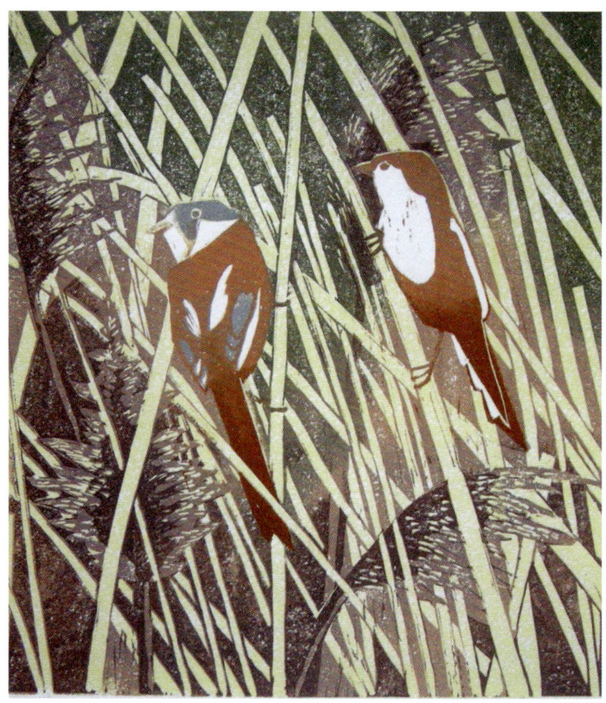

The colour of the birds is enhanced.

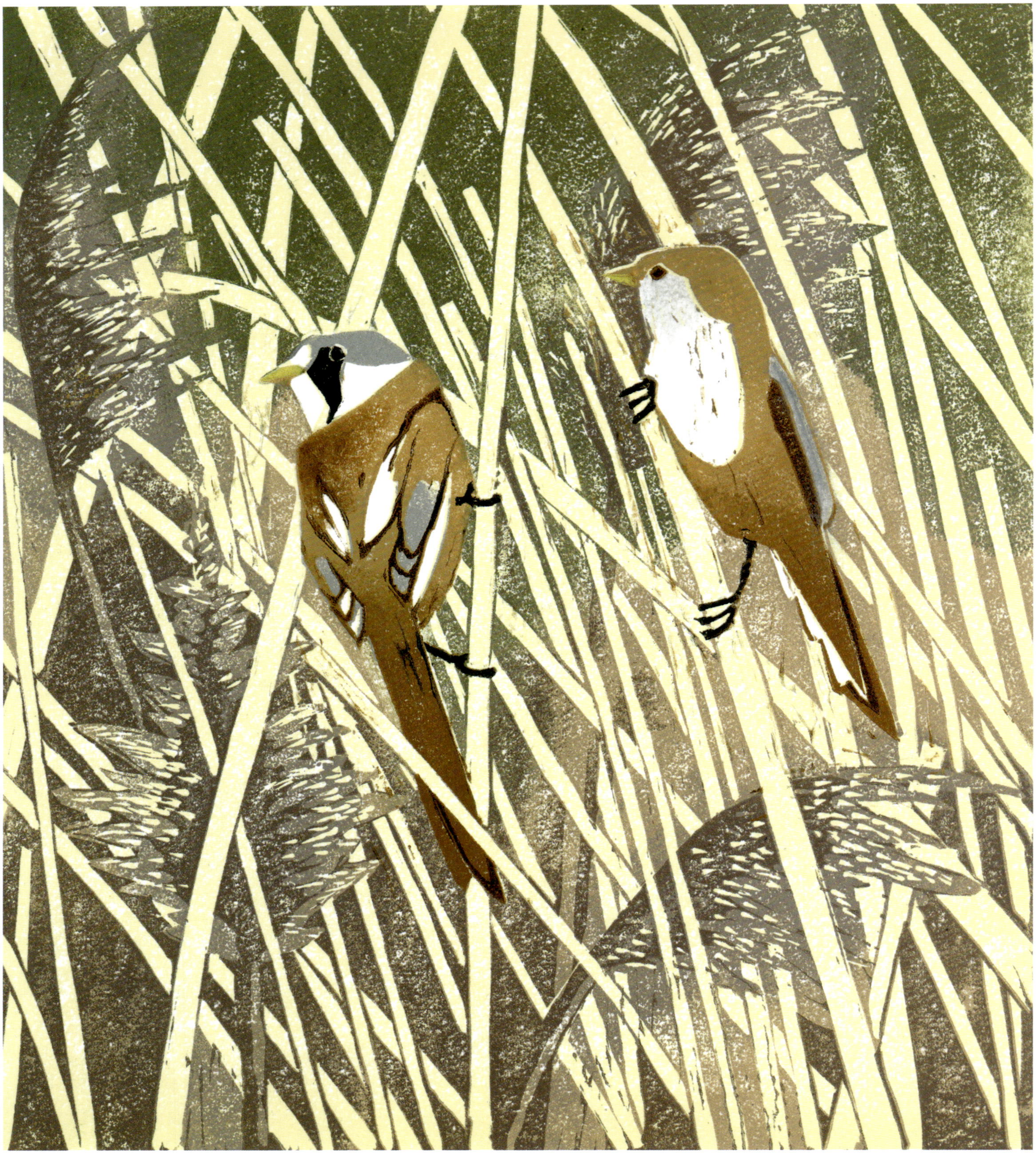

BEARDED TITS,
25 cm x 28 cm, 2011

The finished print.

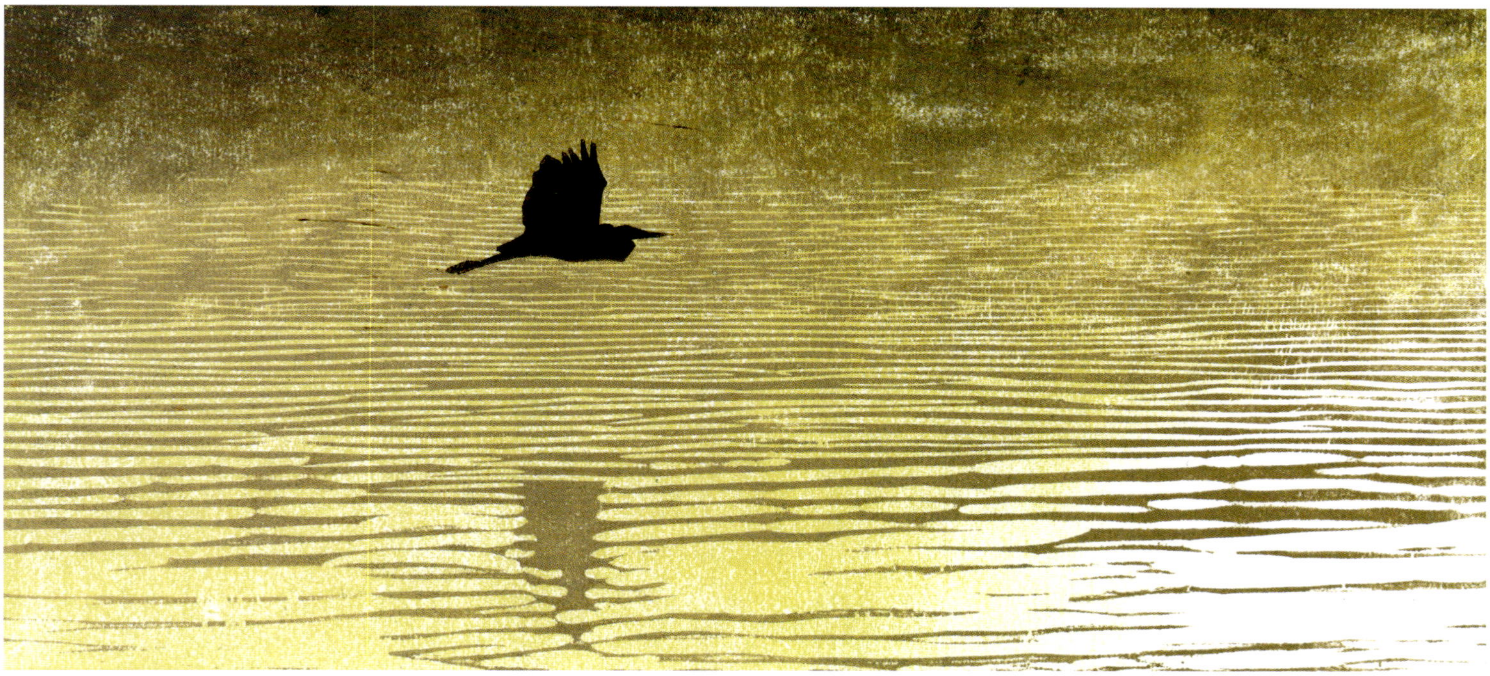

Heron, flying,
27 cm x 13 cm, 2011

This is a reduction woodcut. The restricted palette lends itself to the technique. It is always particularly satisfying cutting water into a woodblock, especially along the grain.

Multi-plate colour

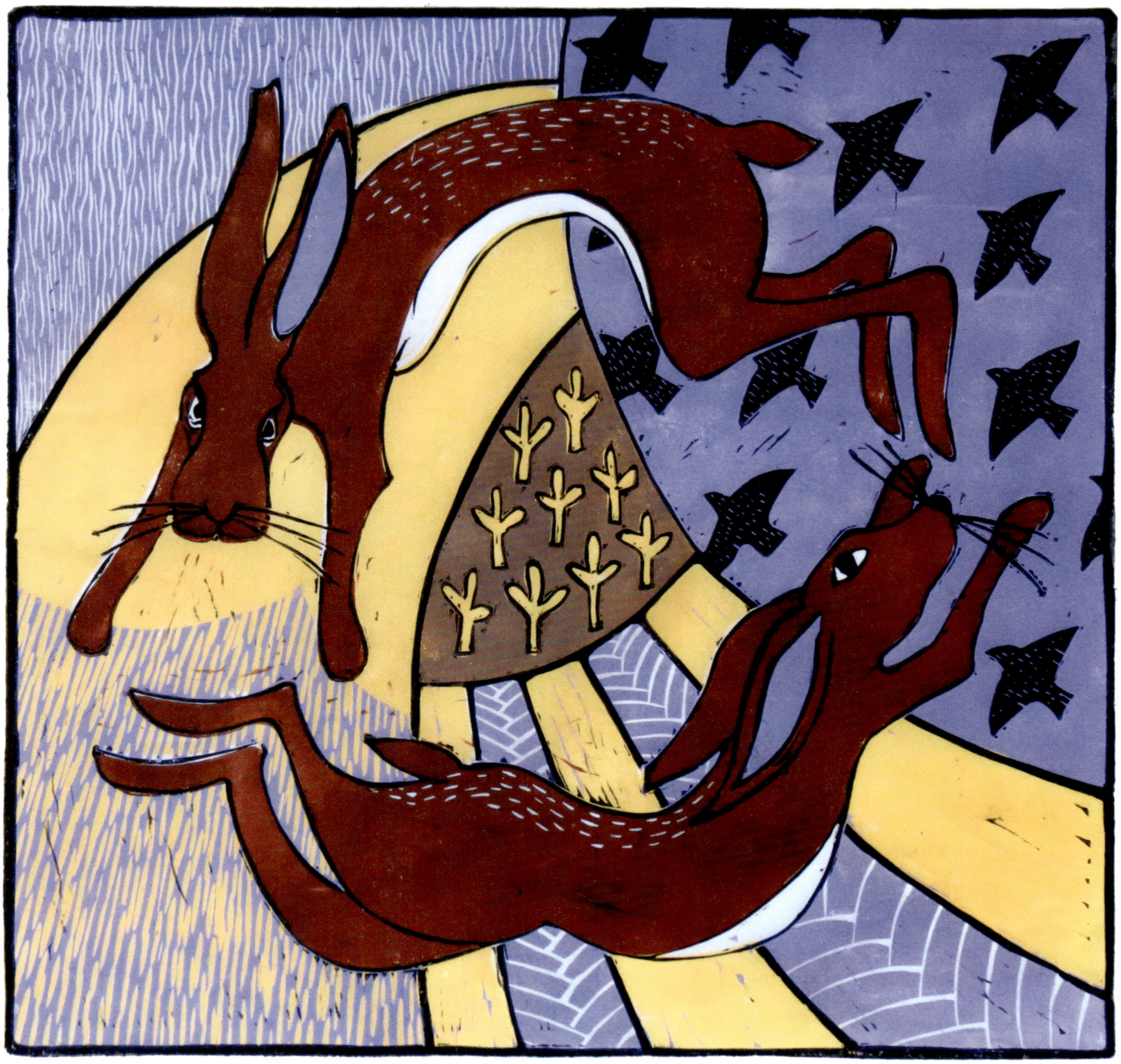

MARCH,
44 cm x 44 cm, 2013

A four-plate linocut, printed using water based inks, this was completed during a 60 hour power cut in March 2013.

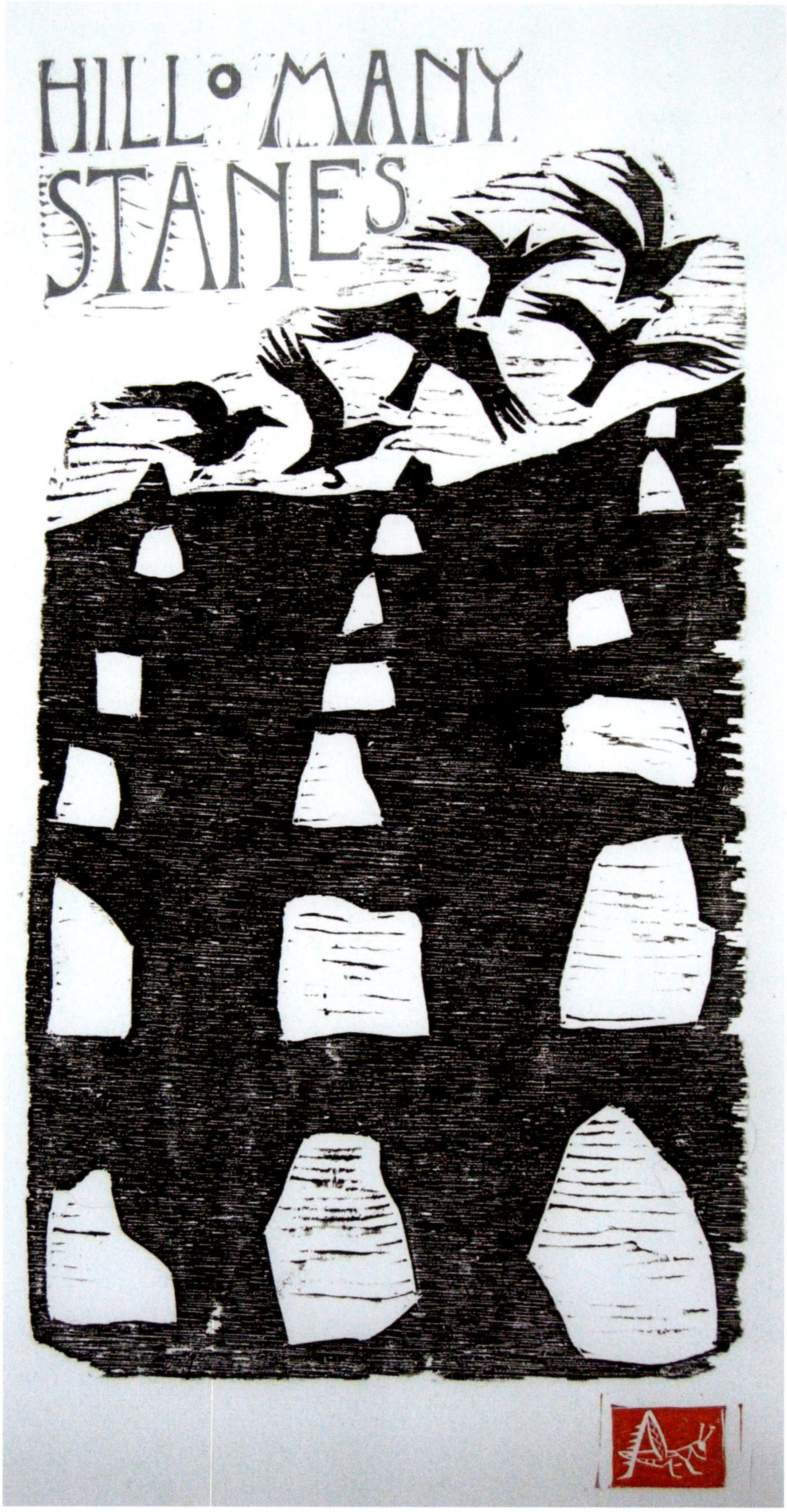

HILL O MANY STANES,
19 cm x 34 cm, 2011

Printed from a piece of driftwood and two separate pieces of lino, the pieces are inked up in silver, red and black and printed sequentially. This ancient monument is in Caithness.

Apart from Japanese woodblock printing, which is discussed in Chapter 6, I have seldom printed from registered, multiple blocks. The registration system is the same and there is more freedom to experiment with colour, but the blocks need to be identical in shape, and as I seldom use pre-cut shapes and sizes, this is quite an undertaking.

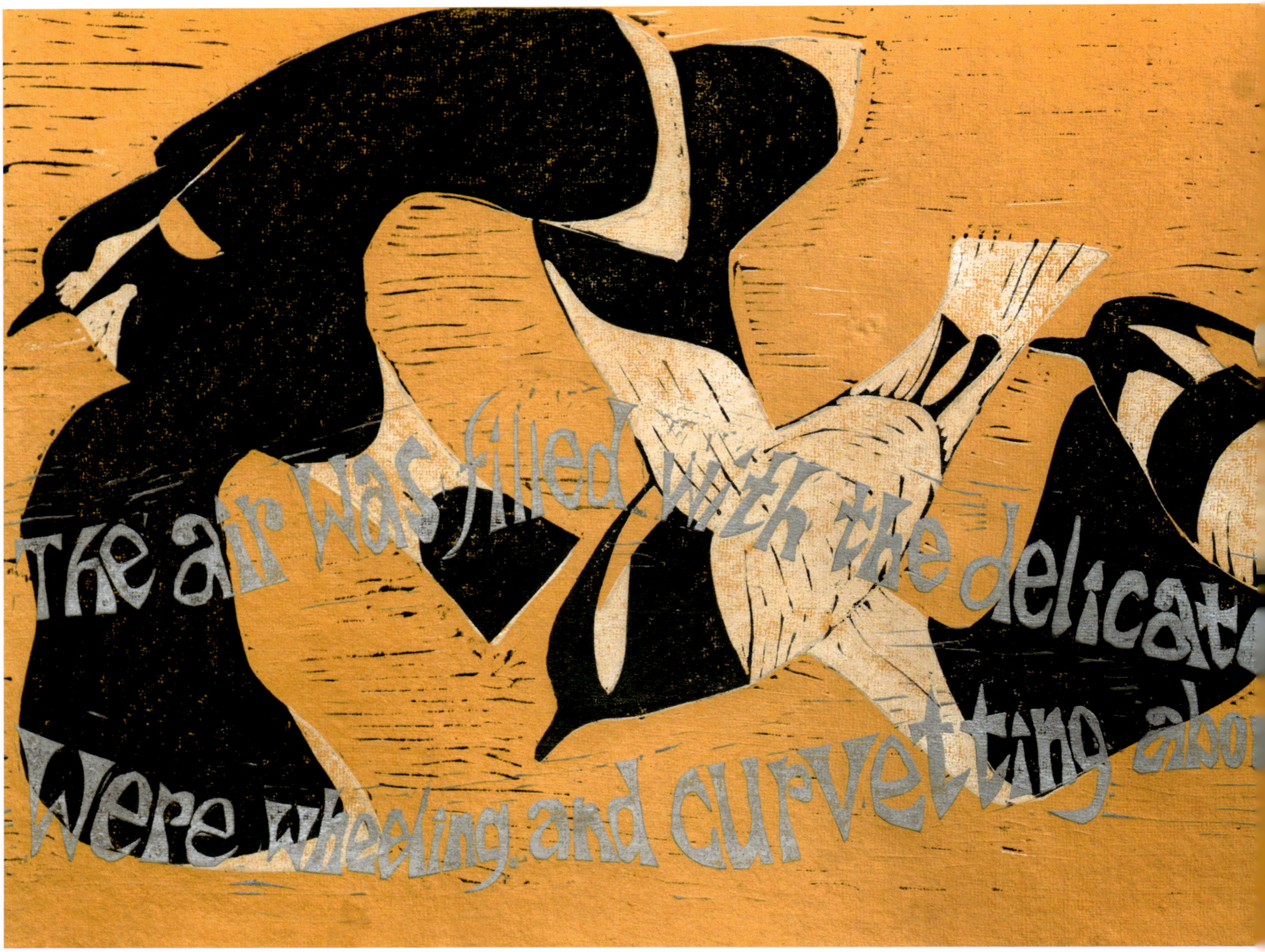

THE AIR WAS FILLED,
75 cm x 27 cm, 2010

This print was inspired by a quote from Paul Nash, which is overprinted in silver across the plate. It is a three block print: black, white and silver, onto coloured paper.

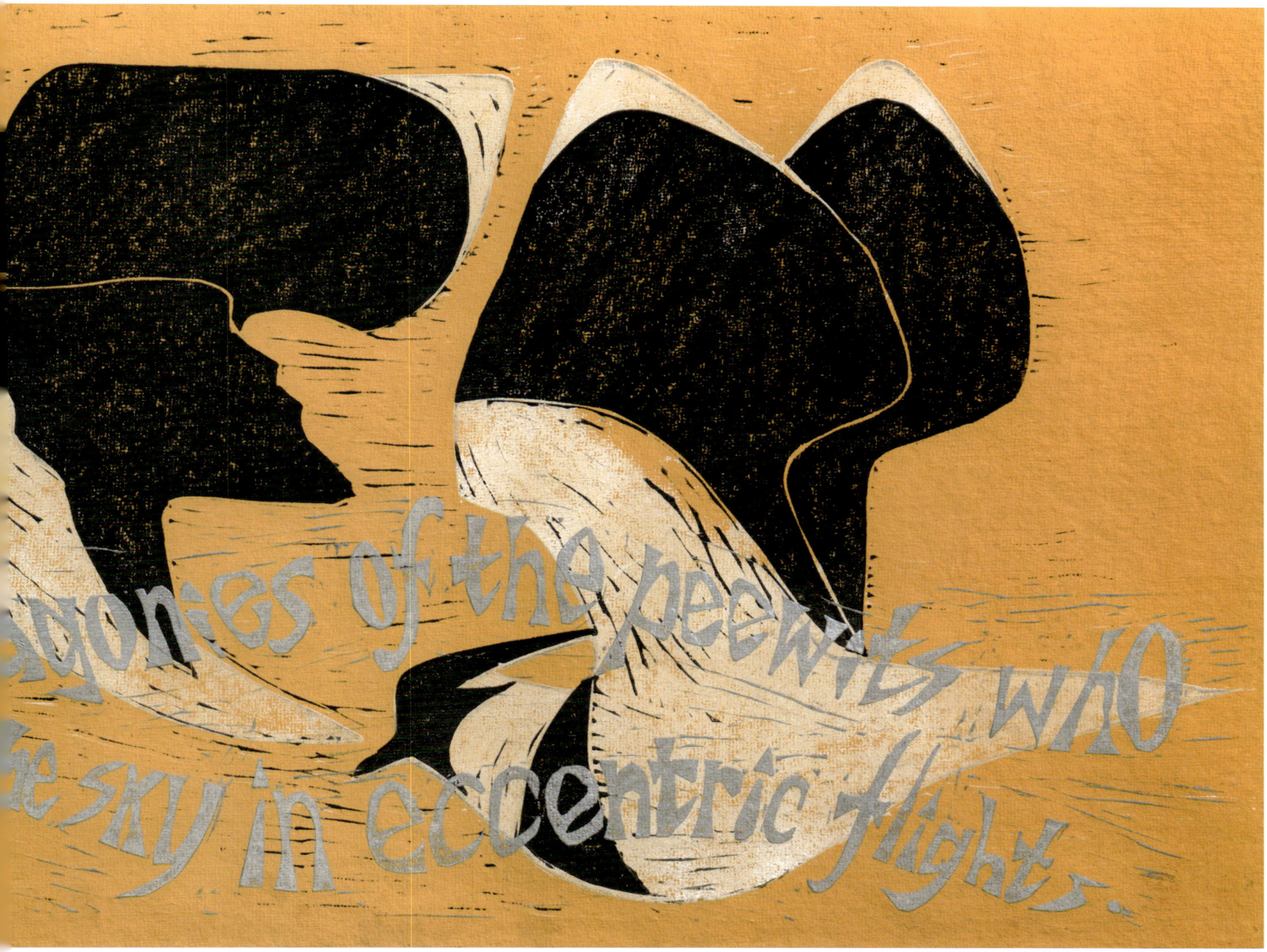
agonies of the peewits who
e sky in eccentric flights.

Jigsaw Prints

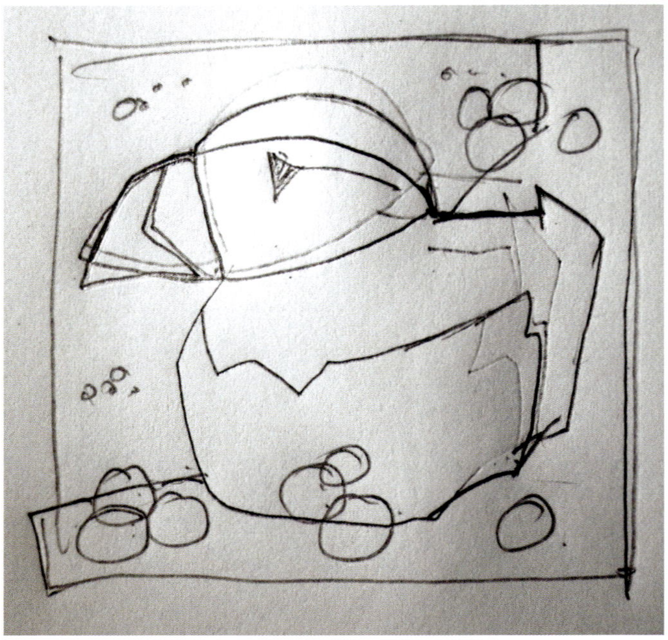

The simple sketch which has been considerably enlarged

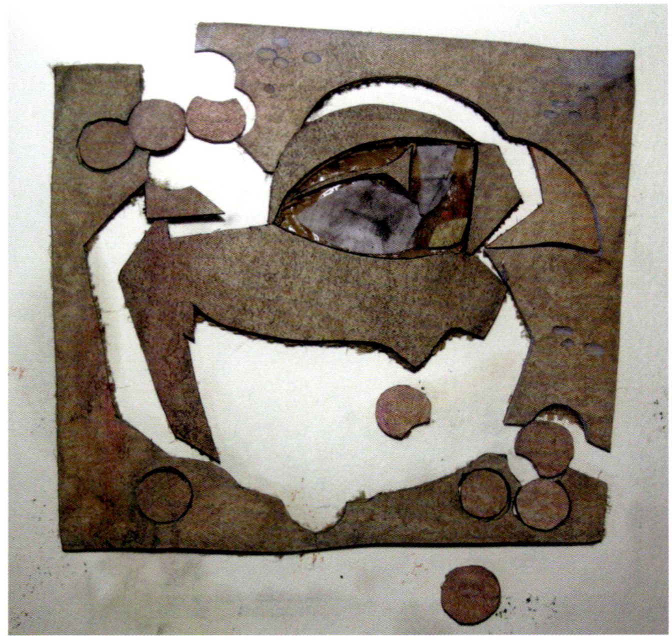

The cut lino pieces

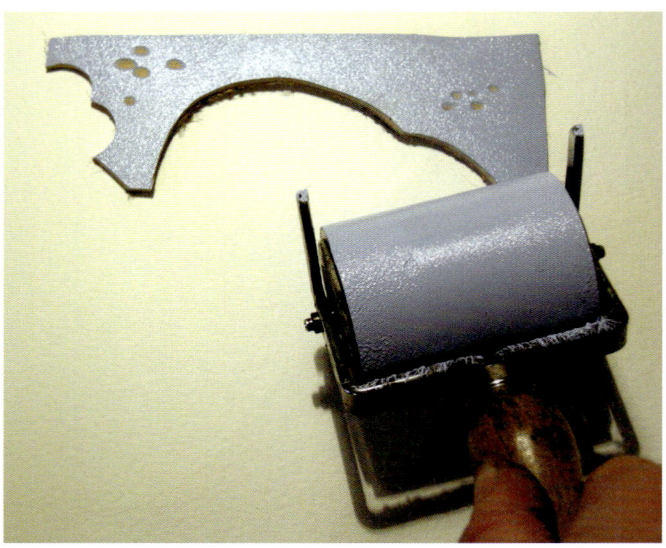

Inking up the sky in blue

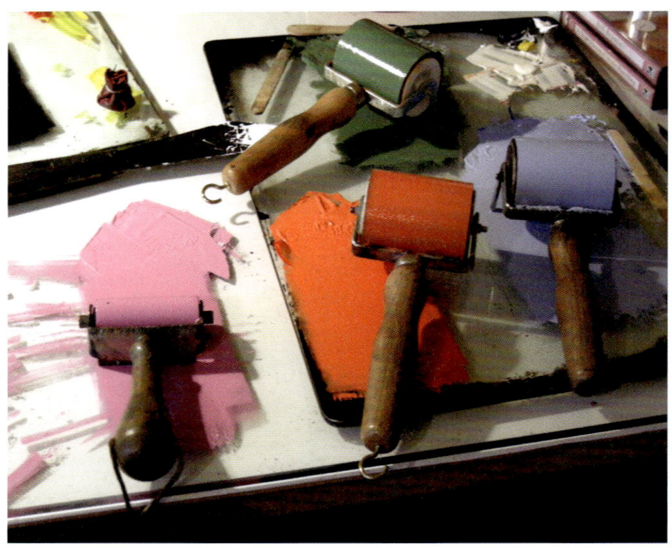

Inking table showing the different coloured inks and rollers

"Jigsaw" prints are made by breaking an image up into its component colours. This technique takes advantage of the ease with which lino can be cut. By creating a simple design in a few colours, it is possible physically to cut the lino into separate pieces, ink up the pieces in different colours, re-assemble them on the press bed and print them in one pass.

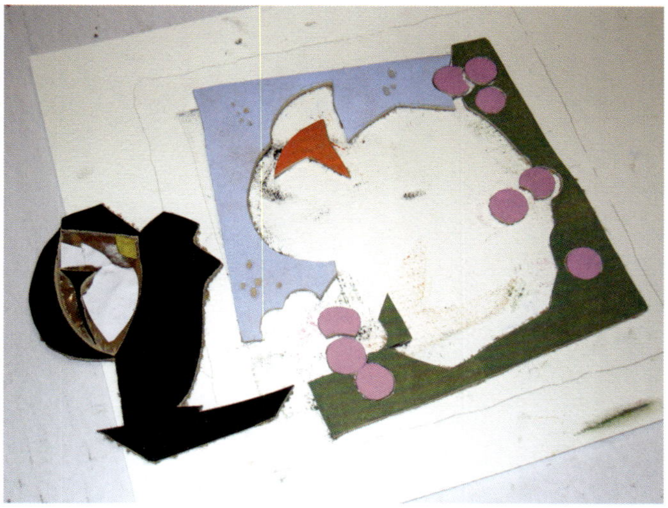

Assembling the pieces on the press bed

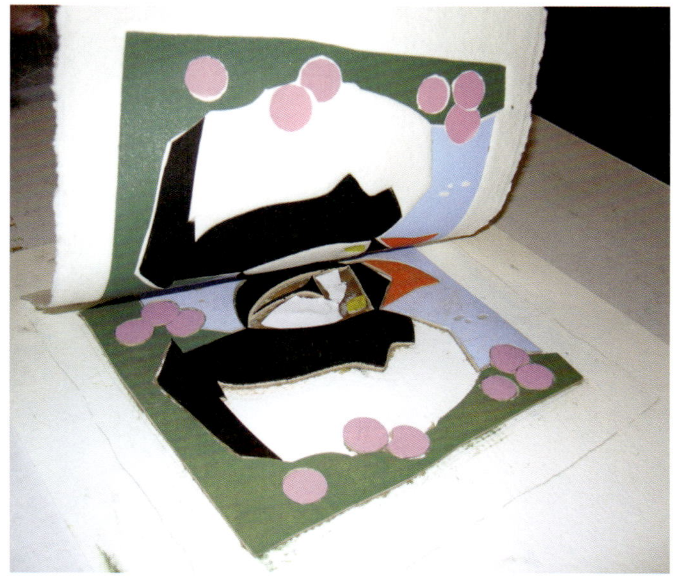

Lifting the print

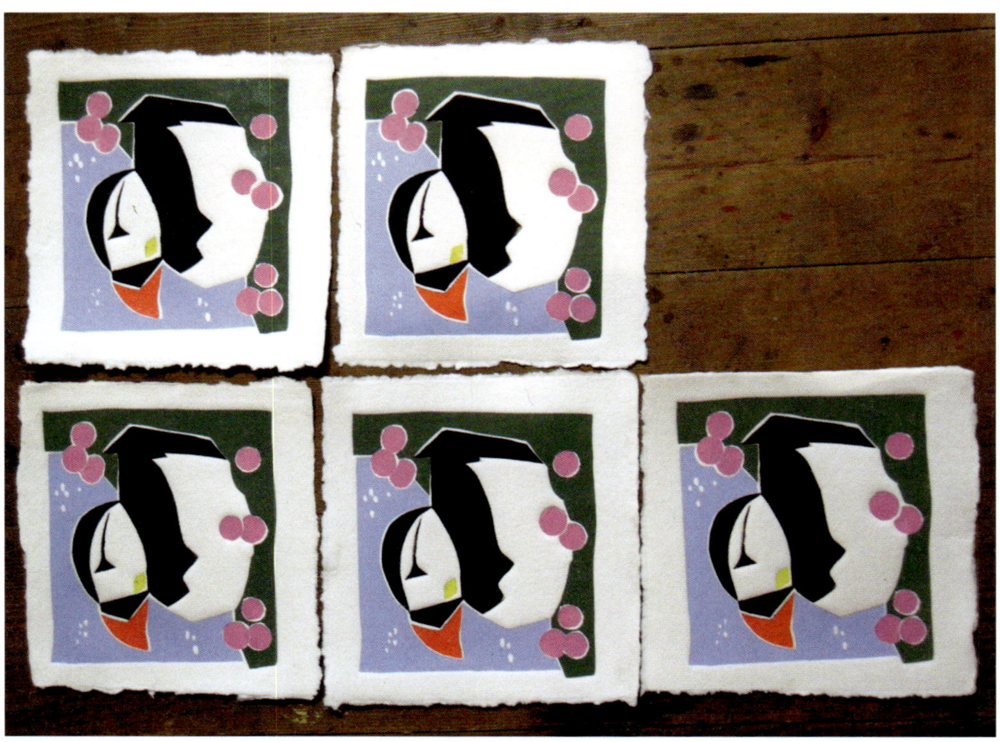

The edition laid out to dry

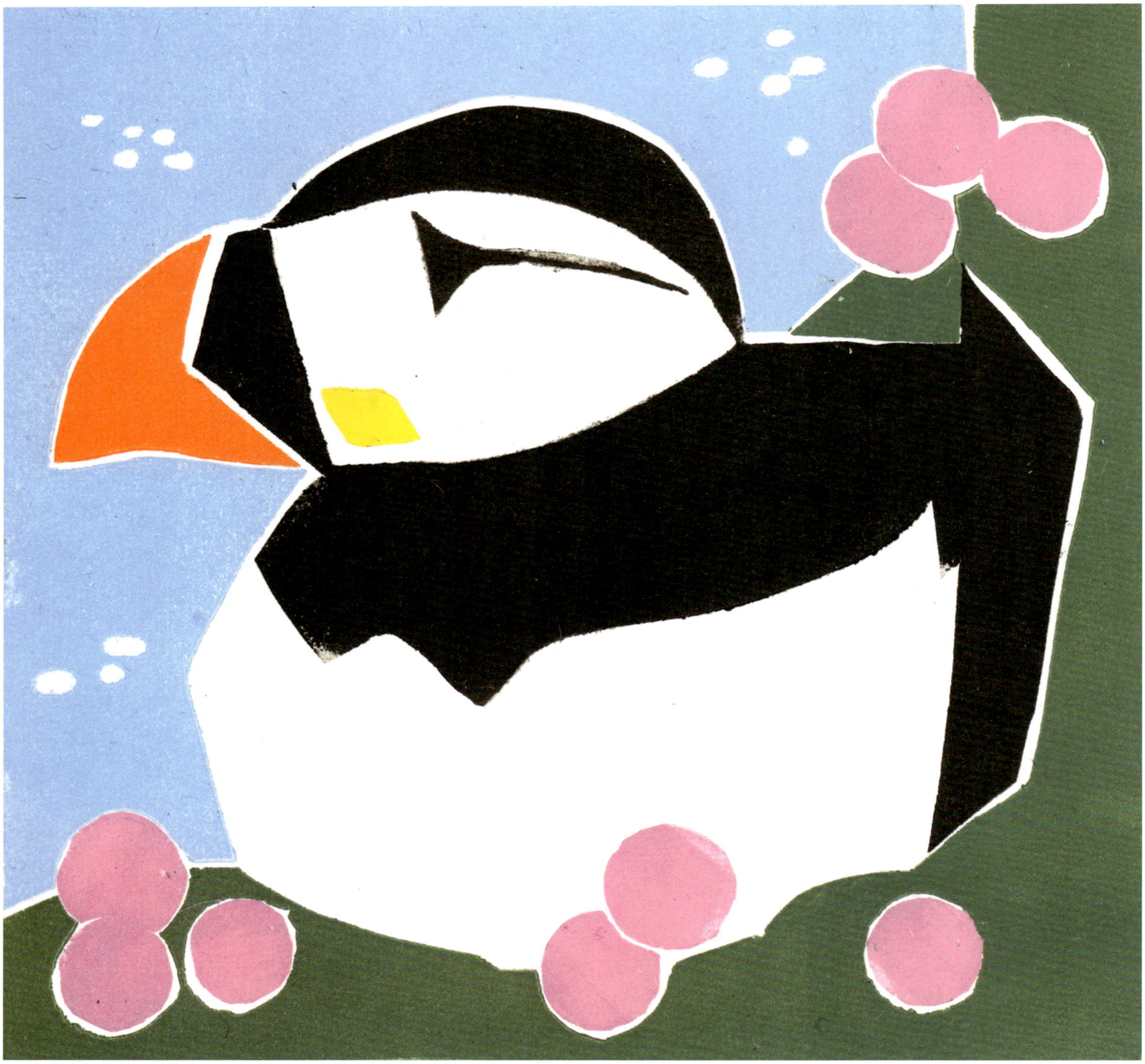

Tammie Norrie,
22 cm x 22 cm, 2012

The finished print. Tammie Norrie is the old Orkney name for the puffin. This one was inspired by puffins on Westray, so it seemed right to give it its local name. The lino has no surface cutting in this print.

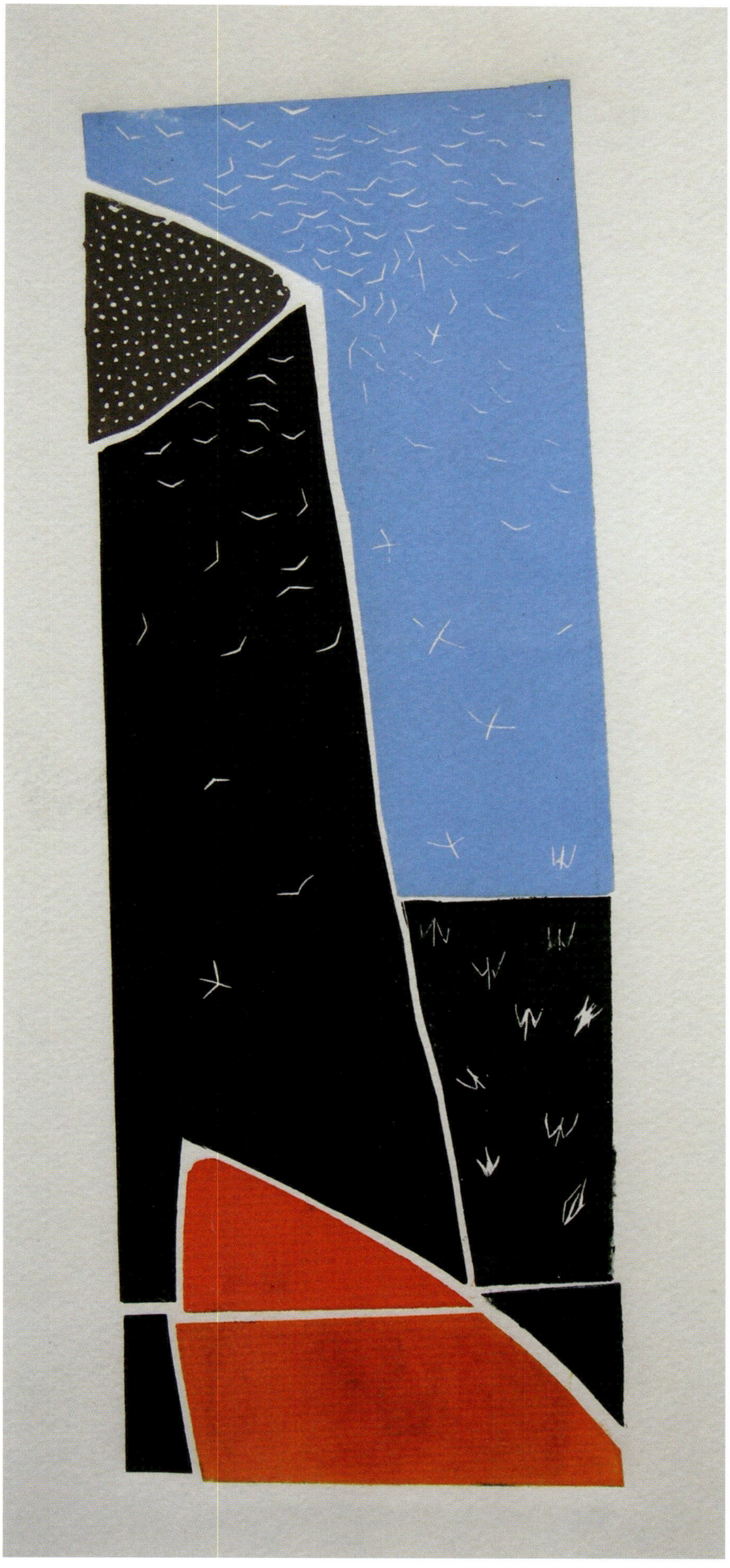

Boat to the Bass,
31 cm x 14 cm, 2010

Inspired by a trip to Bass Rock, this little print incorporates some surface cuts to suggest gannets in the air and dotted on top of the rock.

Sometimes I use poetry with my bird art. I loved poetry at school and college and I try to remember to keep reading it. It so often provides a little doorway into an intense feeling of recognition: that moment of magic when your understanding connects utterly with that of another human being, perhaps dead or a world away. Someone else who loved birds. Recently I was driving to Stranraer when I saw a kestrel hovering and straight away up popped the lines from The Windhover on the frontispiece of this book - "I caught this morning morning's minion" - so that I had to go home and re-read a poem I hadn't looked at for twenty years. Gerard Manley Hopkins also provided the two lines from Inversnaid *which, if they aren't, ought to be a hymn for the conservation movement "Let them be left, wildness and wet, long live the weeds and the wilderness yet". I used them to adorn my print of Forsinard different place, same sentiment!*

Norman MacCaig's many poems about birds touch me in a similar way. He seemed to be able to nail the true colours of any bird with an unswerving and unsentimental eye. There is also a lot of humour and affection in his observations. I used his line from Movements *in my Gannets, Bempton print:*

'When a gannet dives
It's a white anchor falling.'

And the poem continues:

'And when it lands
Umbrella heron becomes a walking stick.'

But there are numerous other fine examples of his unique voice.

'That kingfisher, jewelling upstream
seems to leave a streak of itself behind it
in the bright air.'

From *Kingfisher*

And:

'...by the footlights
of breaking water oystercatchers put on their black-and-white minstrel show, watched by a bandmaster pigeon with built-in epaulettes'

From *July day spectacular*

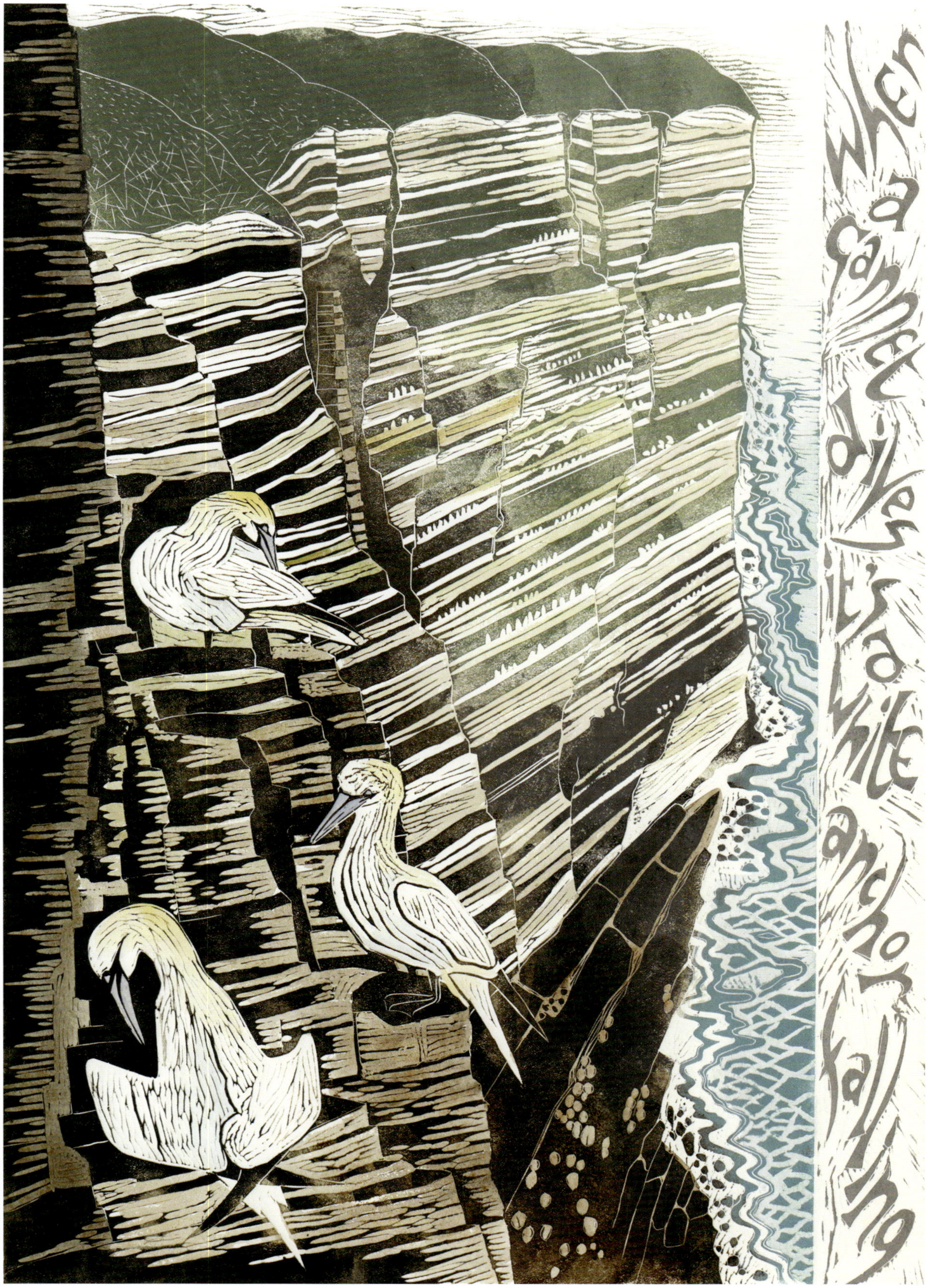

Gannets, Bempton,
53 cm x 79 cm, 2012

This is a two-plate print of gannets at Bempton Cliffs, Yorkshire. The lettering is printed in silver from a separate plate and the words are from the poem Movements, by Norman MacCaig.

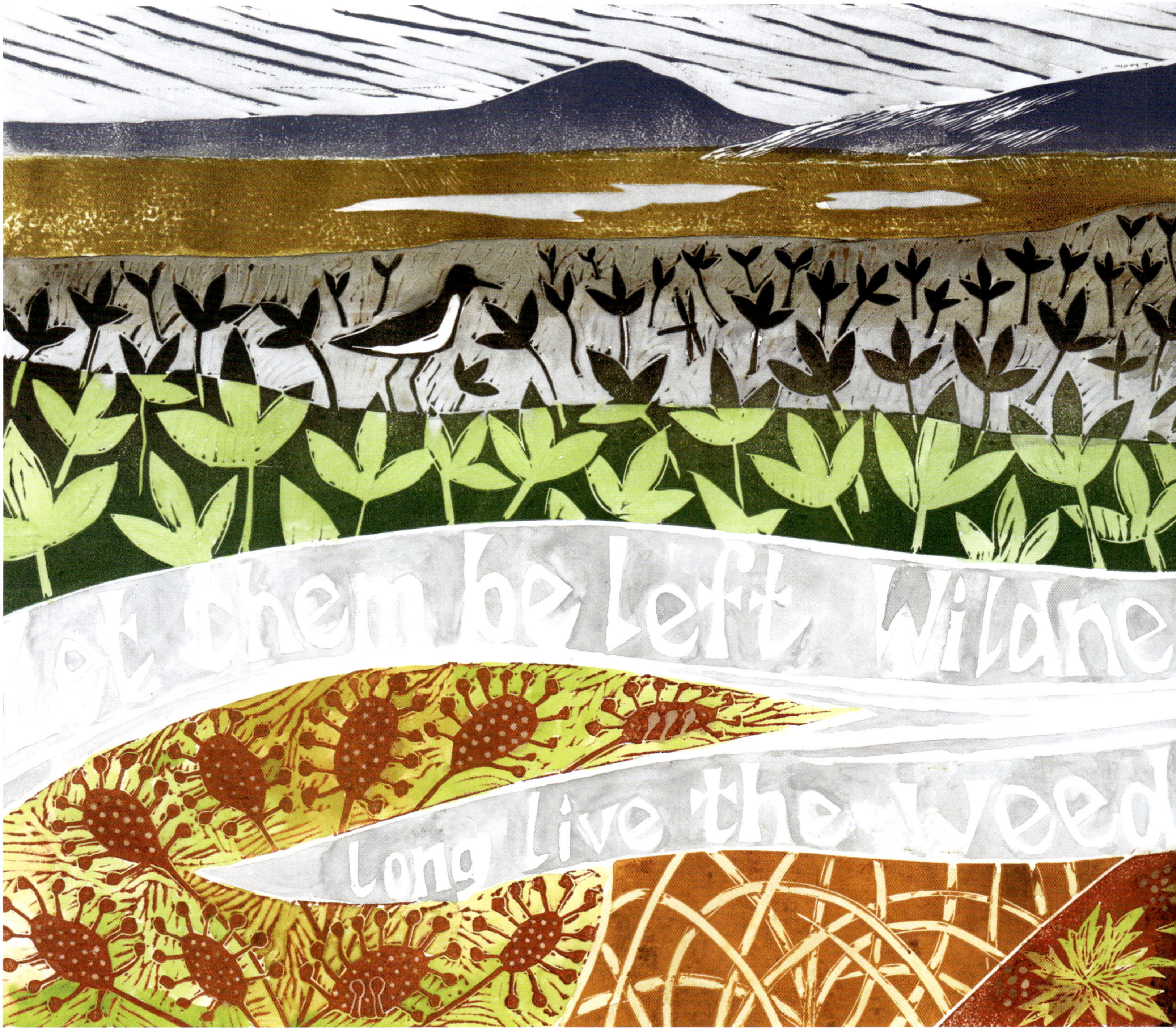

FORSINARD,
70 cm x 31 cm, 2011

Following a trip to the Flow Country in 2010, I wanted to produce a print which captured not only the extraordinary landscape but also the variety of plant and and animal life there. I was particularly struck by the colours of the mosses and lichens. This picture is composed of three horizontal strips of lino for the hills, the bogbean and the writing respectively, plus four pieces across the bottom with the various mosses and the black darter dragonfly. The top two plates are printed in more than one colour, carefully applied with rollers, and the whole thing is also hand coloured. I originally intended the writing to be blind embossed, but it was difficult to read it without side lighting, so this too was hand coloured to highlight the letters. The lines are from the poem *Inversnaid*, by Gerard Manley Hopkins.

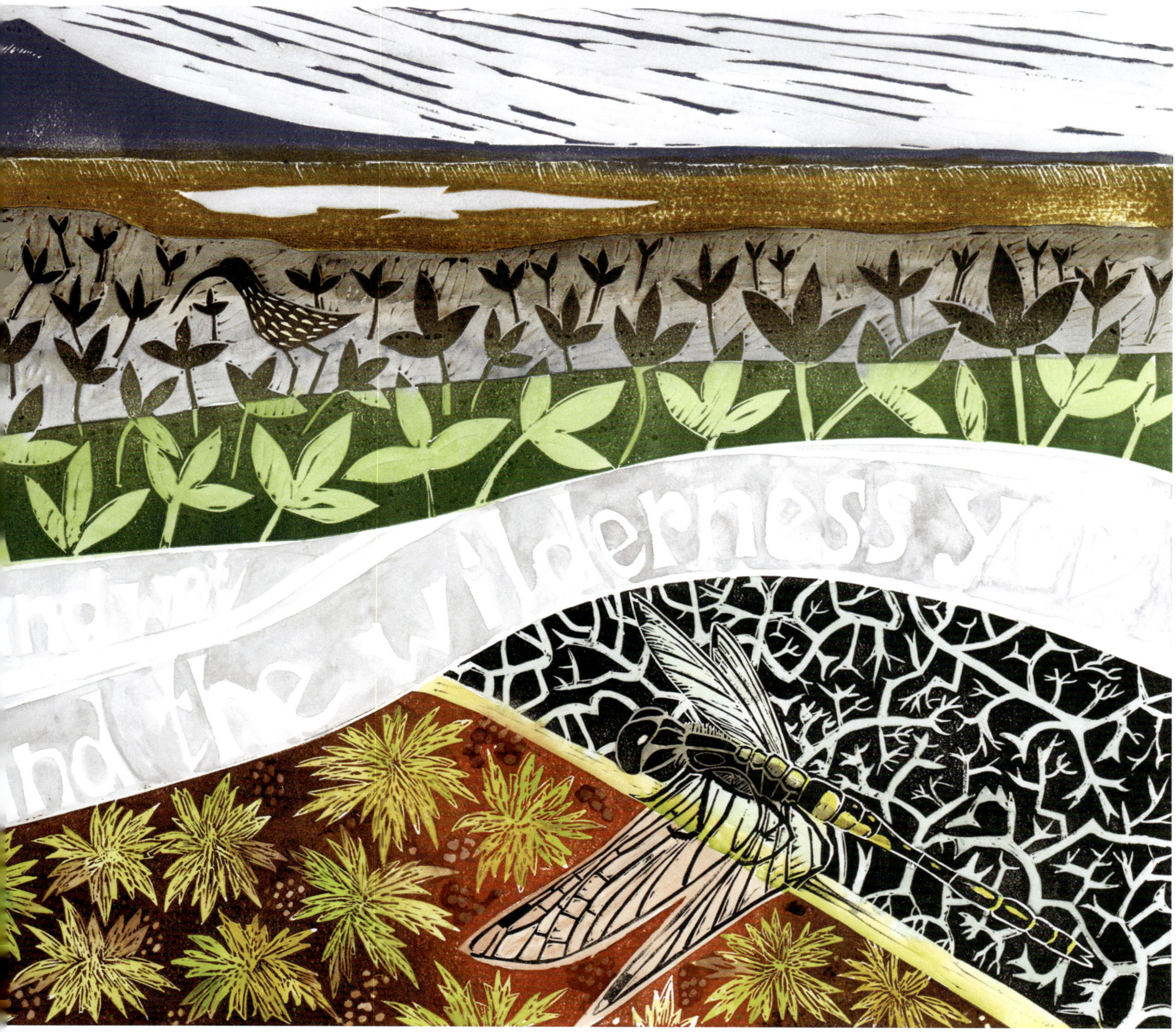
wilderness

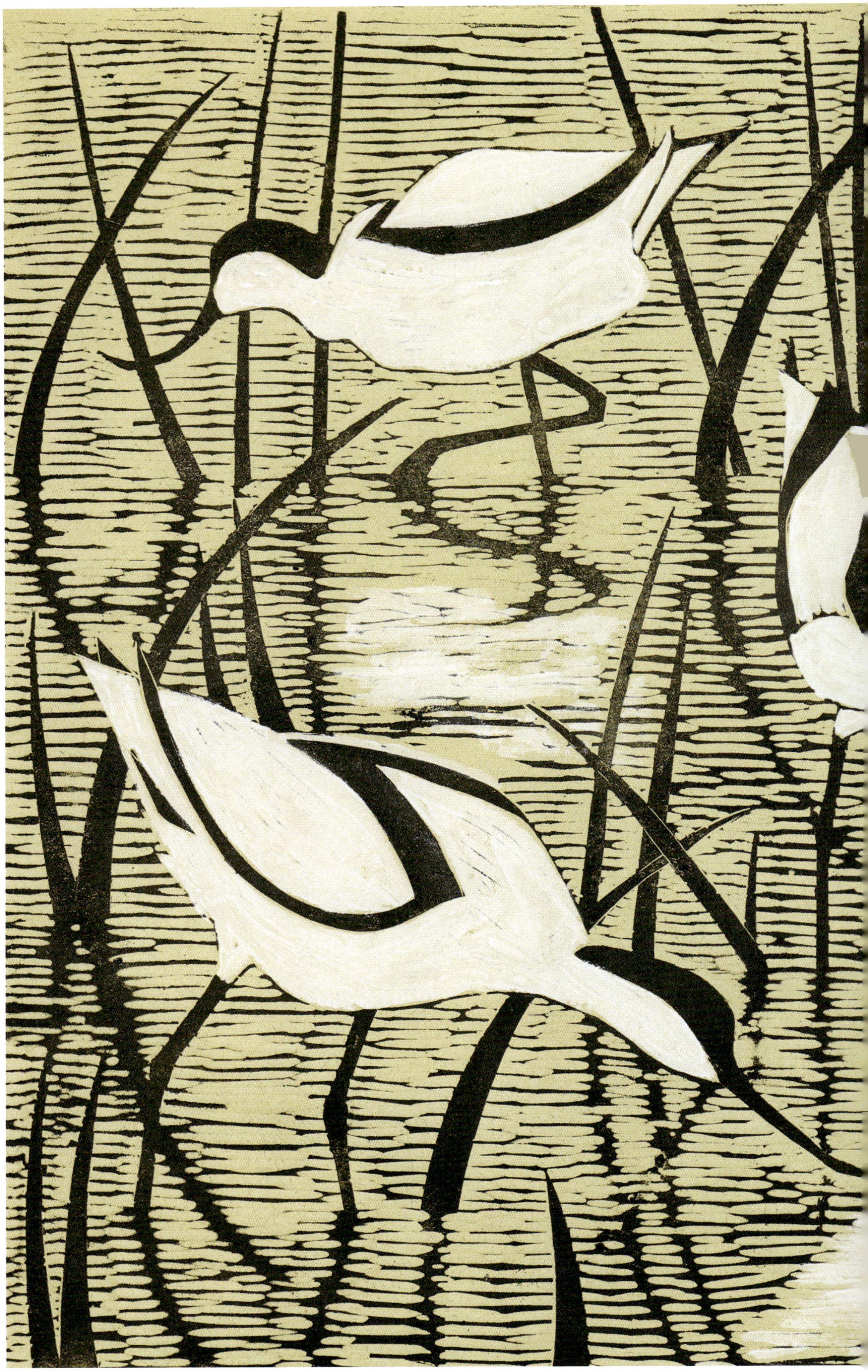

Feeding Frenzy,
70 cm x 50 cm, 2013

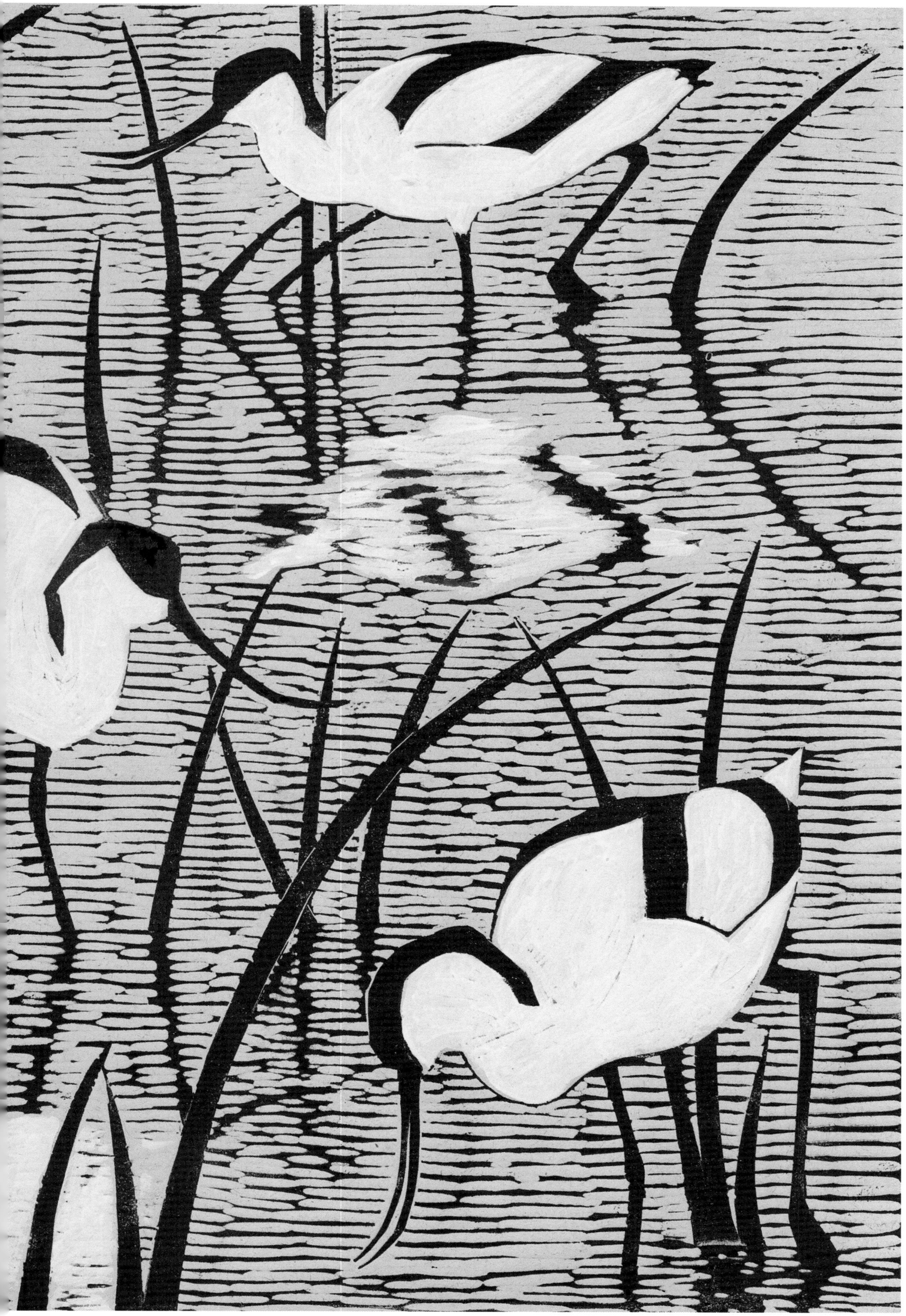

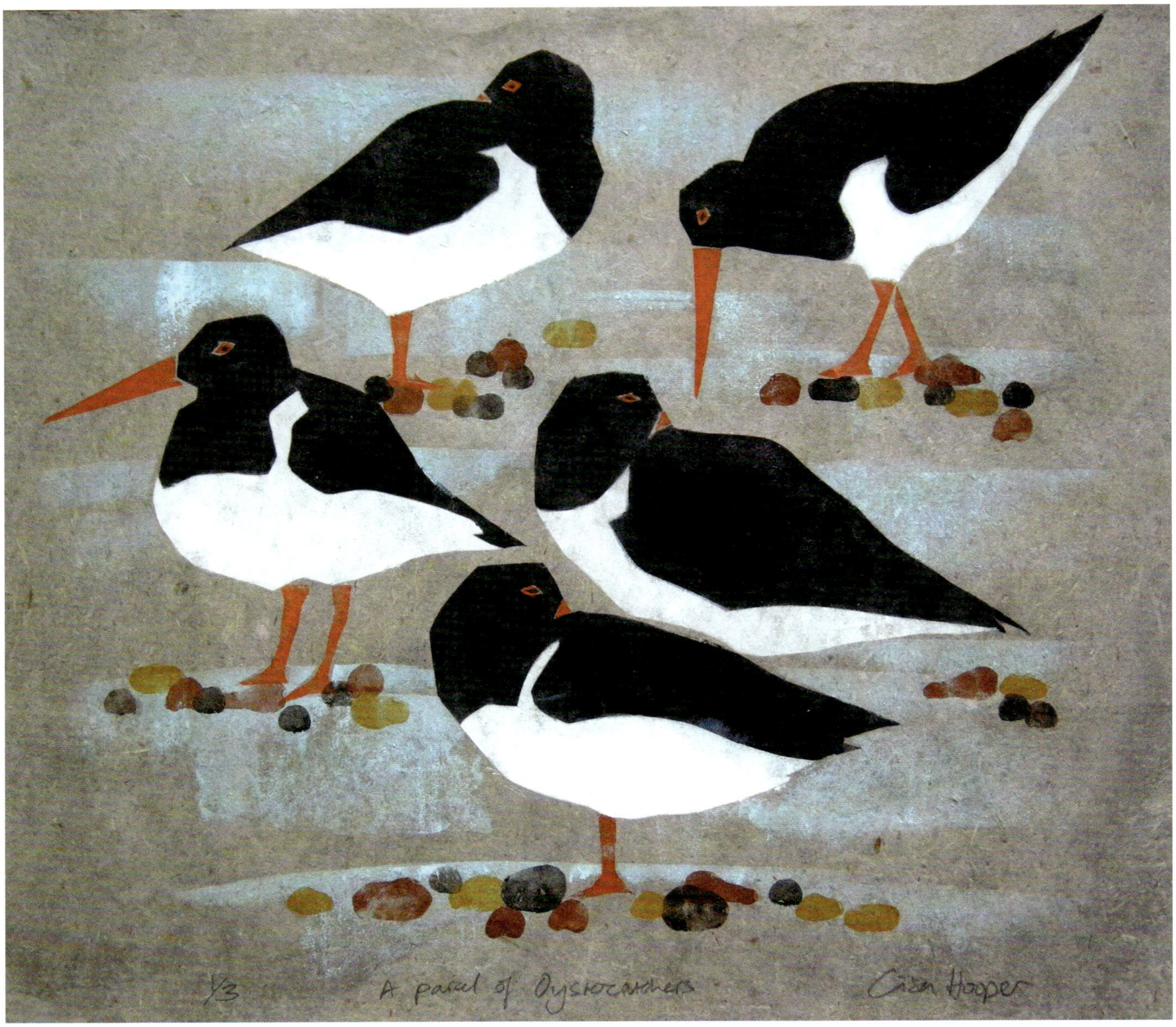

A PARCEL OF OYSTERCATCHERS,
64 cm x 55 cm, 2007

Printed from foam shapes, positioned by eye, with the water added with a roller afterwards.

It is even possible to make simple prints with foam sheets, sold for children's crafts. It is very soft and easy to cut with scissors, and it prints beautifully with light pressure through a press.

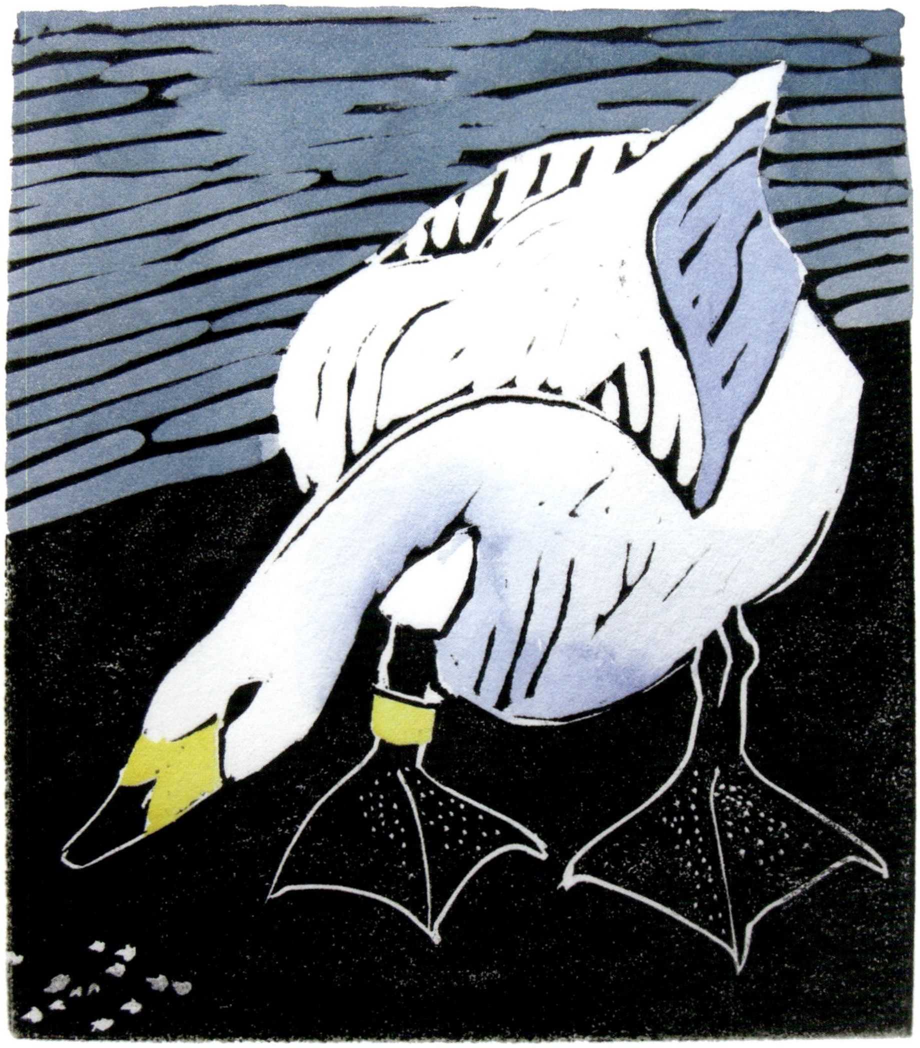

Whooper swan, Caerlaverock,
12 cm x 14 cm, 2010

The feeding station at the Wildfowl & Wetlands Trust Centre at Caerlaverock provides a good opportunity to get close to whooper swans.

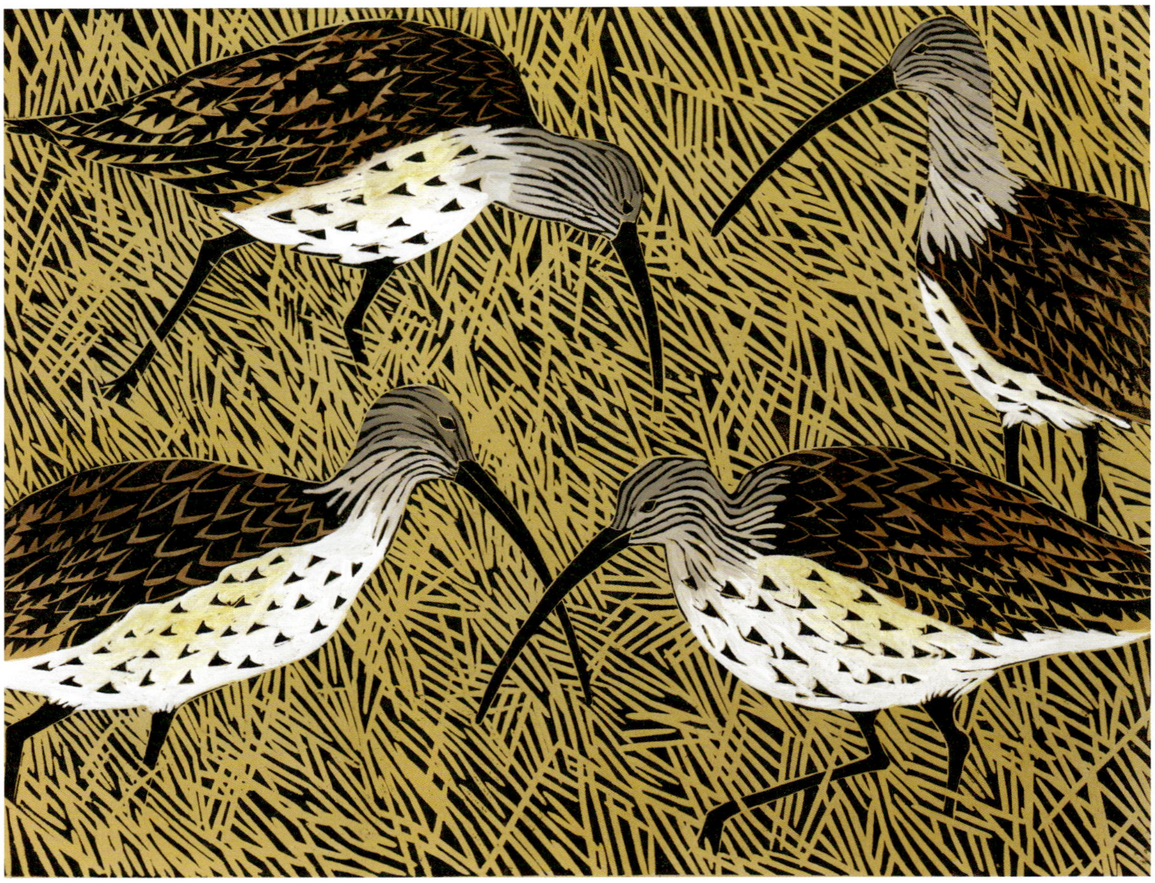

A head of curlews,
51 cm x 66 cm, 2009

Playing with texture - collagraph

'Life Is Serious But Art Is Fun!'

From *The Hotel New Hampshire,* by John Irving

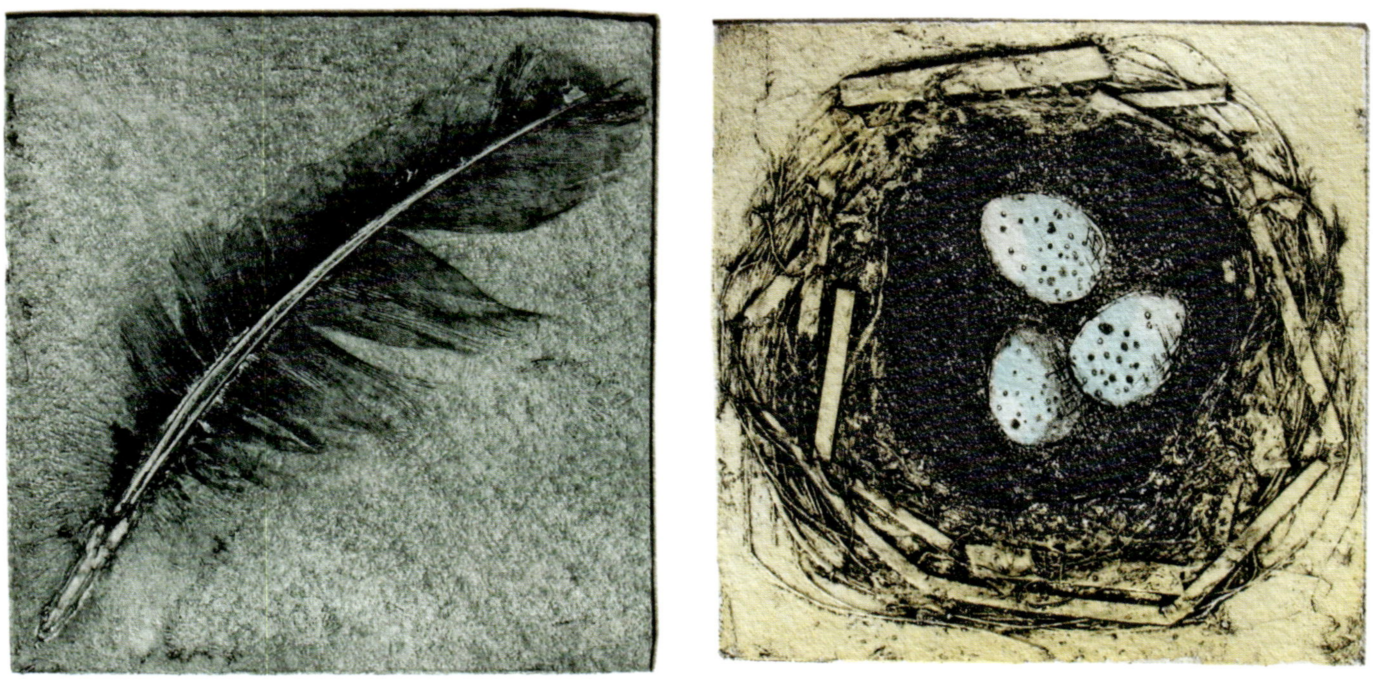

Bird Alphabet pictures: Feather and nest

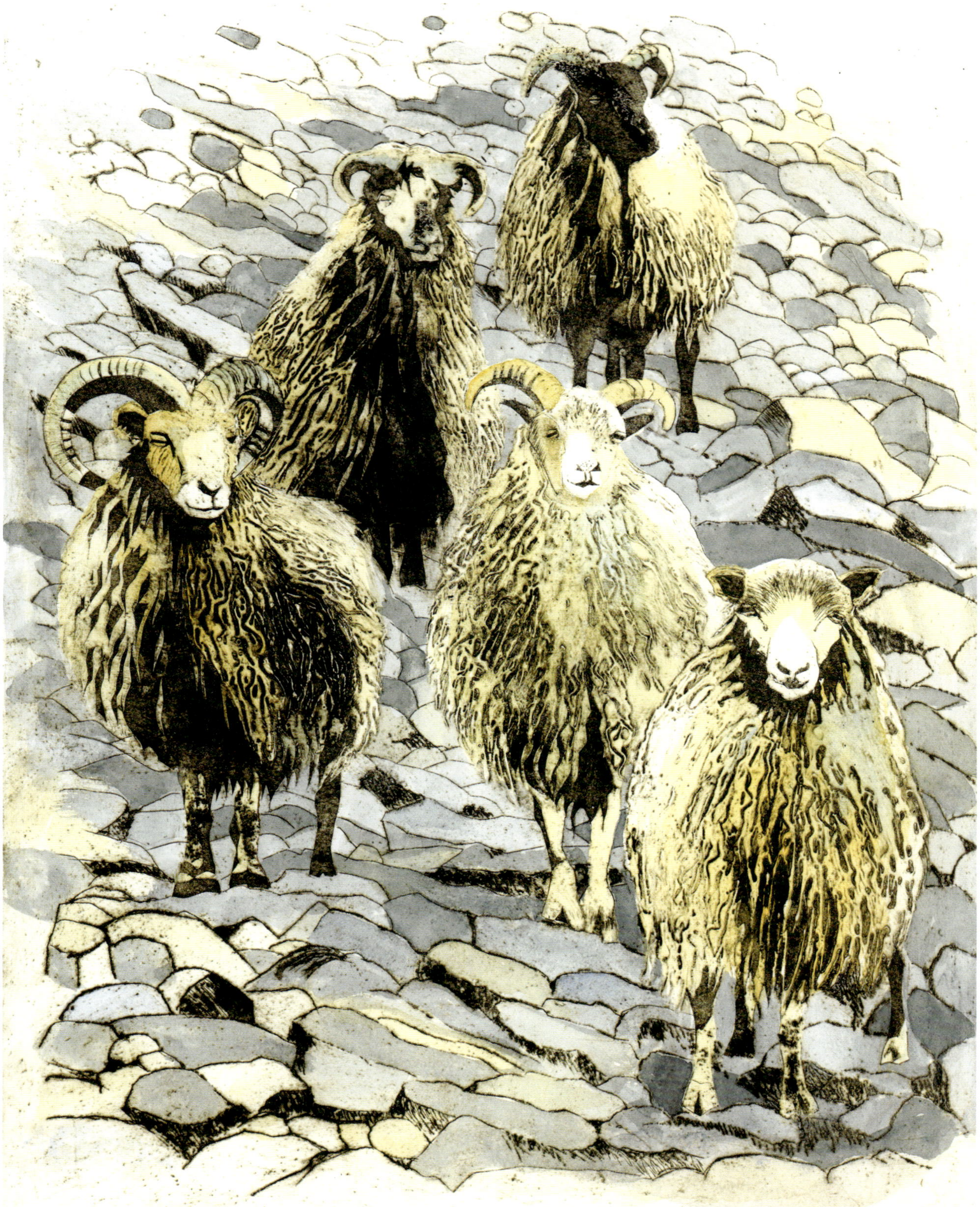

Beyond the Dyke, North Ronaldsay,
46 cm x 59 cm, 2012

This collagraph was made by cutting and engraving mountboard. The sheep's wool was sculpted using PVA. It was printed intaglio and then hand coloured. These are the famous seaweed-eating sheep on North Ronaldsay, which are confined to the beach for most of the year by a six foot stone dyke, which is a national monument. The breed is primitive and semi-feral. In places, their hooves have worn paths into the stones on the beach.

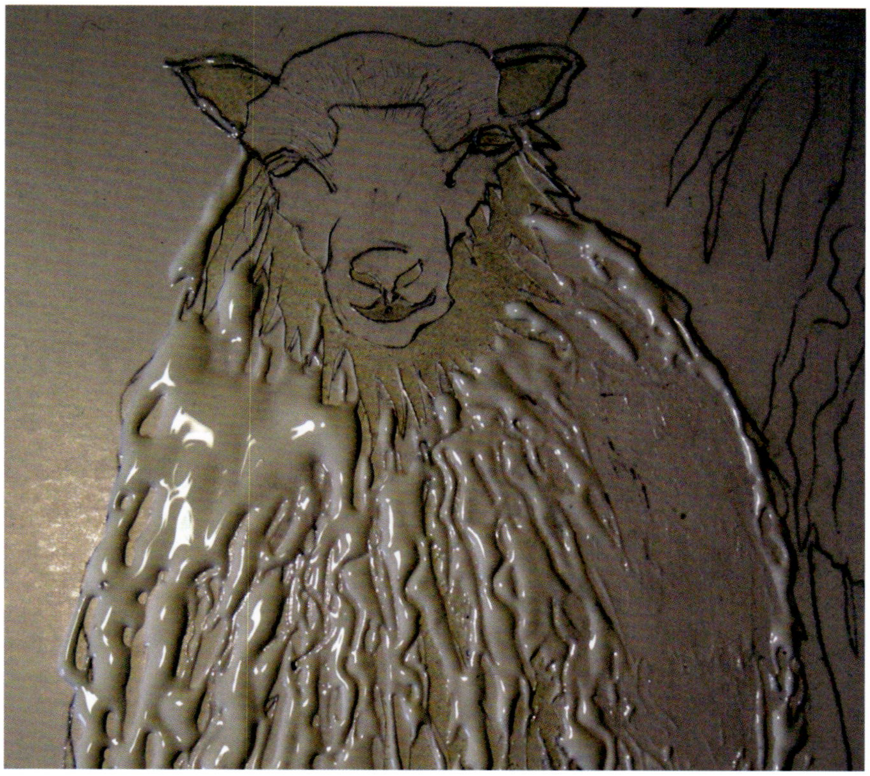

The collagraph plate for the North Ronaldsay sheep, showing the wet glue and also showing where the surface of the board has been peeled away to print the black areas of the face.

A collagraph print is a print taken from a block onto which textures have been added. For example, cloth, cardboard, sandpaper, string, cling film or foil can be glued to a plate to provide a surface from which to print. Carborundum, which is like fine sand, can be mixed with glue and applied to the card, or can be scattered over glued areas of card to provide a tooth for the ink (printing black).

GHOST,
34 cm x 25 cm, 2013

Barn owls are not very common in Galloway, so it's always a real treat to see one. Their white wings at dusk always seem ghostly. This print was made in the same way as the small print of the curlew (Grace) which appears later in this chapter.

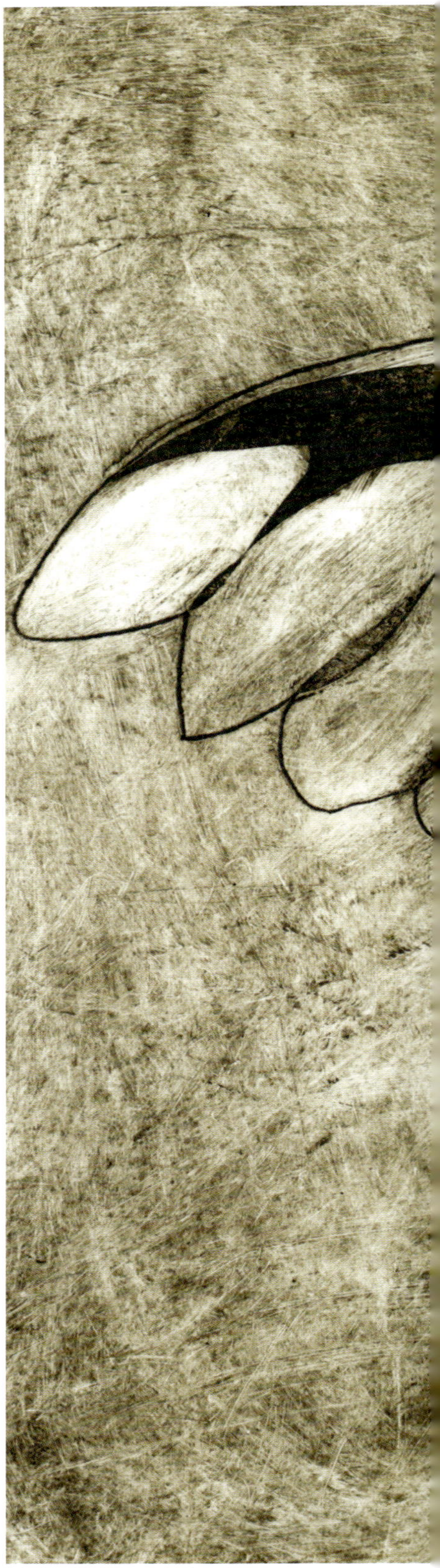

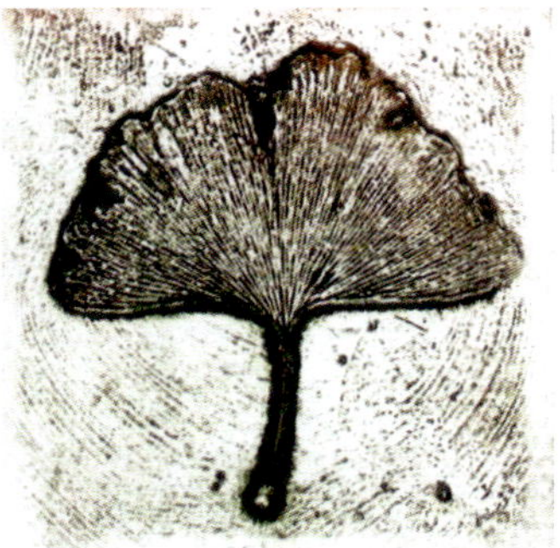

A simple collagraph print taken from a pressed ginkgo leaf.

You can also print from objects such as feathers and leaf skeletons in this way and glue itself can be used to, in effect, pipe textures onto the surface, provided it retains some body as it dries.

In general the textures should not be too thick, as very thick changes in depth get clogged with surplus ink and may also tear or crease the paper.

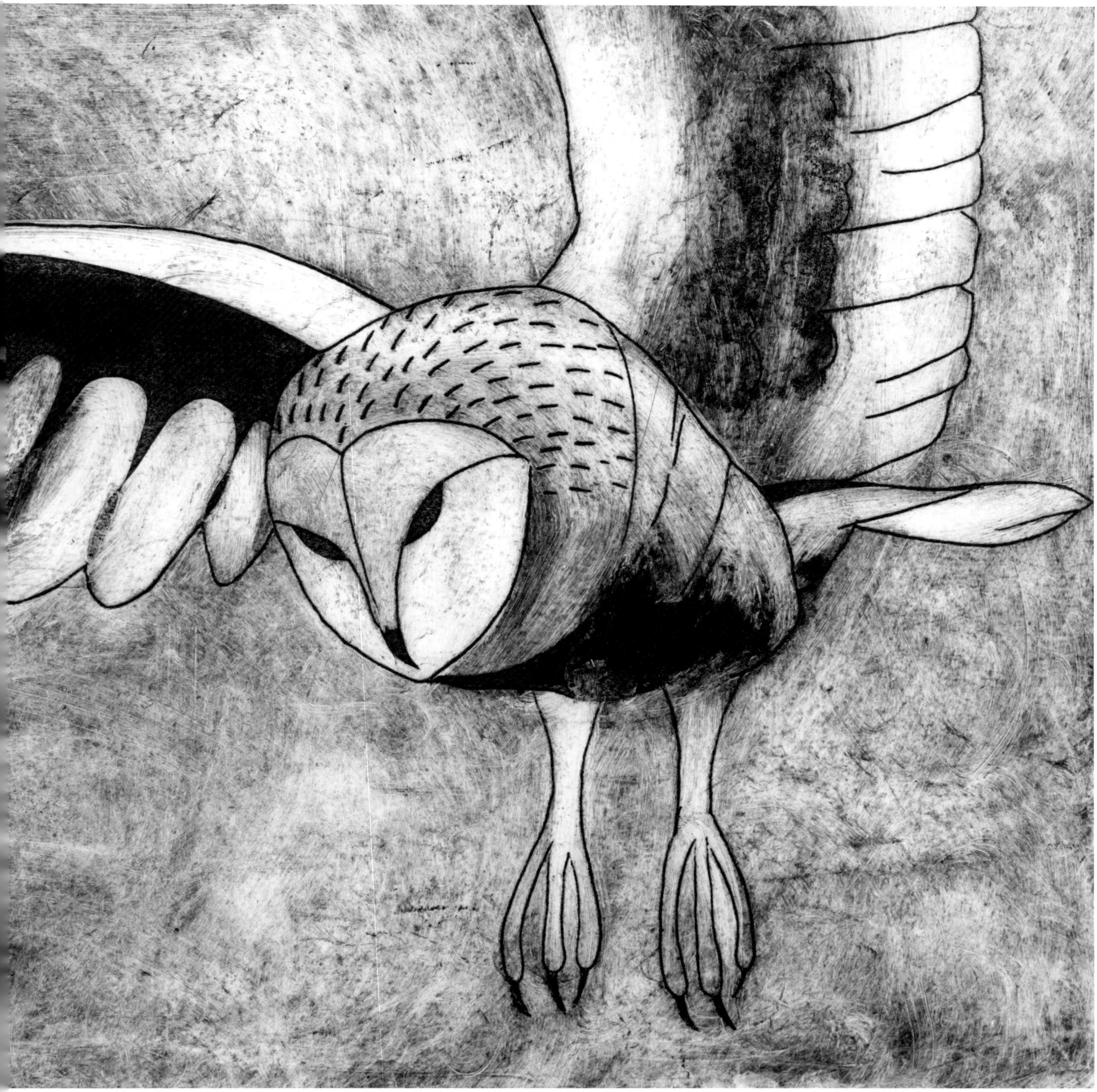

I use mountboard as a support for my collagraphs. The textured surfaces are glued to the board and then, when the glue is dry, the board is varnished a couple of times with shellac. This prevents the glue from adhering to the printing paper and protects the plate. It also makes it easier to clean.

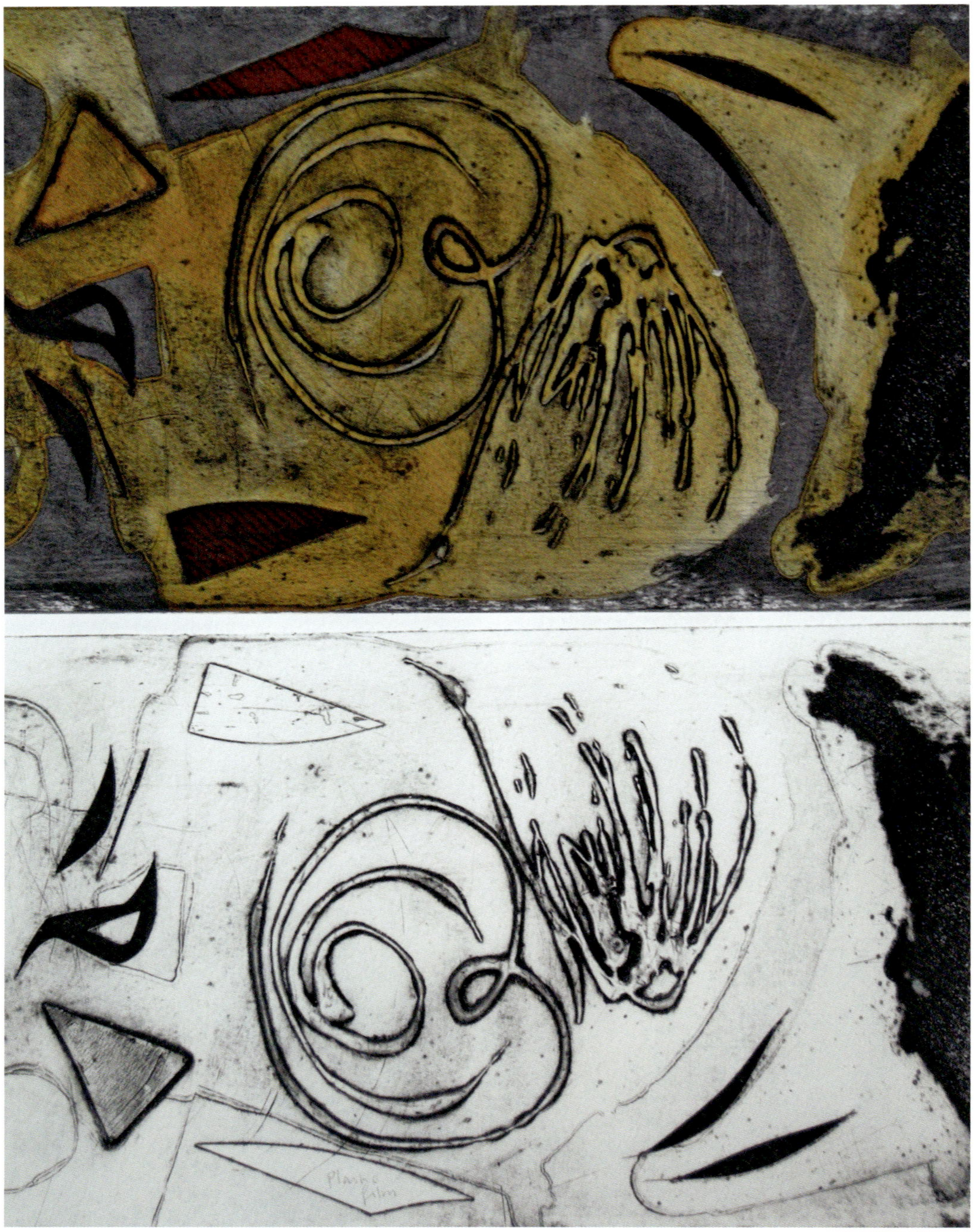

This shows the collagraph "plate" at the top, with the intaglio print below it. Various textures have been tested including glue, plastic, carborundum and surface peeling. The plate is brownish as it has been lacquered with shellac.

Collagraphs can be printed as intaglio prints, or relief prints. In other words, you can either force ink into the surface depressions and clean the top face of the plate for printing it through an etching press, or you can use a roller to ink the raised surfaces and print it with less pressure. You can also do both of course: ink and wipe the indentations in the plate for an intaglio print, then surface roll the top of the plate and print the whole thing through a press. Blind embossings can also be made by printing from a collagraph that has not been inked. It is a very versatile, though sometimes frustrating method of printmaking.

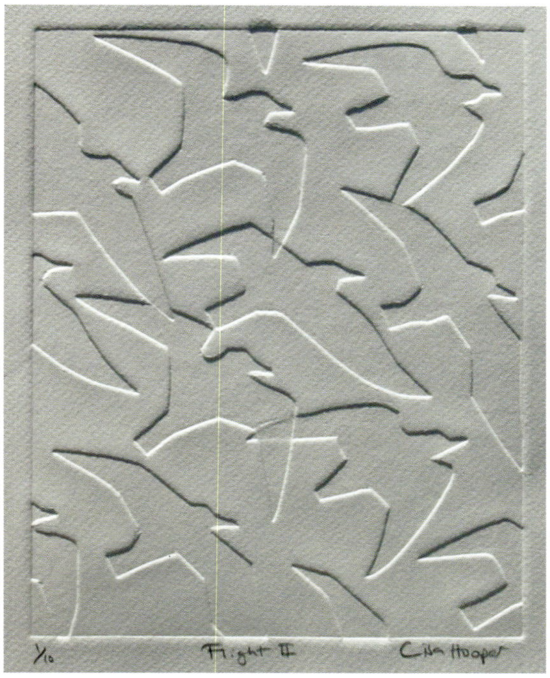

FLIGHT II, (embossing)
16 cm x 20 cm, 2006

The shapes have been cut out of thin card and stuck to the plate before printing onto damp paper through an etching press.

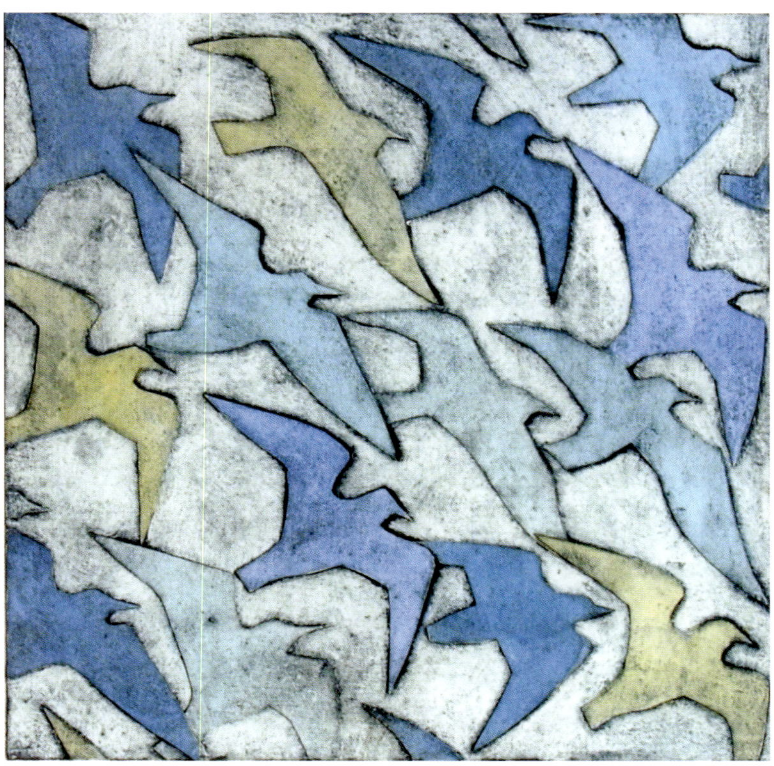

FLIGHT,
21 cm x 21 cm, 2006

This is actually a similar second plate, made in the same way, intaglio printed in blue, and then hand coloured with watercolour.

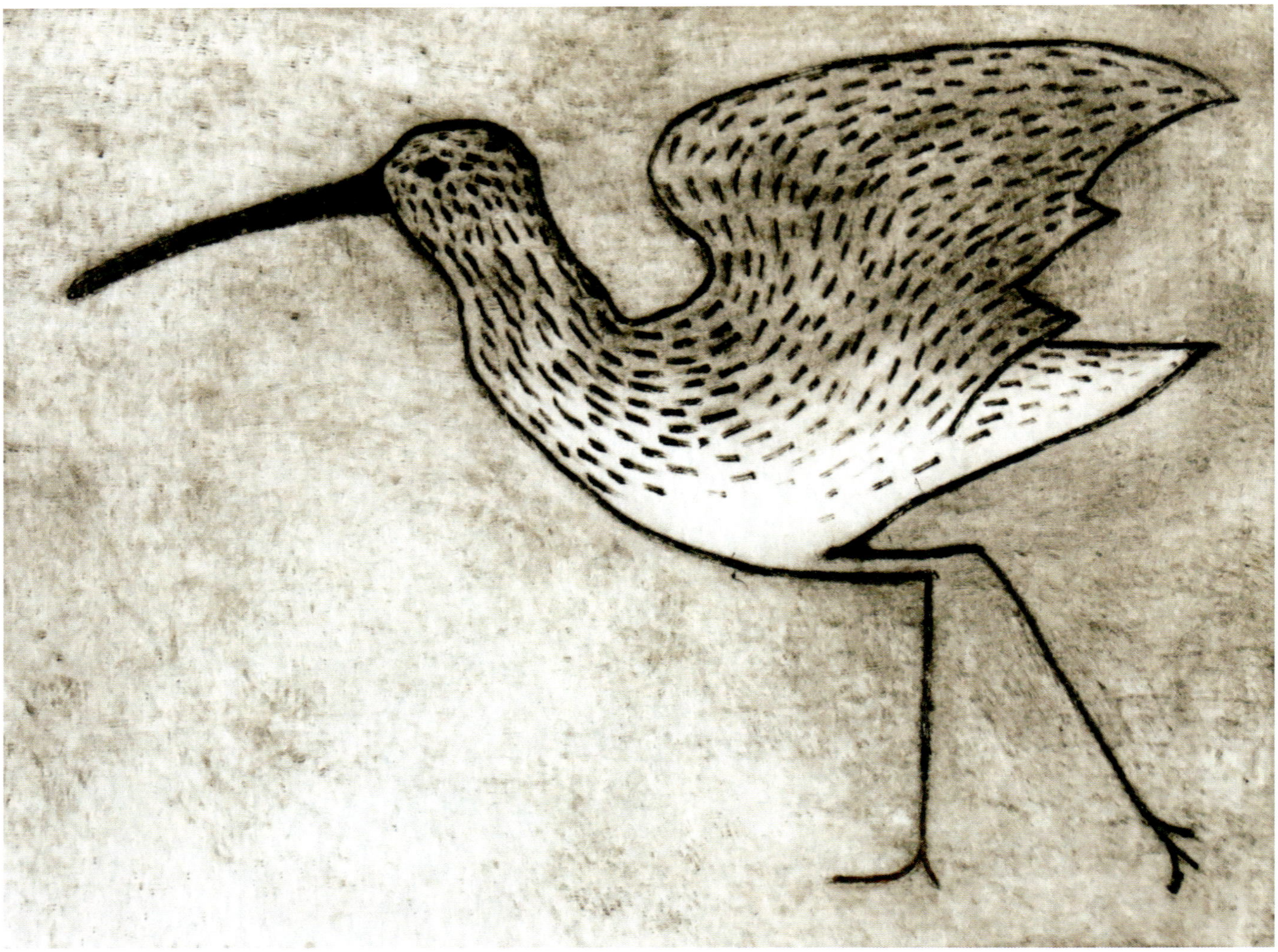

Grace,
18 cm x 14 cm, 2012

This little print was very simply executed by pressing an etching needle into the surface of the card to indent it. It was inked like an intaglio plate and wiped with differing pressure. (the body of the bird was cleaned more than the background). Strictly speaking it is virtually a drypoint print as nothing is glued to the surface, although the dark bill is created by surface manipulation. It was inspired by a curlew on Sanday in the Orkneys.

My collagraphs are all intaglio prints, as they seem to make better use of the textures. I now use a mountboard which has a readily peelable top surface, and where that inner board is exposed an intaglio impression will yield a good black. Plastic or foil will clean fully and yield white. Gesso or acrylic medium can be used to sculpt relief surfaces. Found objects which are thin and textured such as washers or plastic netting can also be used.

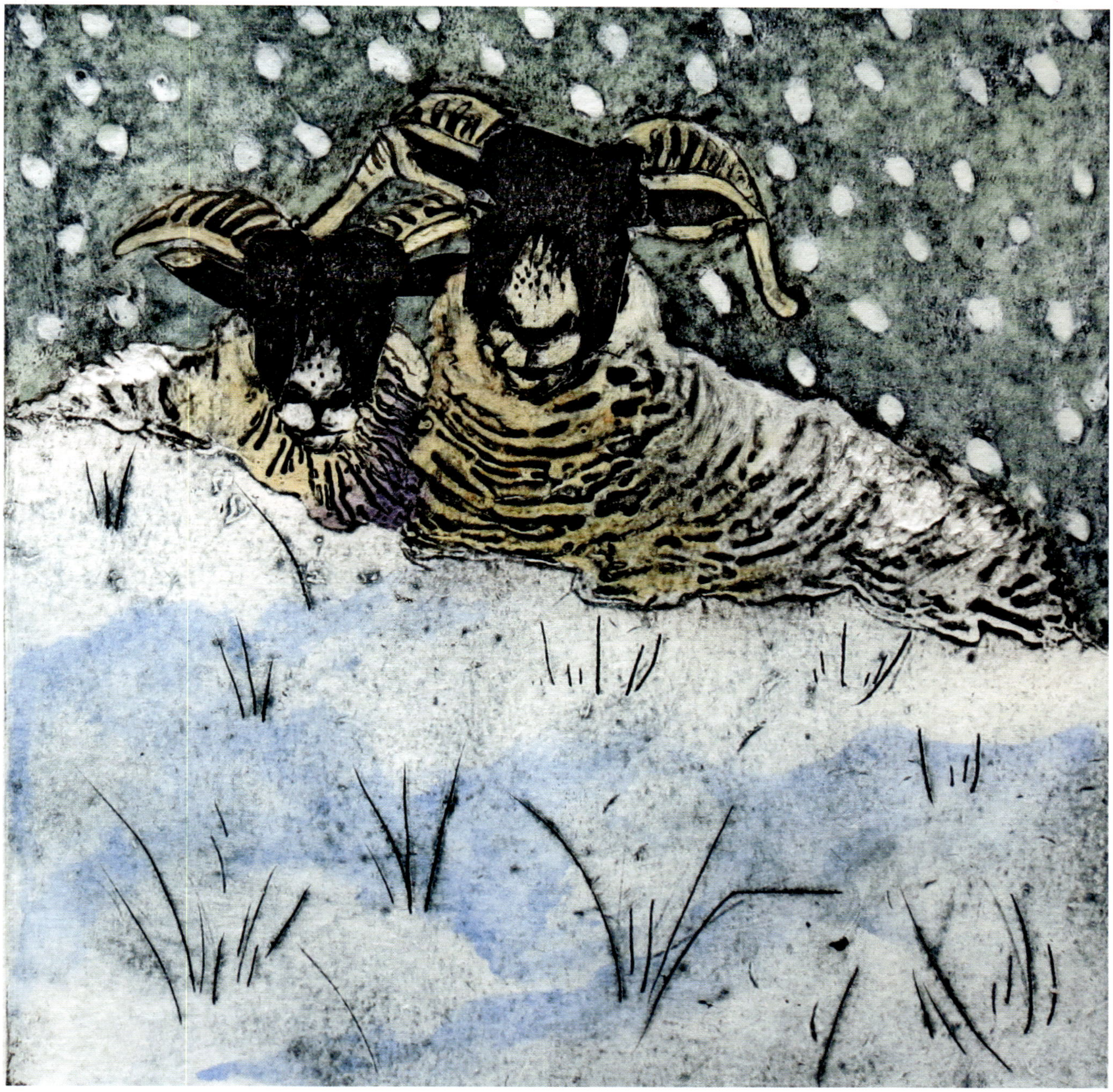

Winter sheep
15 cm x 15 cm, 2012

This has been printed in more than one colour and some hand colouring added.

When inking collagraph plates it is quite difficult to get etching inks into the depressions without slightly thinning it. Rather than using a card spreader I find a stencilling brush or toothbrush helpful to work the ink into the deep surface textures. Wiping the plate is also more difficult and it's easy to overwipe a collagraph, which can result in a dull print. Selective wiping is usually necessary to obtain the desired result. You can of course cut into the plate, use an engraver on the surface and cut plates of different shapes and sizes very easily.

The North Ronaldsay sheep in this chapter are a reminder of many happy days spent on Orkney. Increasingly, living in Scotland, we simply drive north for our holidays (and my inspiration), rather than go to the trouble of flying off anywhere. There is something enticing about the north; its remoteness, its emptiness, the frontier spirit of those making a living off marginal lands. The birds themselves seem to be more plentiful and confiding. It's easy to idealise but life in these places seems to be less of a scramble, less of a crush. Even Dumfries and Galloway, which is remote rather than particularly northern, is a gentler place than those I left behind.

Freestyle - monotypes and monoprints

'This is what I want to learn: to notice, but not analyse... You can do the organising and redrafting, the diagnosing and identifying later, but right now, just be open to it, see how it's tilting nervously into the wind, try to see the colour, the unchancy shape - hold it in your head, bring it home intact."

Kathleen Jamie, *Findings*

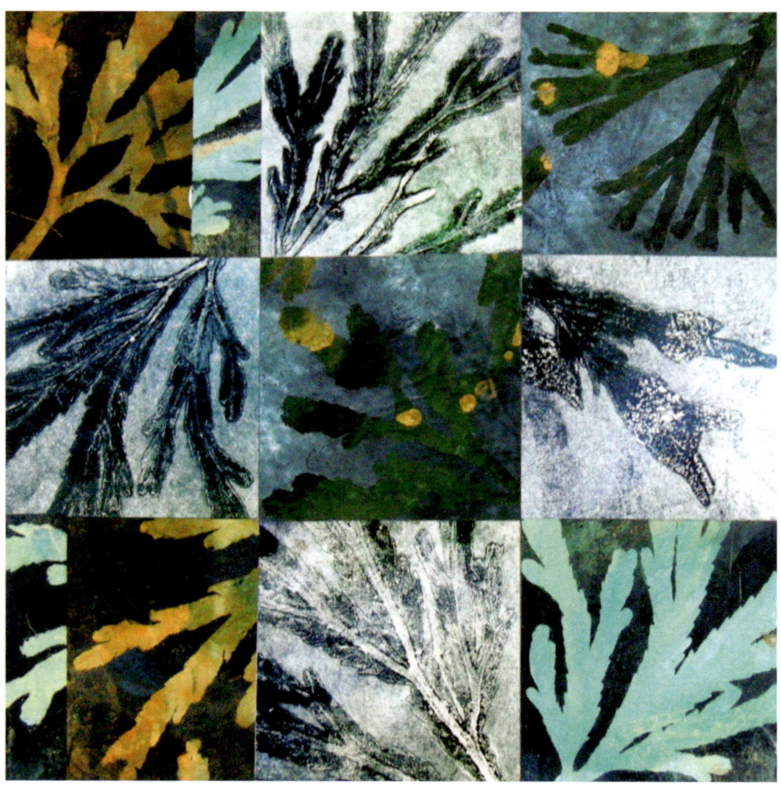

Example of a composite print of seaweed, using pre-painted papers.

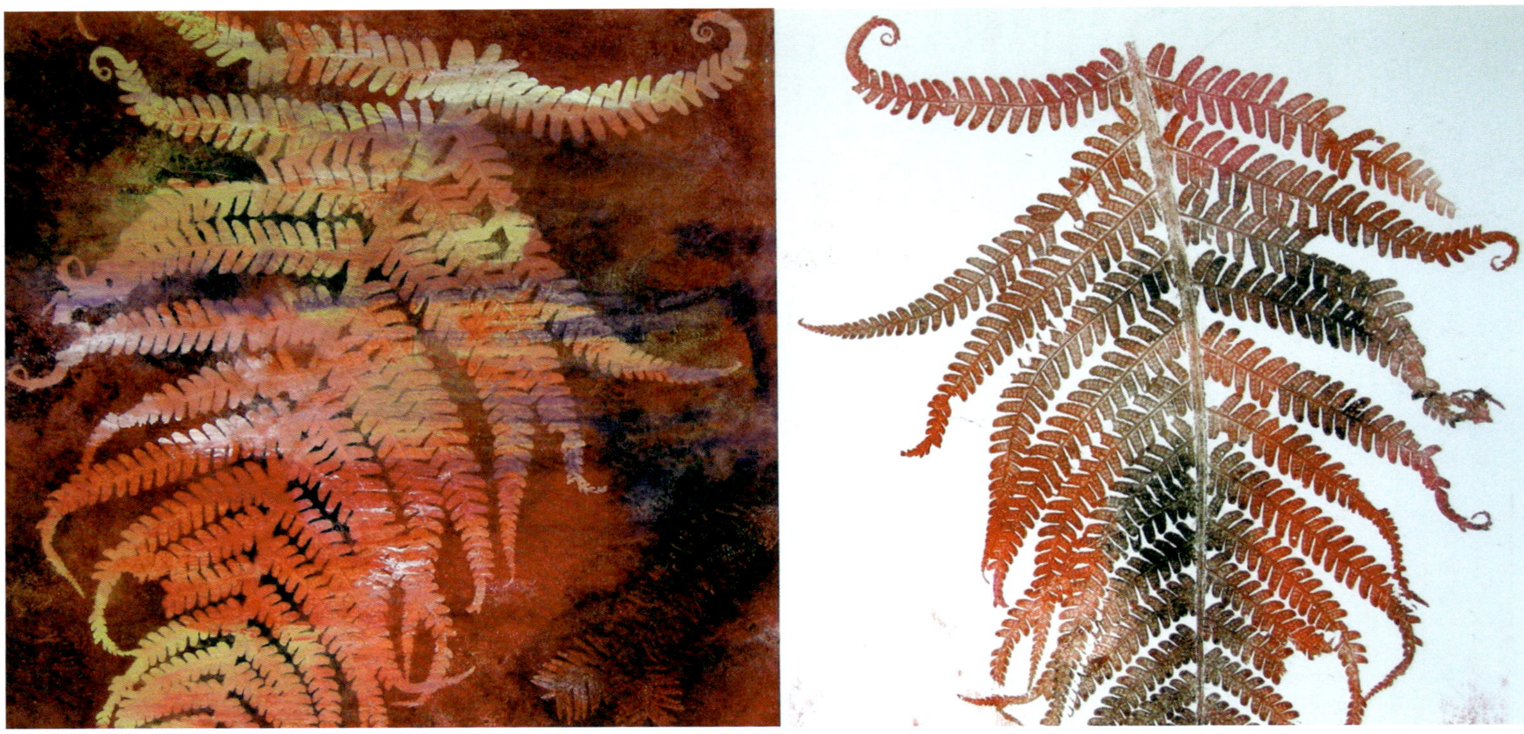

FRONDS,
70 cm x 37 cm, 2008

Monotypes and monoprints are frequently confused. Both are prints made from a flat surface onto which painterly marks have been made, and from which one unique print only can be made, but monoprints contain elements which are repeatable (such as stencilled parts) which mean that small editions of very similar prints can be made.

To make a monotype or monoprint, you need a flat surface from which to print. This can be cardboard, zinc, perspex or other flat non-absorbent surface. I mainly use perspex sheets. These can be cut and filed to shape, then it is a good idea to use sandpaper to put a key onto the printing surface.

Printing from a single coloured ground

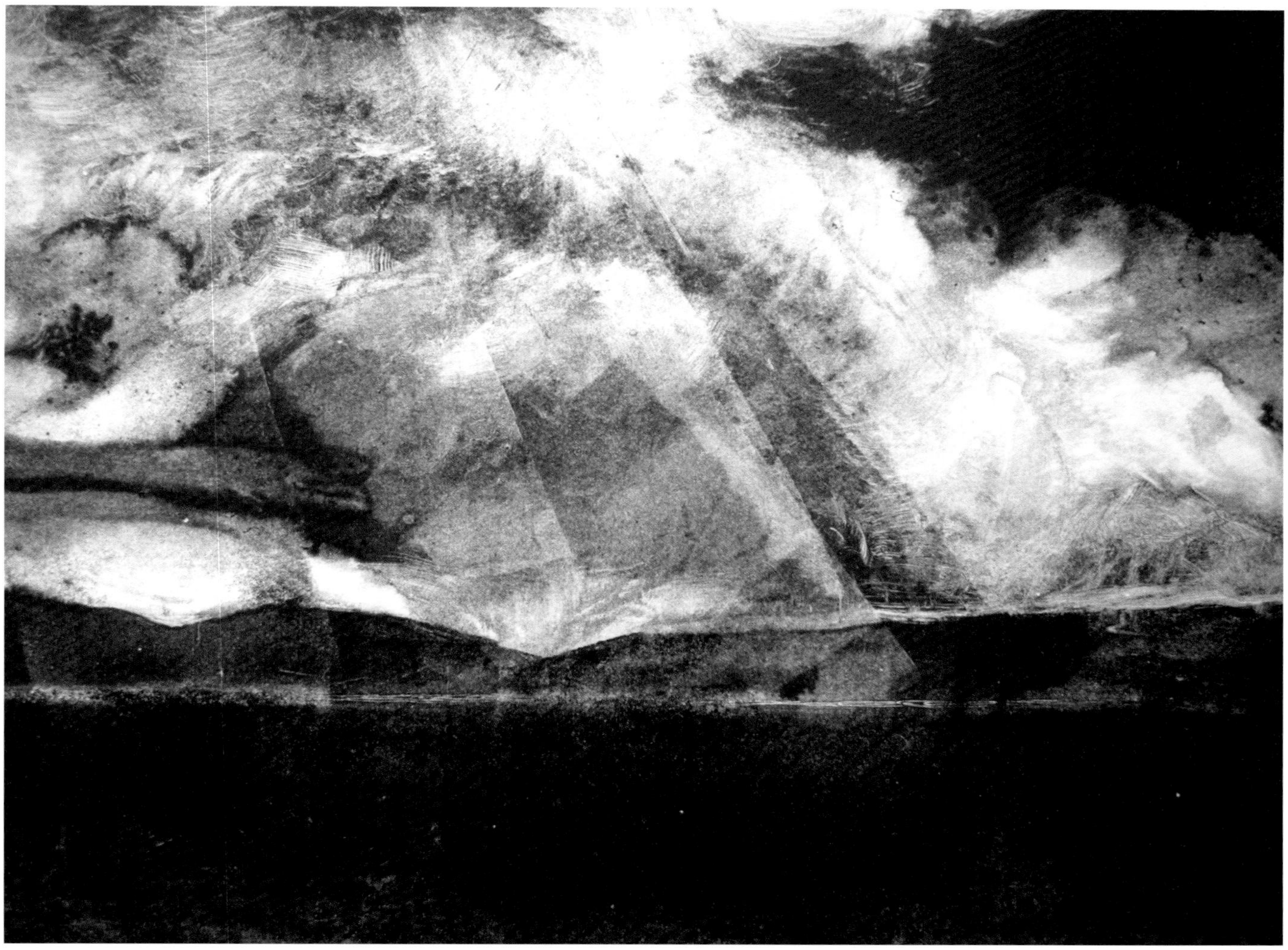

MULL OF KINTYRE FROM ARRAN, DETAIL, 2008

If you simply roll ink onto the plate and draw into it, or press different textures into it, you can create a monotone image which will print through a press

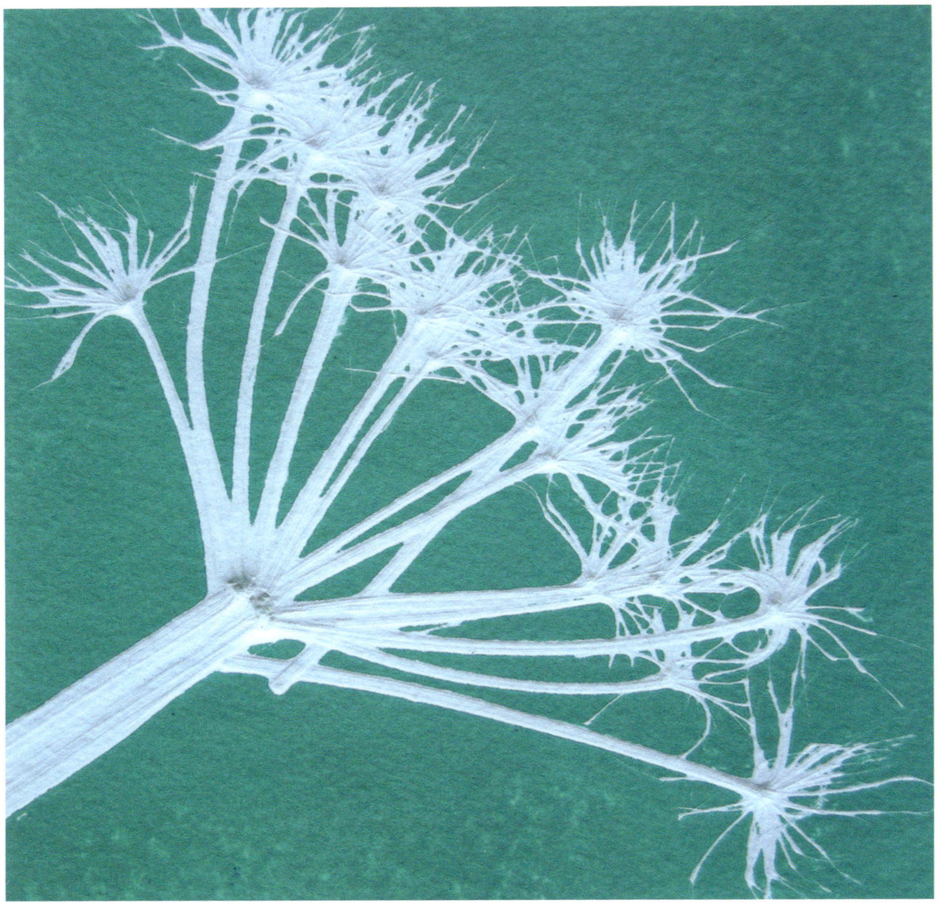

An impression from a hogweed seedhead.

A development of this involves laying a stencil between the inked plate and the paper, which will yield a perfect impression. Leaf skeletons work particularly pleasingly.

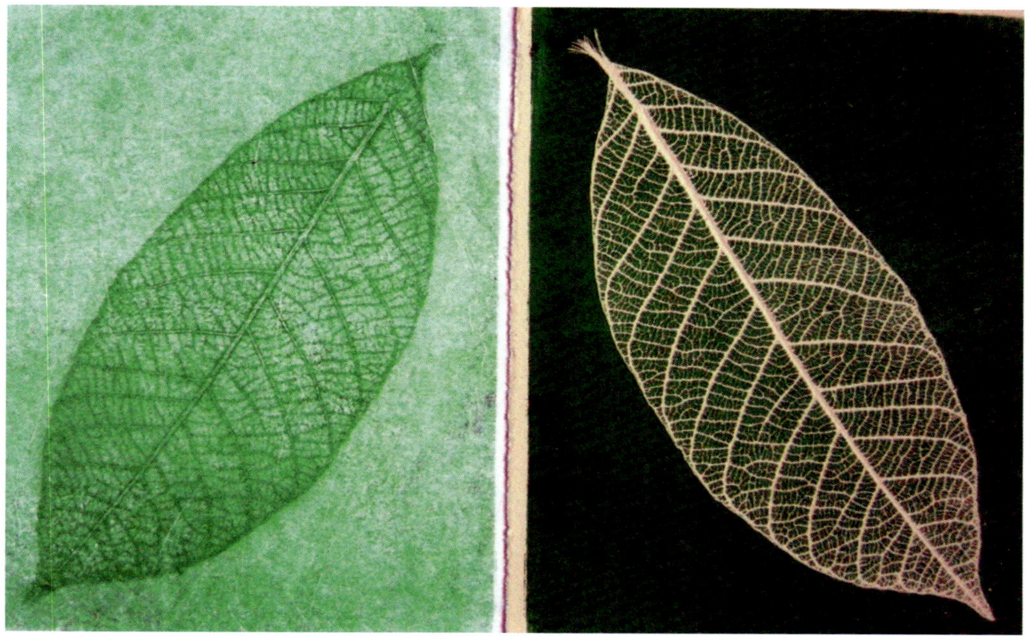

This shows a stencilled print on the right and a "ghost" print on the left. To make a ghost print the leaf is peeled off the inked plate after printing and a second print is taken from the plate. Where the ink has been pulled off by the plant material an impression is left, which prints. The plant has also been inked on its underside and by turning it ink face up, a positive impression can be made. This is how the positive frond in the print at the beginning of this chapter was printed.

Printing from multi-coloured grounds

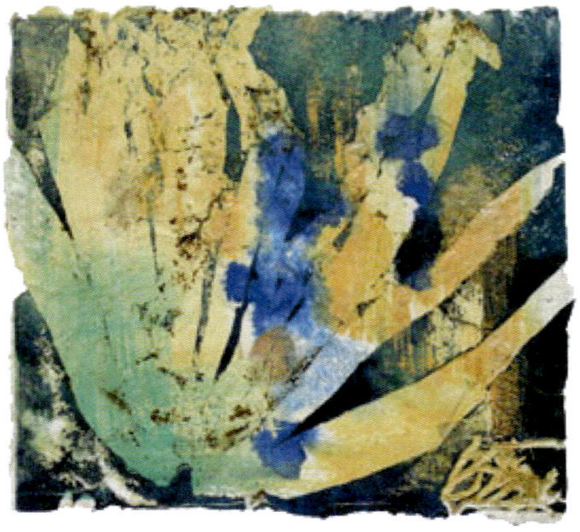

Oarweed
25 cm x 25 cm, 2008

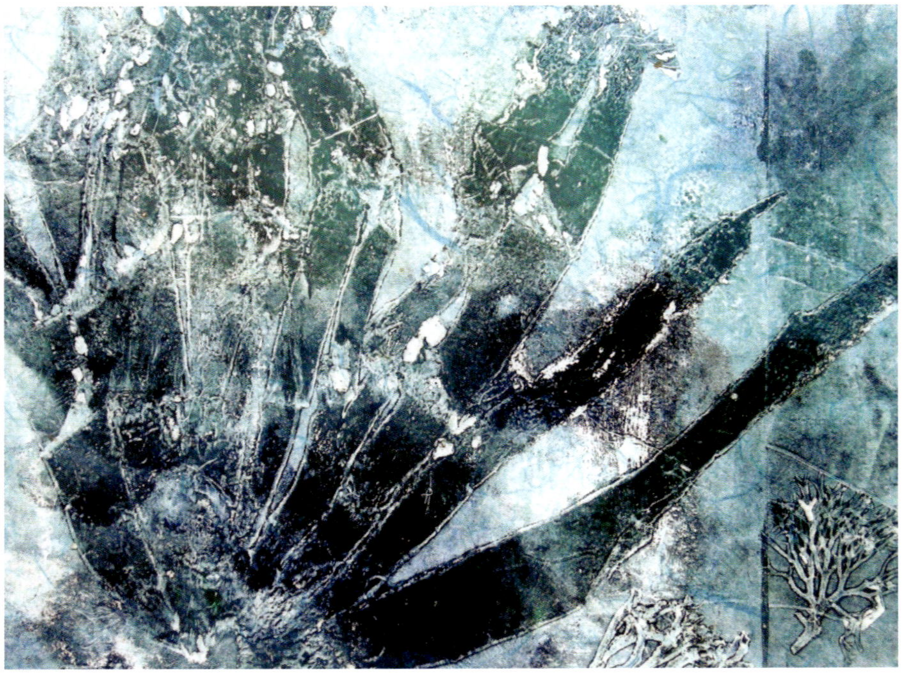

By removing the plant material and printing a second time, the marks left under the leaves will print as veins etc. This second pull is called a Ghost print.

I found that by pre-painting coloured papers (using acrylic inks which are insoluble once dry and are available in metallic colours as well) I could get interesting effects by using contrasting inks on the plates and sandwiching plant materials between the two.

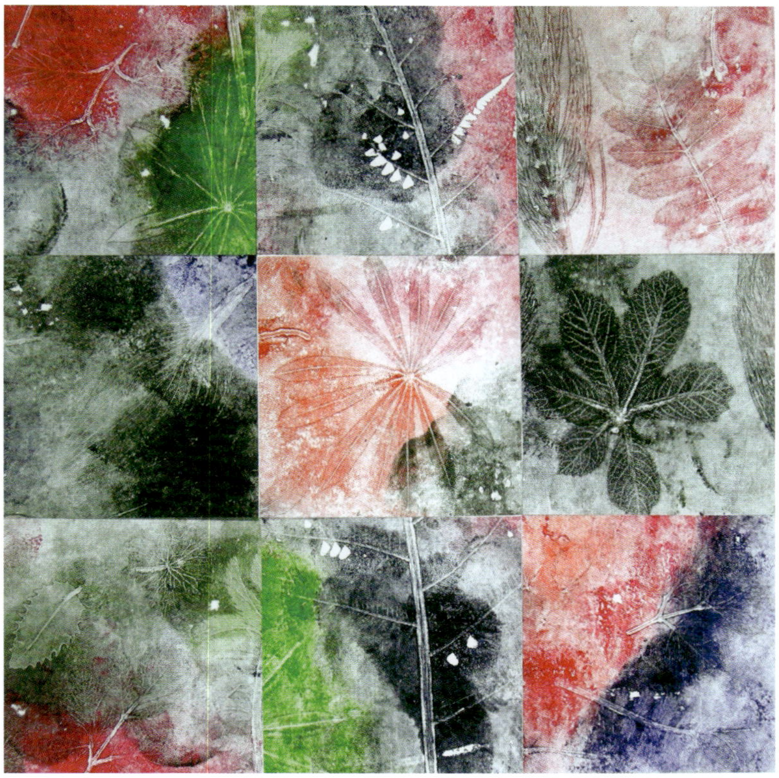

Garden Ghosts
55 cm x 55 cm, 2009

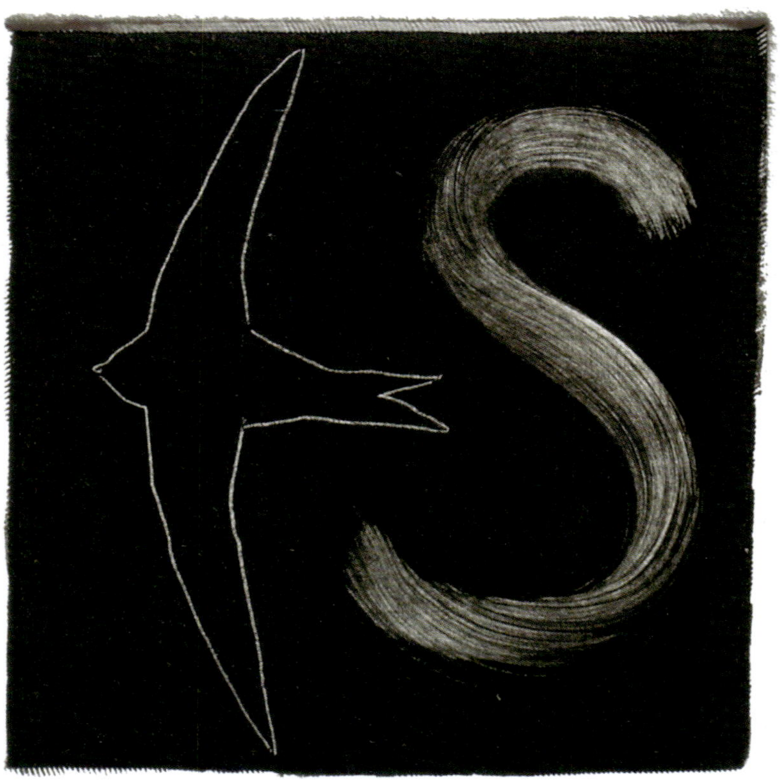

Bird Alphabet pictures: Swift
11 cm x 11 cm, 2006

Printing from real objects can be quite exciting and is a very old form of printing. Monotype prints of plants are extraordinarily accurate, almost like herbarium specimens. Recently, I was astonished to read about the history of printing from nature. It seems there is a centuries old and worldwide tradition of printing directly not just from plants and algae (eg seaweed) but also from dead animals including fish. The somewhat Pythonesque Japanese art of fish printing, known as Gyotaku is described at some length in Roderick Cave's book, Impressions of Nature: *a history of nature printing (The British Library, London, 2010), but is not something I have tried!*

Drawing onto a ground

If you ink up a plate in one colour or a series of colours, then gently lay a sheet of paper over it and draw on the back of the paper, lines will transfer onto the paper where you have drawn. By planning and drawing the design and going over it more than once you can achieve some interesting effects. Any pressure on the paper will result in ink transfer, so you have to be careful not to press onto the page, except with the pen or pencil you are using.

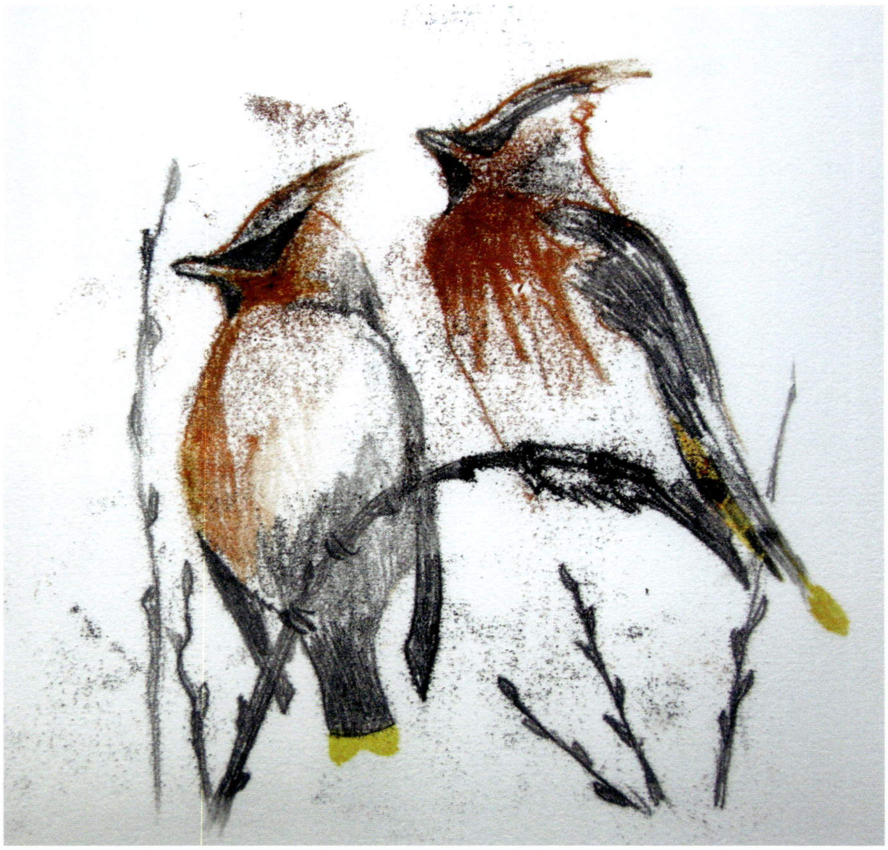

UNTITLED
25 cm x 25 cm, 2011

These two monotype sketches of waxwings were produced by drawing onto the back of the paper with an inked plate underneath. Several colours were used.

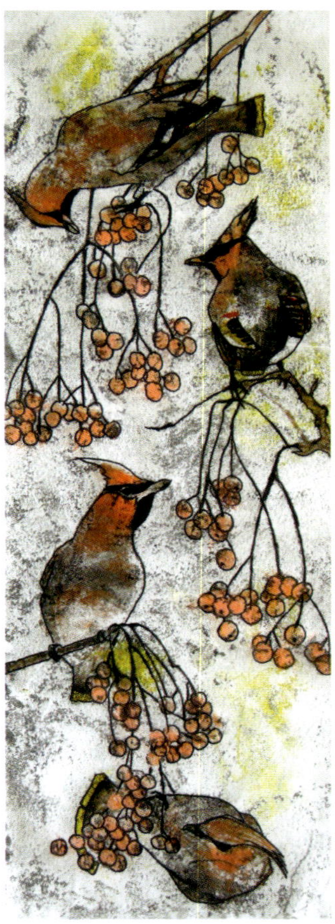

WAXWINGS,
22 cm x 58 cm, 2012

Using a roller to draw/paint

It is possible to create a design using a roller and perhaps a brush or two, from which to print. You need several rollers, some very small, and quite a bit of patience to do this, as the roller is quite a crude drawing tool, but the effects can be pleasing.

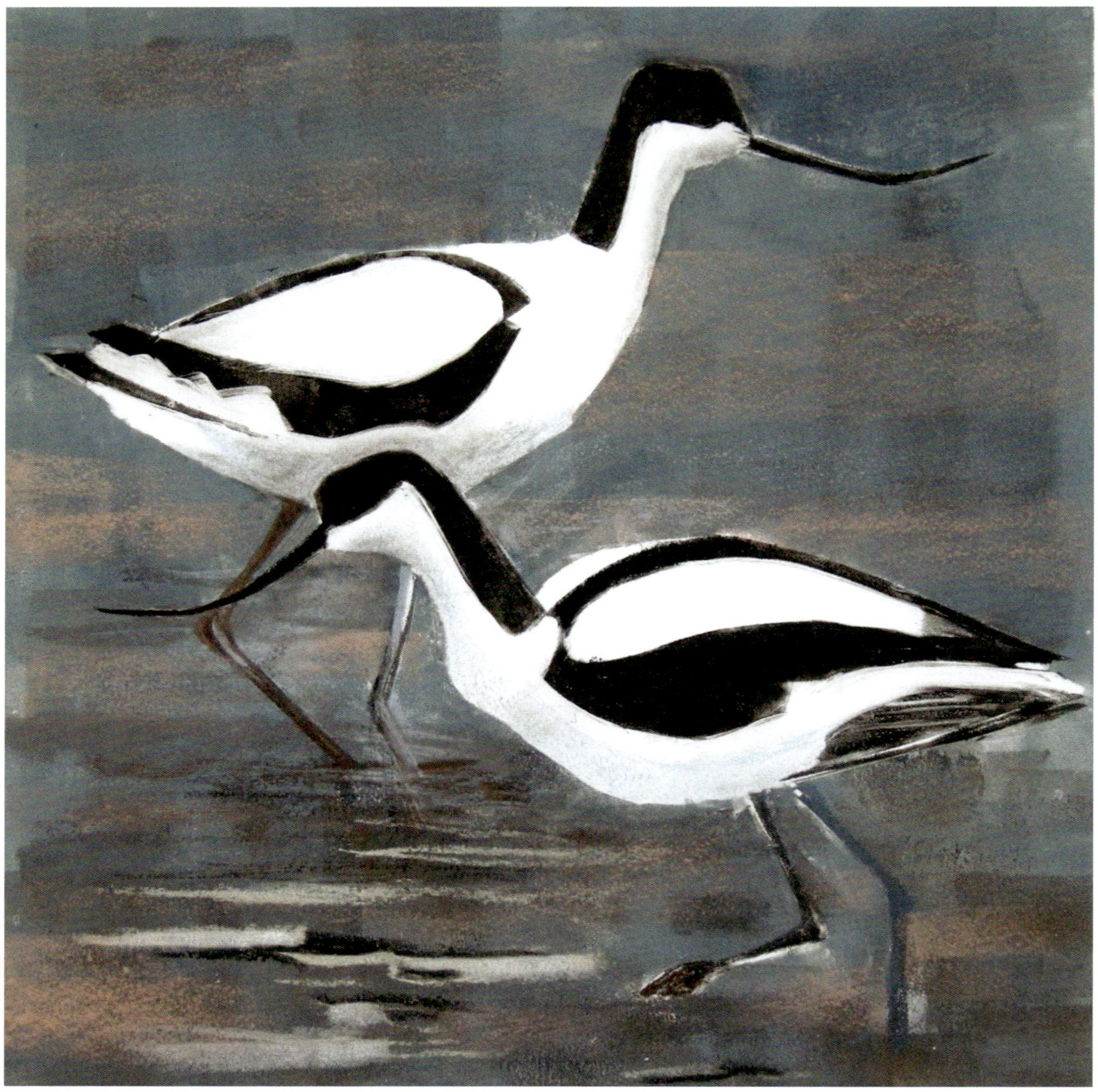

AVOCETS,
35 cm x 35 cm, 2011

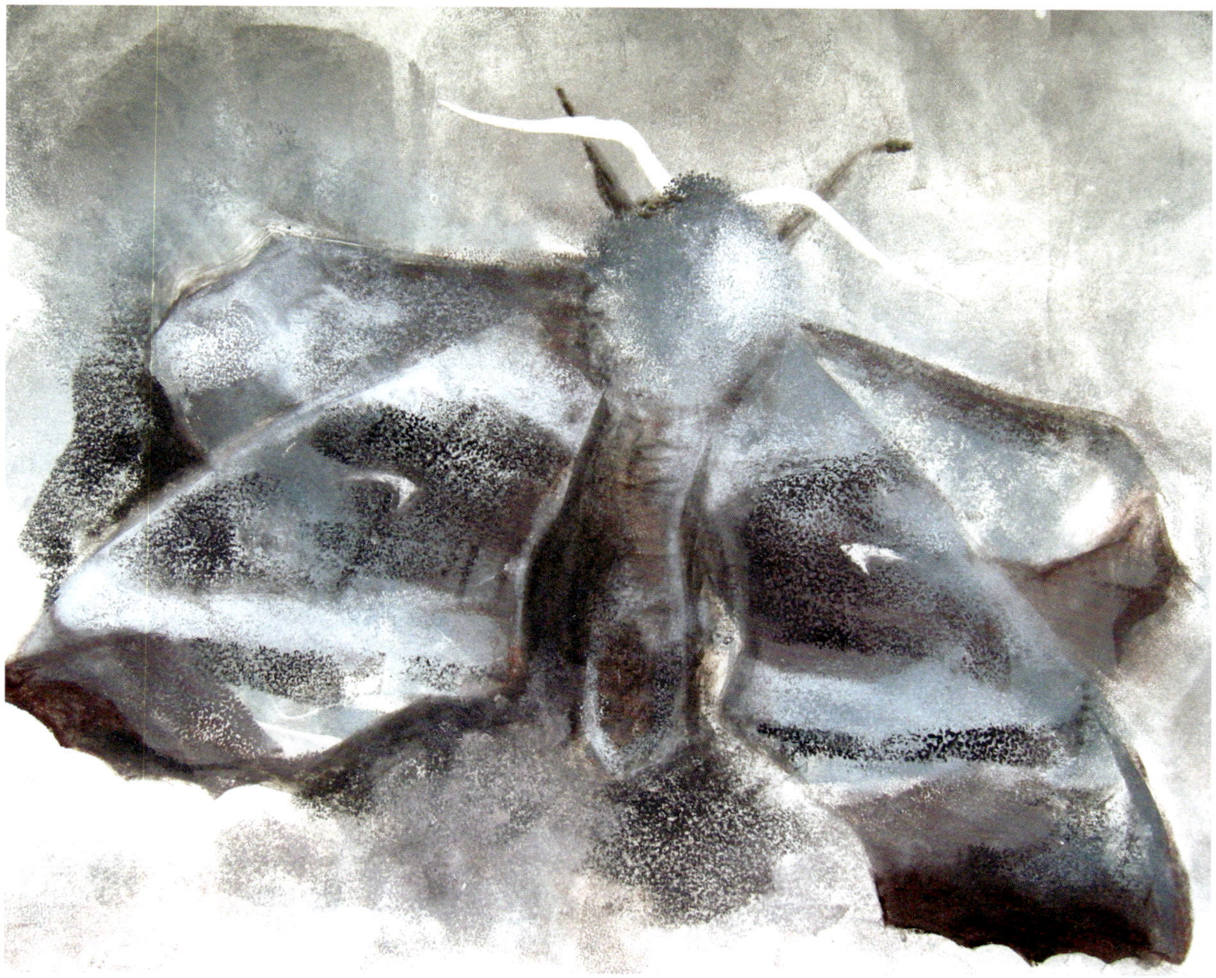

Poplar hawk moth,
36 cm x 32 cm, 2010

You can also use combinations of these techniques. For instance by using rollers and stencils I was able to make the print of Wigtown Harbour.

WIGTOWN HARBOUR,
29 cm x 38 cm, 2007

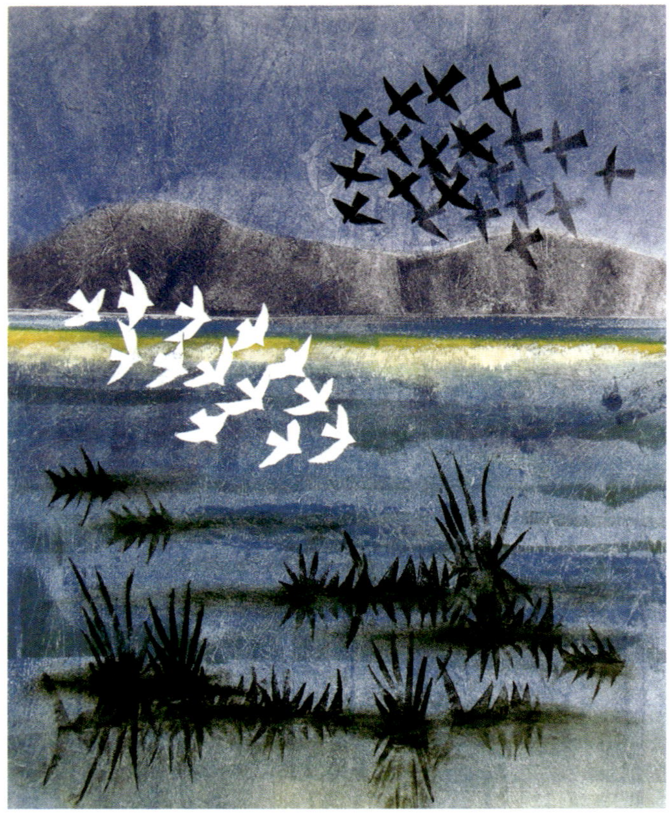

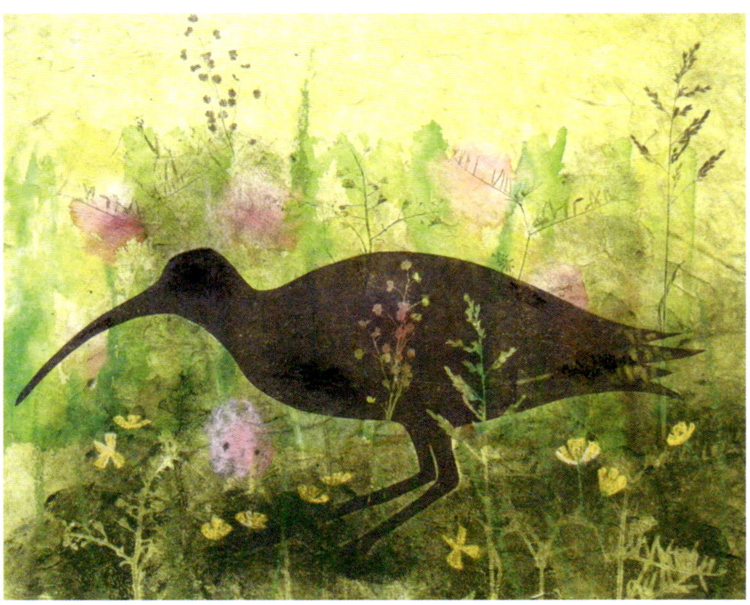

SUMMER QUARTERS,
37 cm x 29 cm, 2008

By using a stencil and a roller, in combination with grasses and plants as stencils I made this print of a curlew in a meadow, inspired by a summer visit to the Yorkshire Dales. This is technically a monoprint, because of the use of the stencilled shape of the curlew. By lifting the plants off the inked plate and putting them ink side onto the paper and running through the press a second time, I was able to get a positive impression of some of the grasses, which helped to add depth to the print. The paper was also pre-painted.

Monotype is a very painterly technique suited to small or single editions.

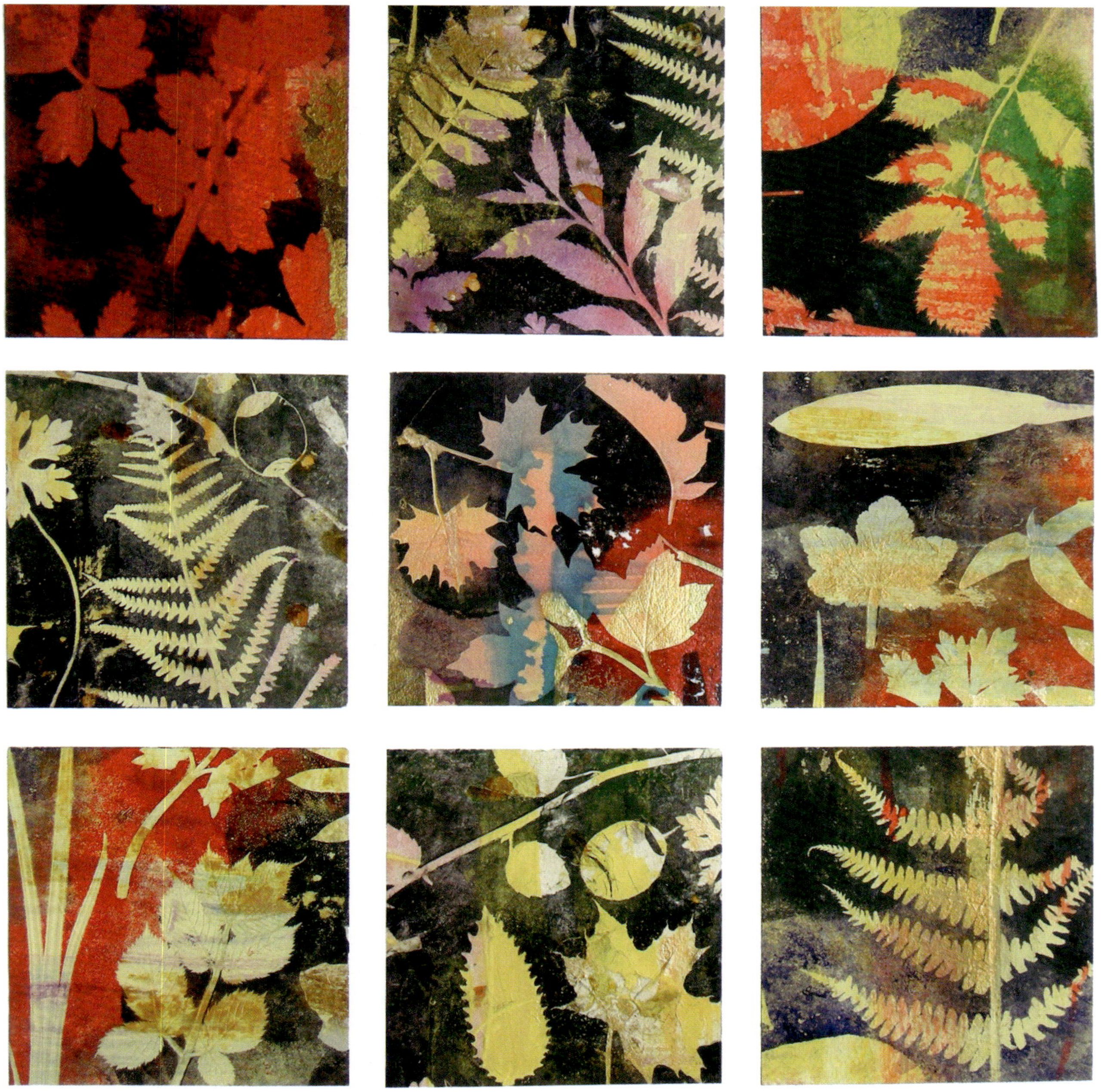

Garden Window,
50 cm x 50 cm, 2008

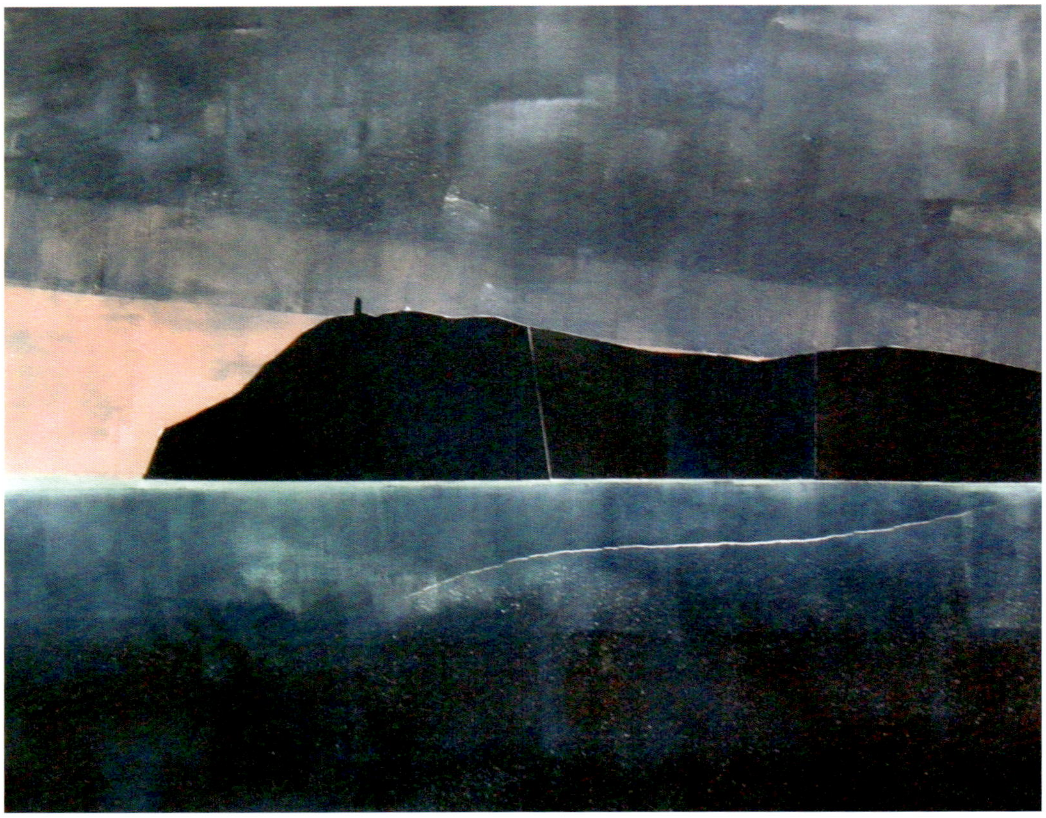

The Mull,
38 cm x 39 cm, 2007

The view of the Mull of Galloway from Port William, where I live.

Japanese woodblock printing

'The wren Looking here, looking there, - "Dropped something?"'

The Wren, Issa Kobayashi (1763—1828)
Japanese Haiku translated by R H Blyth

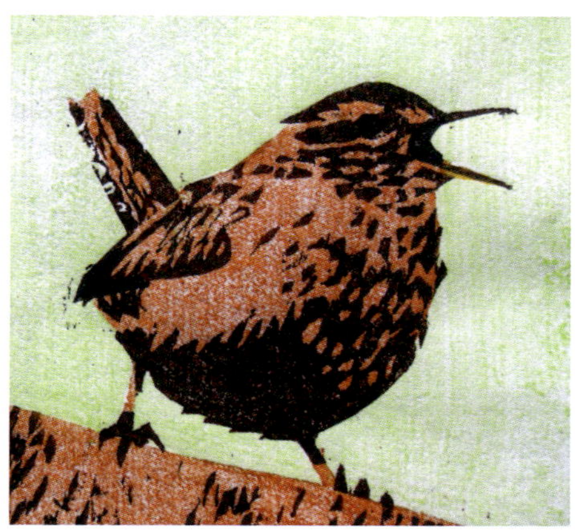

Wren,
8.5 cm x 8.5 cm, 2011

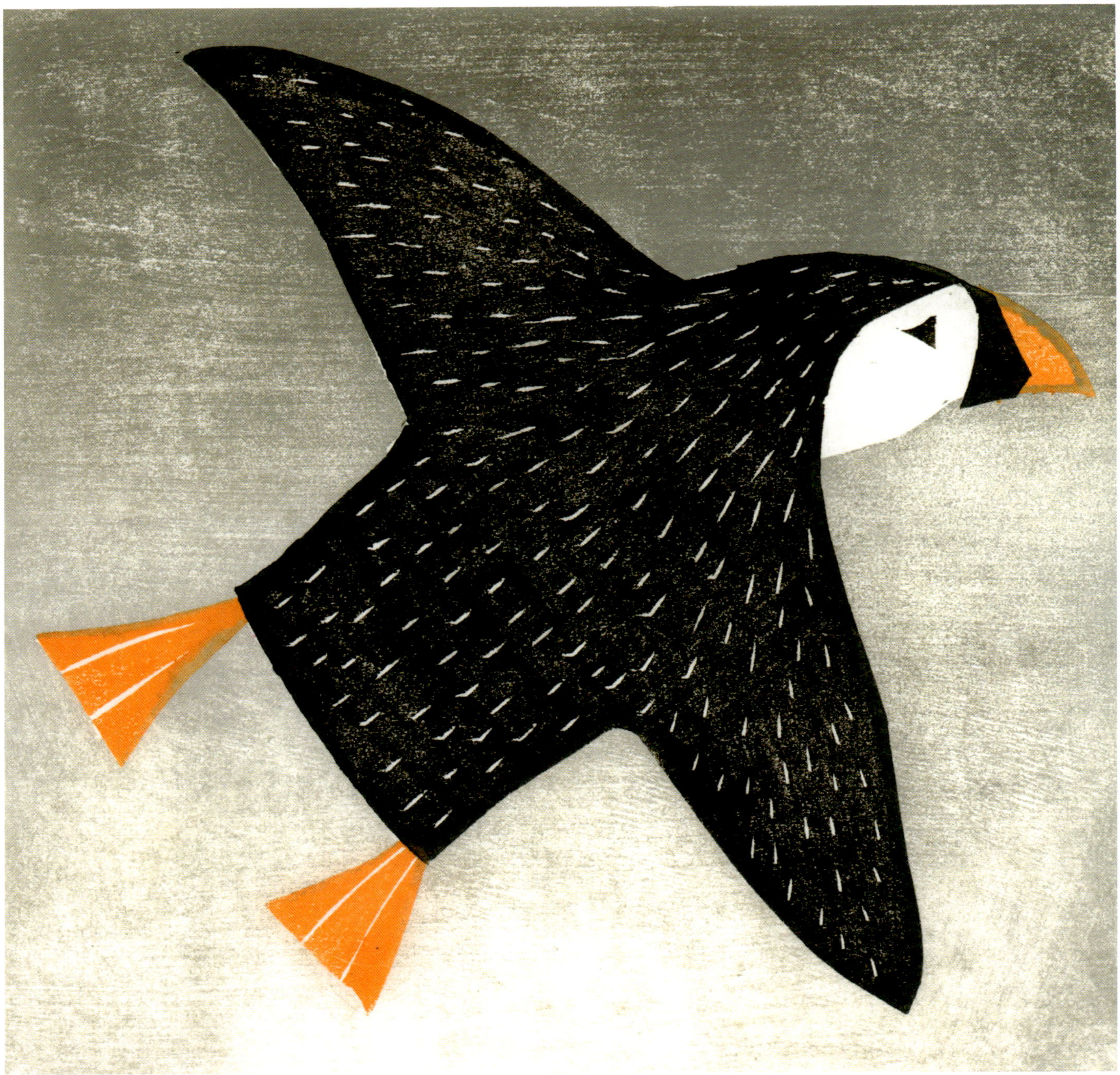

The physical inspiration for this print was a morning spent watching puffins at the Castle of Burrian, on Westray, Orkney. Their short flights struck me as rather comical and I wanted to capture this in a print. However, there is also a strong Inuit influence on this print seen in the pattern on the body and the very spare drawing.

The evolution of woodblock printing or Mokuhanga in Japan differed in lots of ways from European printing. It is believed to have existed in Japan for more than eleven centuries, and originated in China. In the seventeenth and eighteenth centuries, when books other than scriptures began to be produced, there was a flowering of the art and the first multicoloured prints were made.

When I am demonstrating the technique, people often ask "What's Japanese about it?" A summary of the main features follows:

- in general one block is cut for each colour, often with a black key plate
- traditionally Cherry wood was used
  there is a system of registration called "Kentō" which is unique to Japanese woodblock printing
- the inks used are water-based and applied with brushes
- rice paste is used as an extender
- therefore techniques for grading and blending tones on the block are different
- the paper has to be damp and is prepared overnight
- the paper is generally quite thin and absorbent with good wet strength and usually contains a high proportion of mulberry fibre ("Kōzo")
- the back of the paper is hand burnished using a Japanese baren and relatively little pressure.

Sometimes I really enjoy the challenge of honing down an image of a bird to its essentials. Although I have said that I don't like images of birds with no context, I have occasionally sought a kind of purity of expression with my bird art, which has dictated little or no background interference. These prints are inspired by Inuit art, which at its best portrays the birds and animals important to Inuit everyday life with a timeless and pure simplicity. I have gathered a small collection of Inuit art books and I often gain inspiration by poring over the plates. My puffin Japanese woodblock is an example of a print which started as a childlike doodle, seeking to capture the slightly silly look of a flying puffin (a leg at each corner) and finished up as rather a strange hybrid: a Japanese woodblock print, inspired by Inuit art. My curlew collagraph, Grace, I would put in a similar category. Both say something real and observed about the birds and both are identifiable to species level. They suggest an environment of some sort (the sands of Sanday, the grey sky of an Orkney day) but there is much less information about context than usual, which forces the viewer to focus on the bird exclusively.

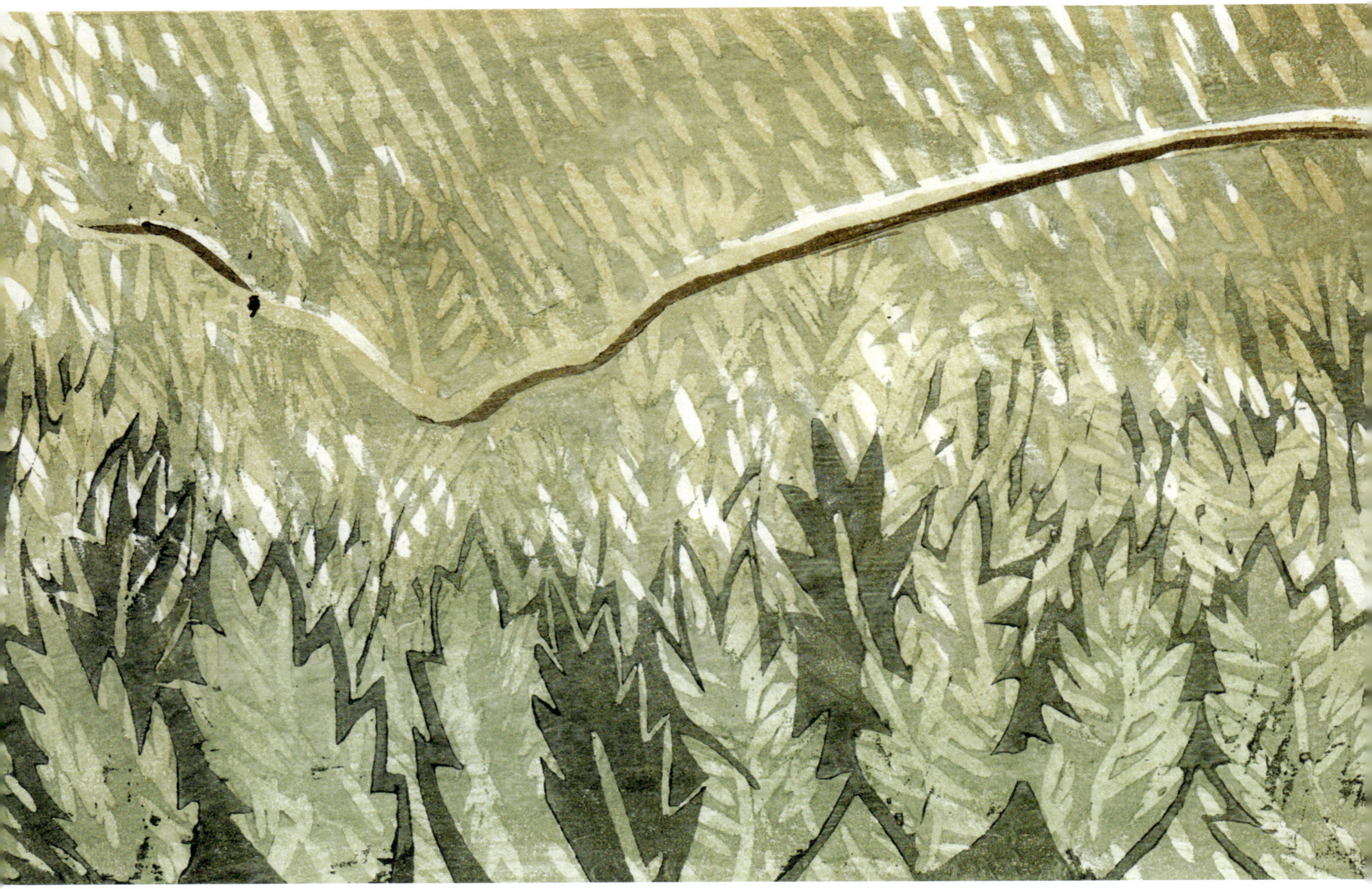

Sedge warbler, Blakeney,
52 cm x 17 cm, 2011

Inspired by numerous sedge warblers on the Blakeney marshes, this Japanese woodblock uses five plates.

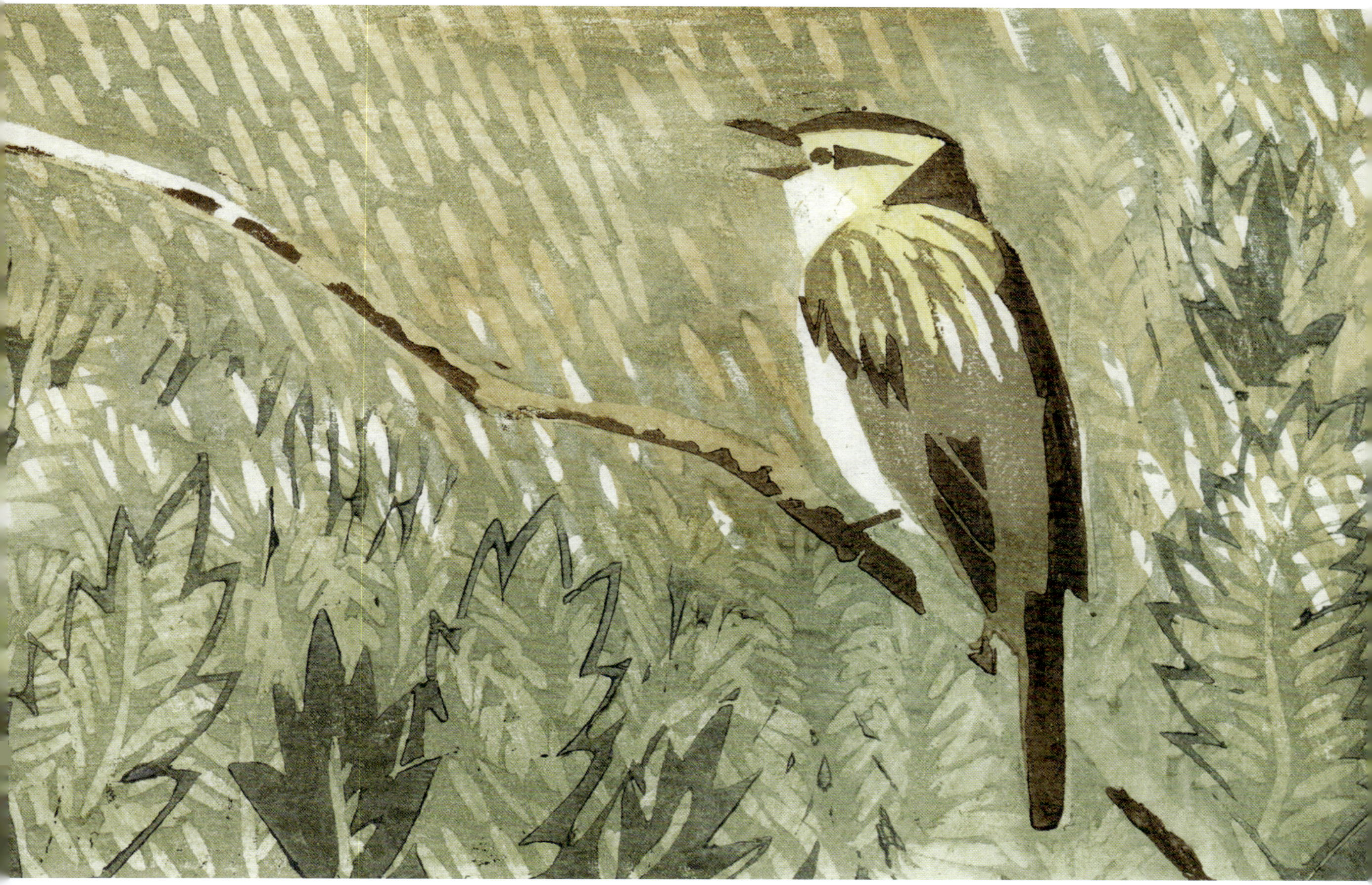

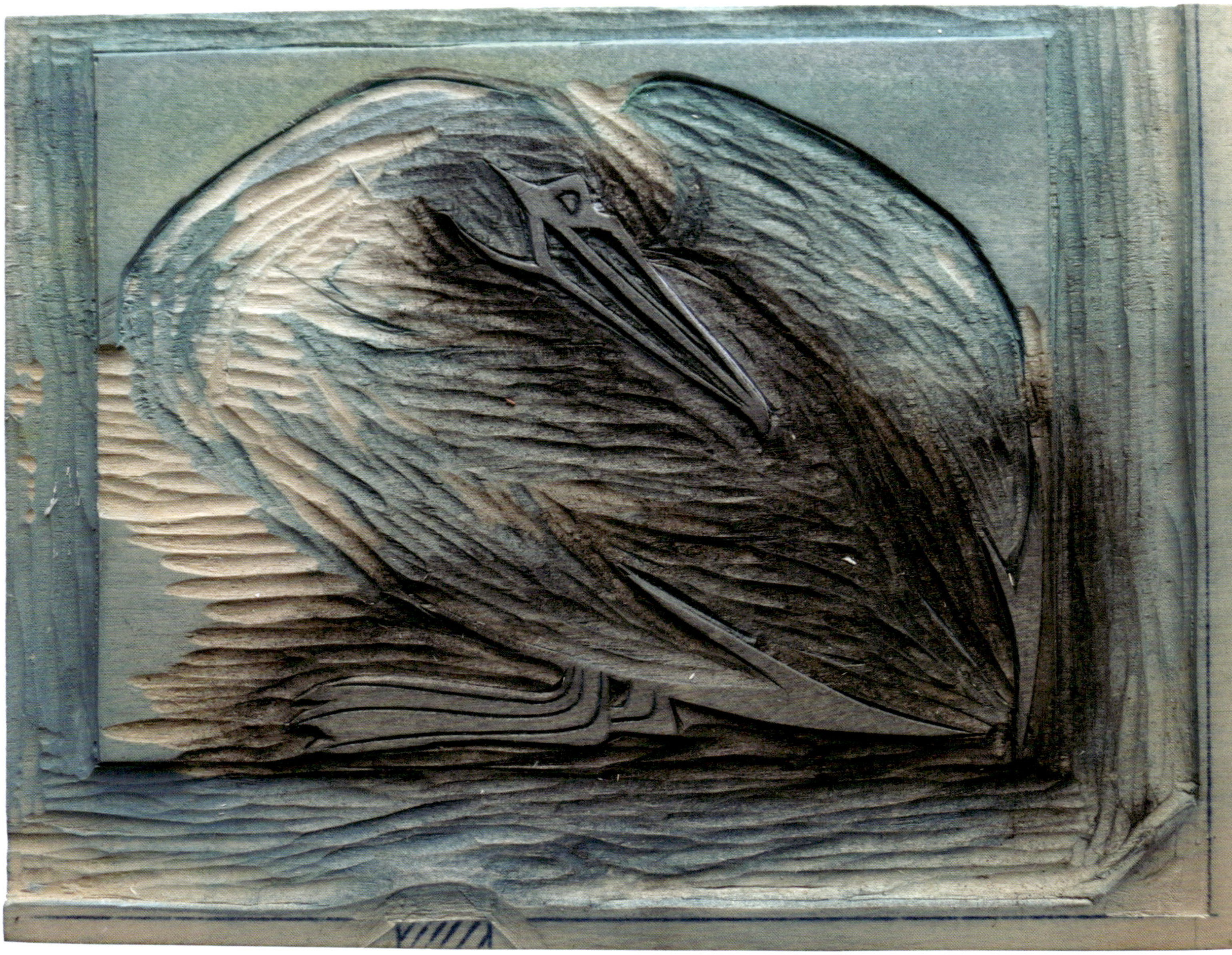

This plate shows the registration marks on a reduction plate used to print the gannet on page 139.

In common with other types of printmaking, the first step is to design the print. This means making a drawing and a colour separation plan for the print. The aim is to use the smallest number of plates possible, bearing in mind not only that two or more colours can be printed from one plate (provided a 2 cm or so gap separates them), but also that the transparent inks can be overlaid to create extra colours. In general, I find that four or five plates will suffice. In order to register properly, the plates need to be identical. The plates also need to be about 4 cm larger than the picture area on at least two sides, to accommodate the registration system.

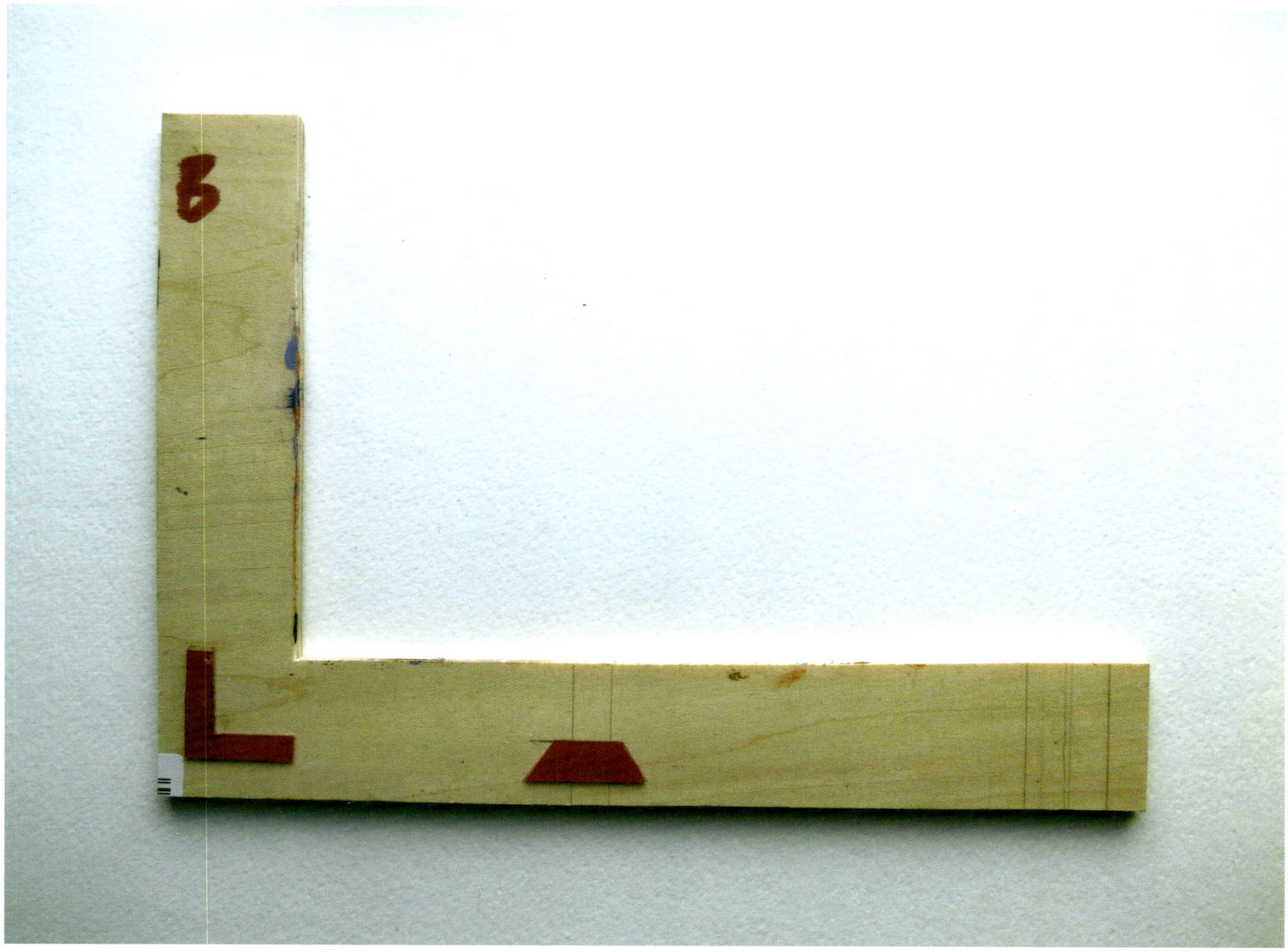

This is an alternative registration device, external to the plate, known as a kentōban. It is the same depth as the block and the block sits against it. The paper rests on raised tabs and the kentōban is removed when the paper is in position, prior to burnishing.

This system, particular to Japanese woodblock printing, involves cutting a right angled depression into the corner of each block and one further stop along the bottom edge. These are used to position the paper in the same position relative to each block, so that the colours print in register. Therefore they have to be marked onto the master tracing and transferred to each block very carefully. They have to be cut accurately and the paper sheets must also be prepared with a good right angle in the corresponding corner.

Autumn Feast,
22 cm x 56 cm, 2011

This is quite a large Japanese woodblock and did give me a few headaches with registration.

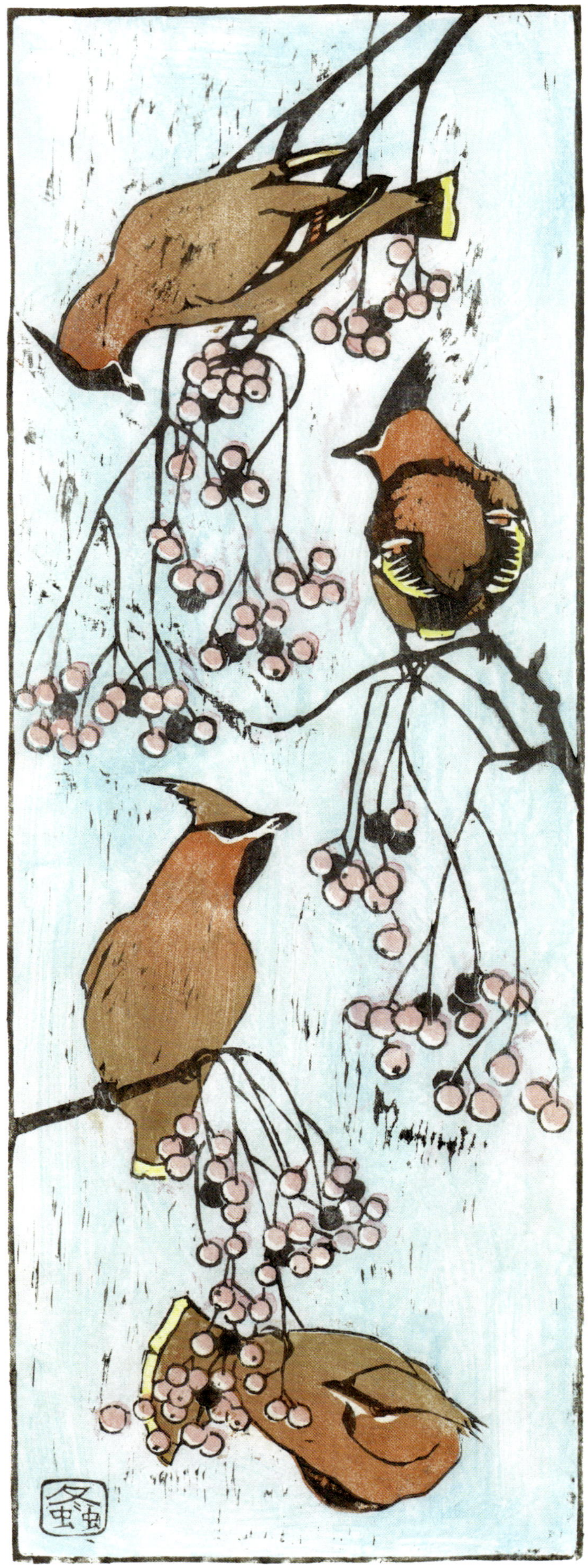

I was encouraged to try Japanese woodblock printing at the British Birdfair one year, by wildlife artist Matt Underwood, who had been teaching himself the technique from a book by Rebecca Salter. The fact that it was an environmentally friendly technique and also quite a portable one, requiring no press, made it attractive. In fact I already had most of the materials I needed and was used to cutting woodblocks. So it was a shortish step, although I was surprised by many of the idiosyncracies of the printing process. It is also quite a quick medium in the sense that, once the blocks are cut, the whole print can be completed in an hour or so – there is no drying time between printing. This means you can be more experimental with colour. Both of us then attended a Summer School in Japanese woodblock printing, at Edinburgh Printmakers, with Paul Furneaux, who has studied in Japan.

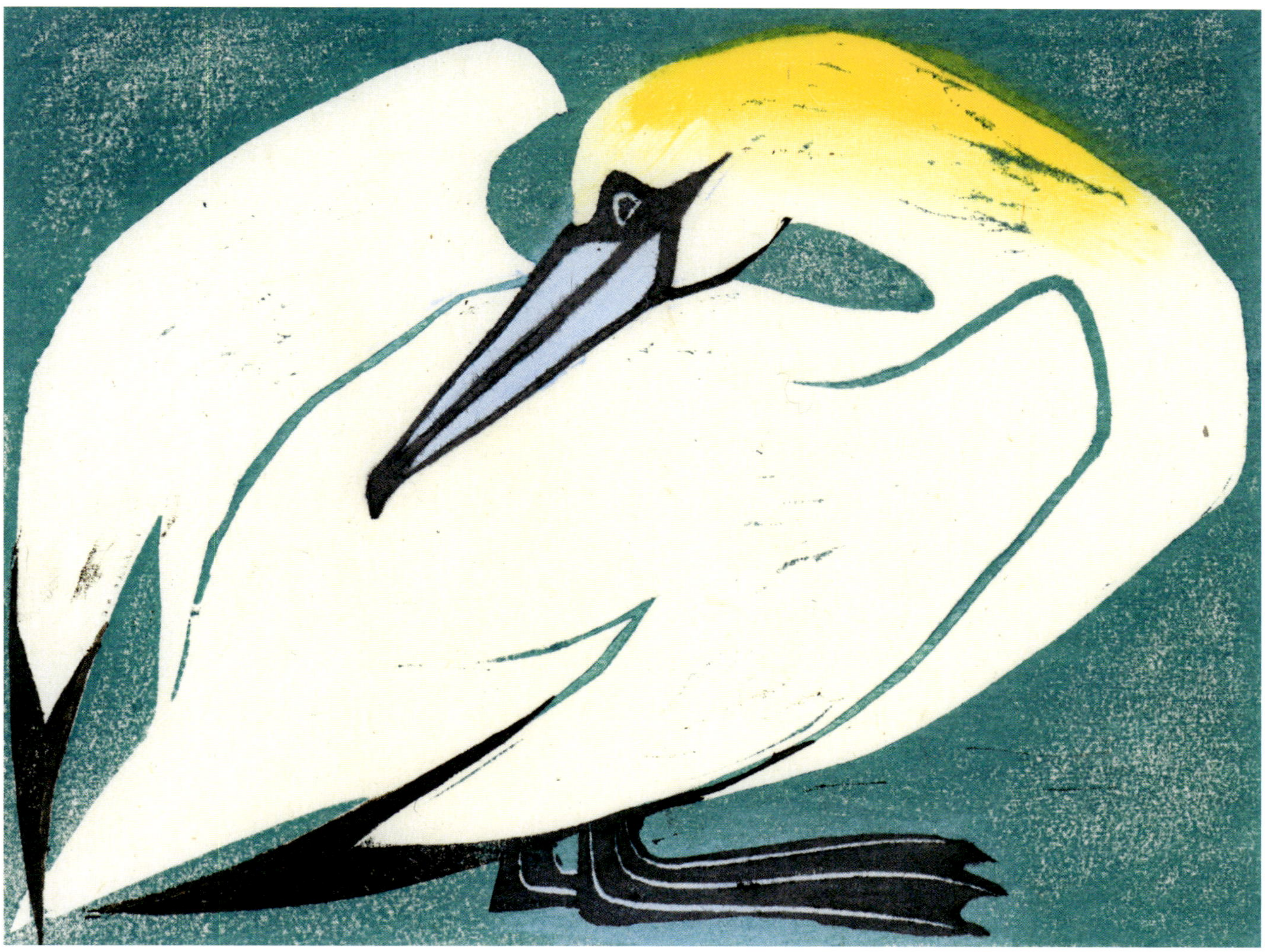

Gannet,
15 cm x 10 cm, 2012

This print was an exercise in reduction printing, undertaken at the Japanese woodblock printing Summer School at Edinburgh Printmakers in July 2012.

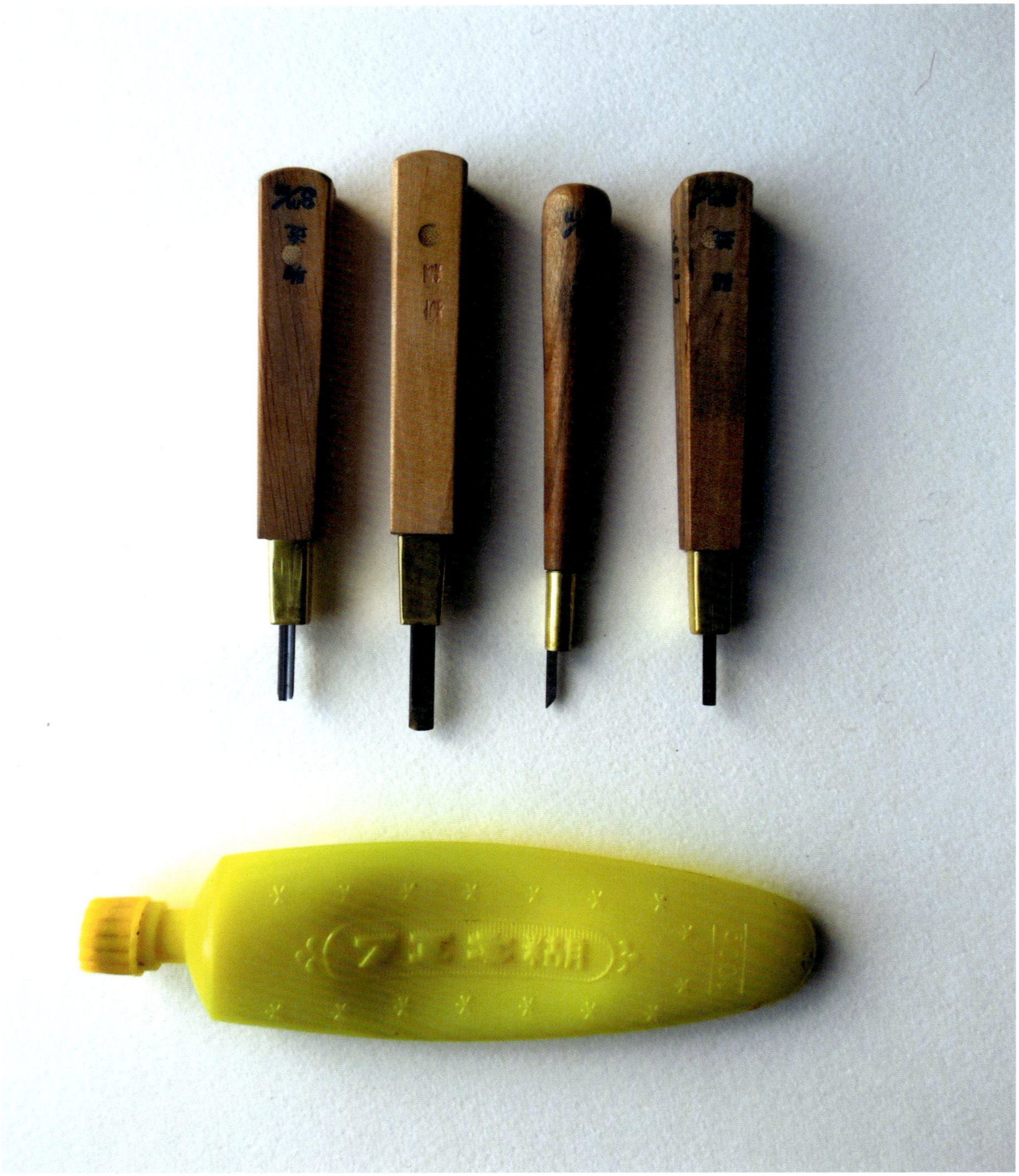

Japanese tools and a tube of Nori paste

I use carbon paper to transfer the most detailed drawing, usually the black or key plate onto one of the plates from the tracing. You can either use the same tracing to draw the other coloured areas onto the remaining plates, or you can use the first print from the black plate to do this. In both cases small complementary overlaps may be used to cover registration issues. Extreme care is needed to make the drawings accurate, and to cut them without making small alterations to the lines.

I use side grain wood blocks sold for woodcuts, or Asian ply and a combination of European and Japanese tools to cut them.

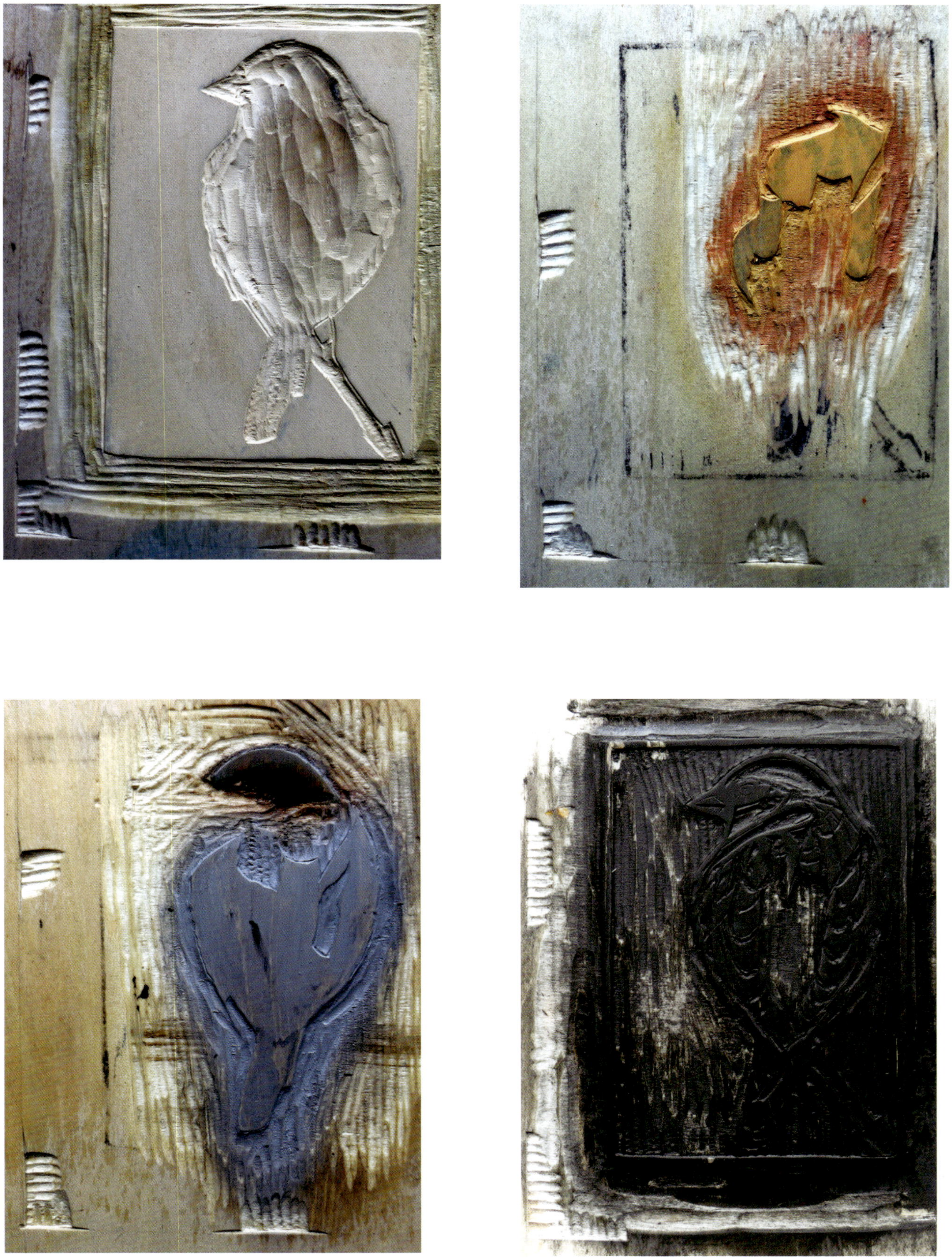

Four blocks for printing a house sparrow. The brown and grey inks are blended on the block. Note the rather crude kentō marks and the remains of the offset black print on the orange plate (131 b)

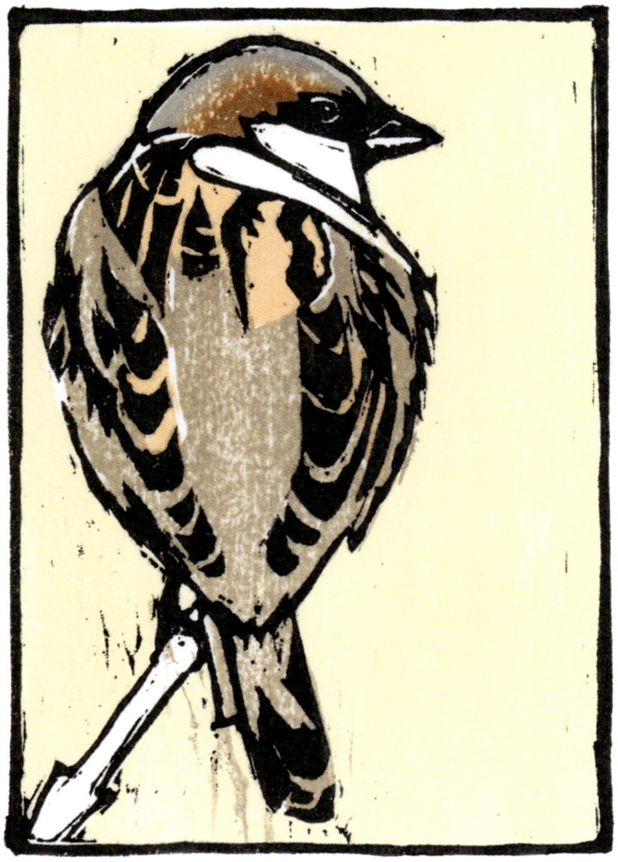

House sparrow,
8 cm x 11 cm, 2011

My first Japanese woodblock print.

The paper has to be prepared the day before printing. The basic method is to place the sheets of Japanese paper between layers of wet newspaper and to leave them overnight. This results in the paper becoming uniformly damp, so that it will receive the ink properly.

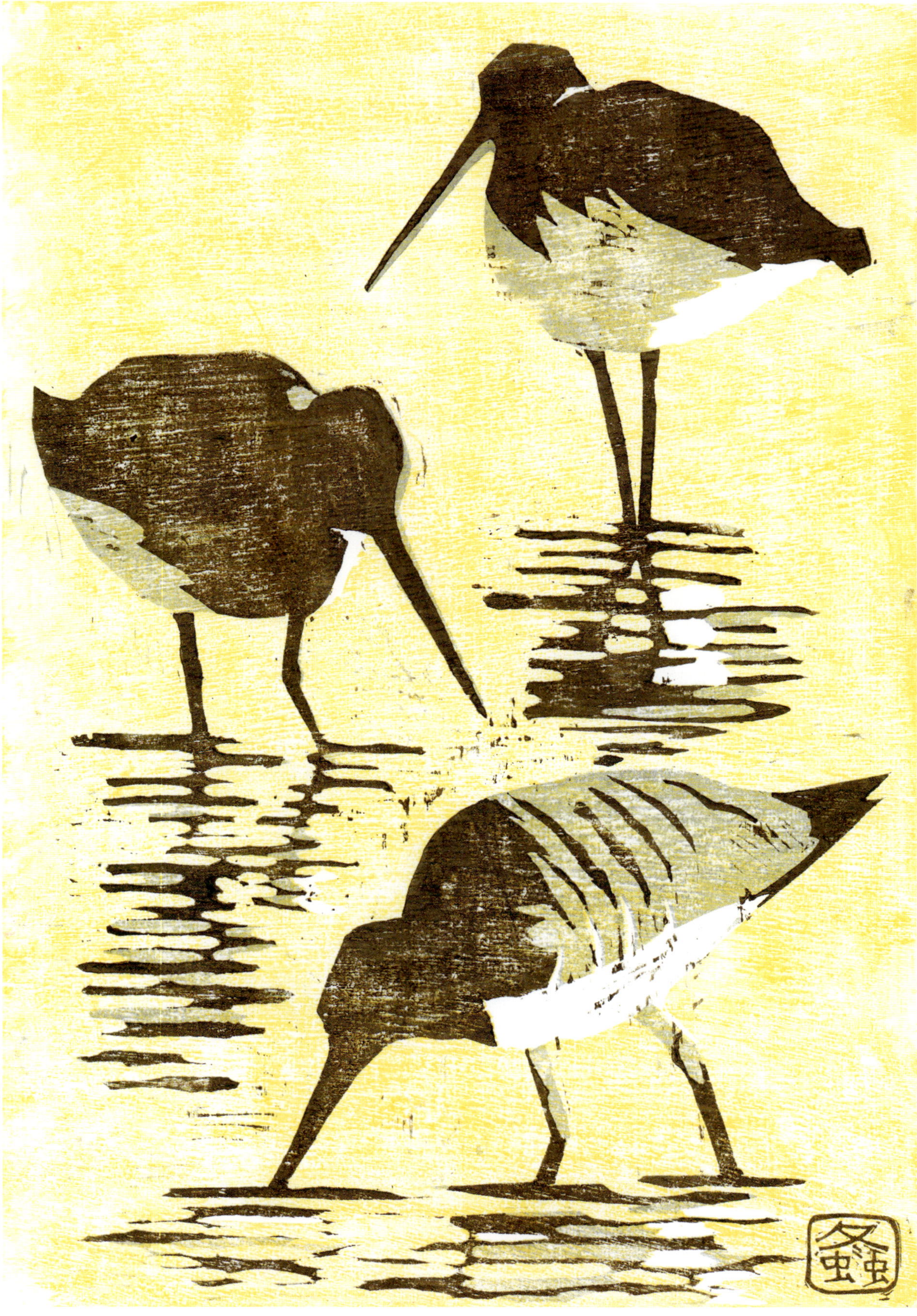

Godwits,
25 cm x 36 cm, 2011

This is a reduction print, made on floor ply which is very hard but has interesting grain.

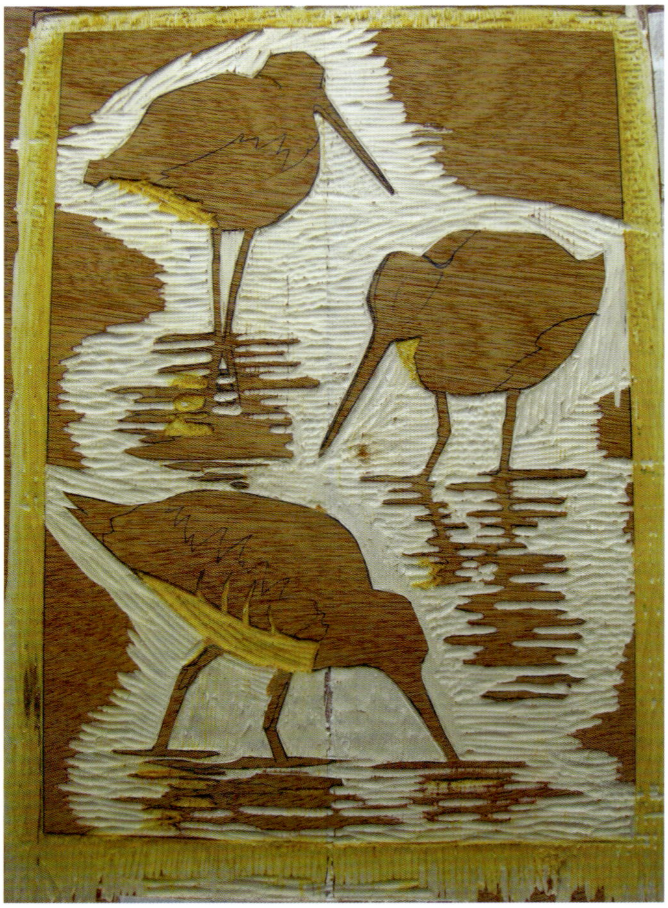

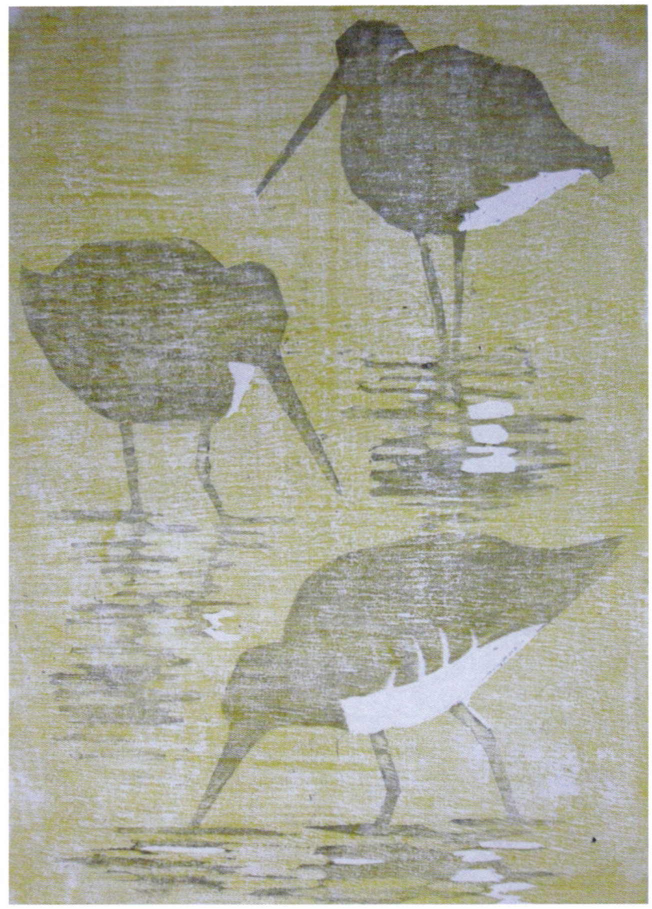

The block for the Godwits partly cut away and an early printing stage (two colours).

I start by deciding on a printing sequence; usually light to dark. I then wet the first block with a water mister and leave it for a few minutes, then dab dry. Watercolour or gouache paint is applied direct from the tube or with a paintbrush if pre-mixed. A larger brush is used to distribute the paint evenly and ensure there are no blobs of paint in detailed cut areas. The paper is carefully lowered, smooth side down, into the corner of the kentō, lining it up with the second mark. After gently lowering it, the paper is covered with a piece of baking parchment and then burnished firmly with a baren.

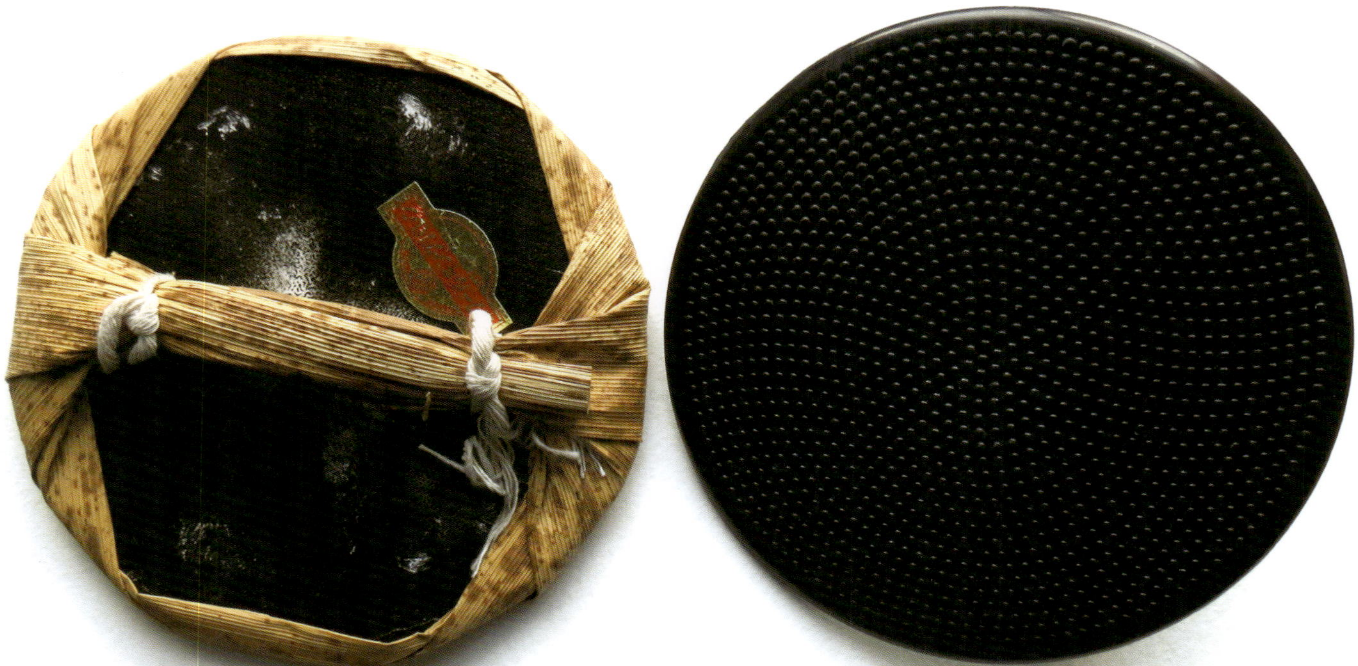

Two different barens: a traditional bamboo leaf covered baren and a plastic baren.

Printing bokashi:

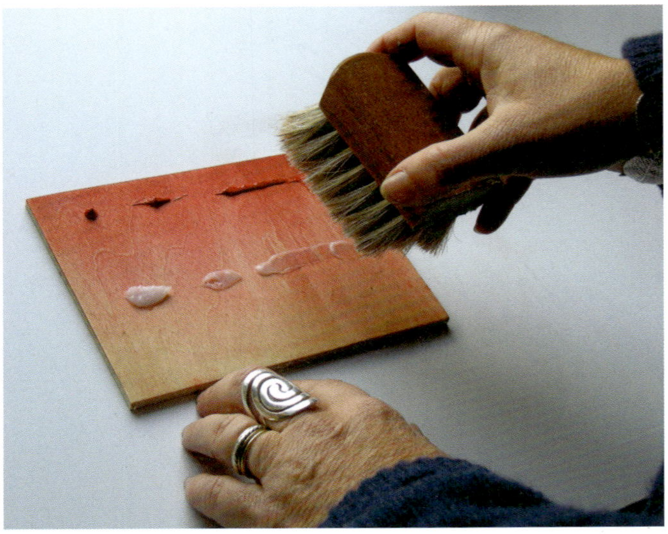

The paint is applied to the top of the moistened plate and the nori paste is applied across the middle of the plate.

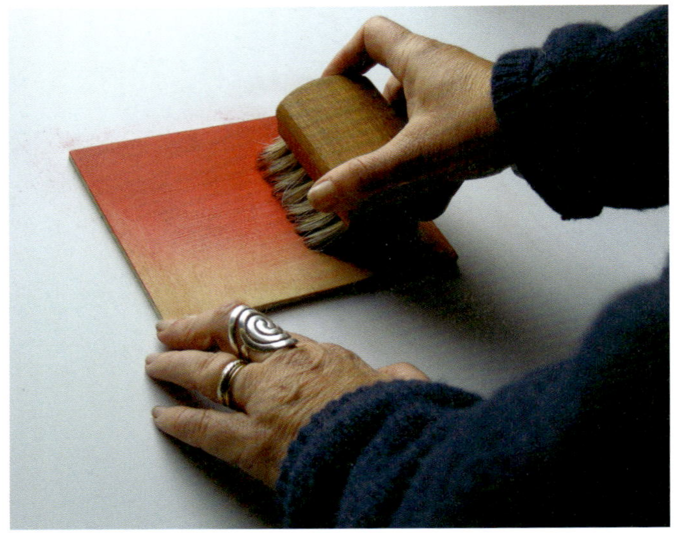

A good quality horse hair brush is used horizontally to blend the paint and paste, drawing the colour down across the plate in an even blend.

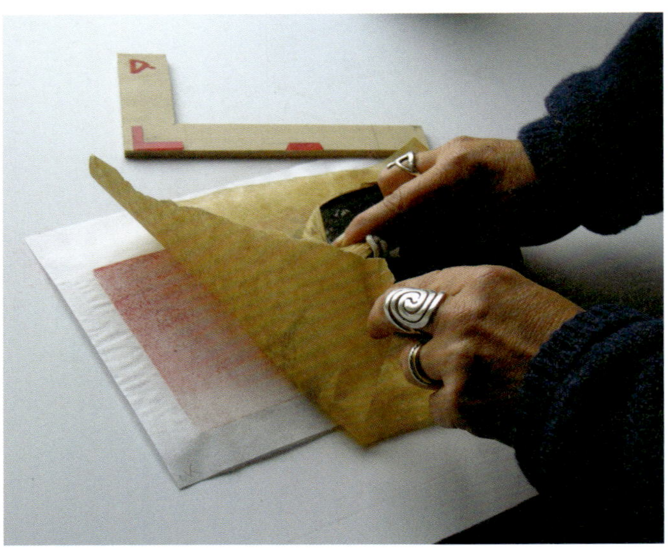

The plate is burnished through a piece of baking parchment onto the dampened paper.

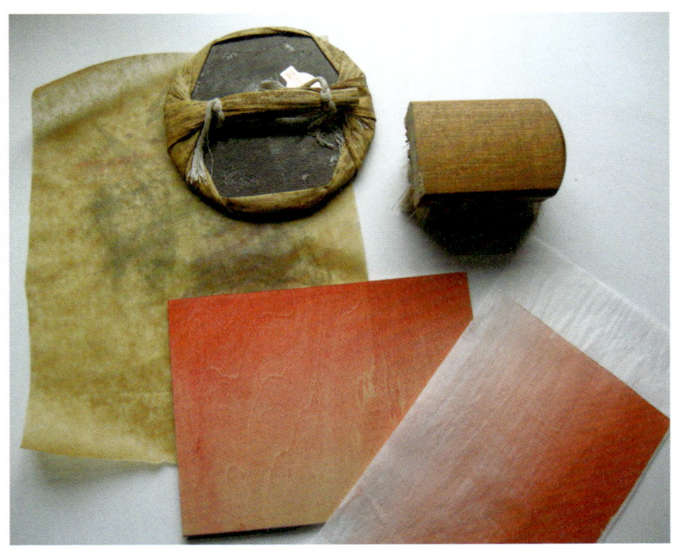

The final print, plate and tools.

The colour will come through the paper. Nori (rice flour) paste can be used on the block to create blends or fade effects. Fading washes are known as bokashi.

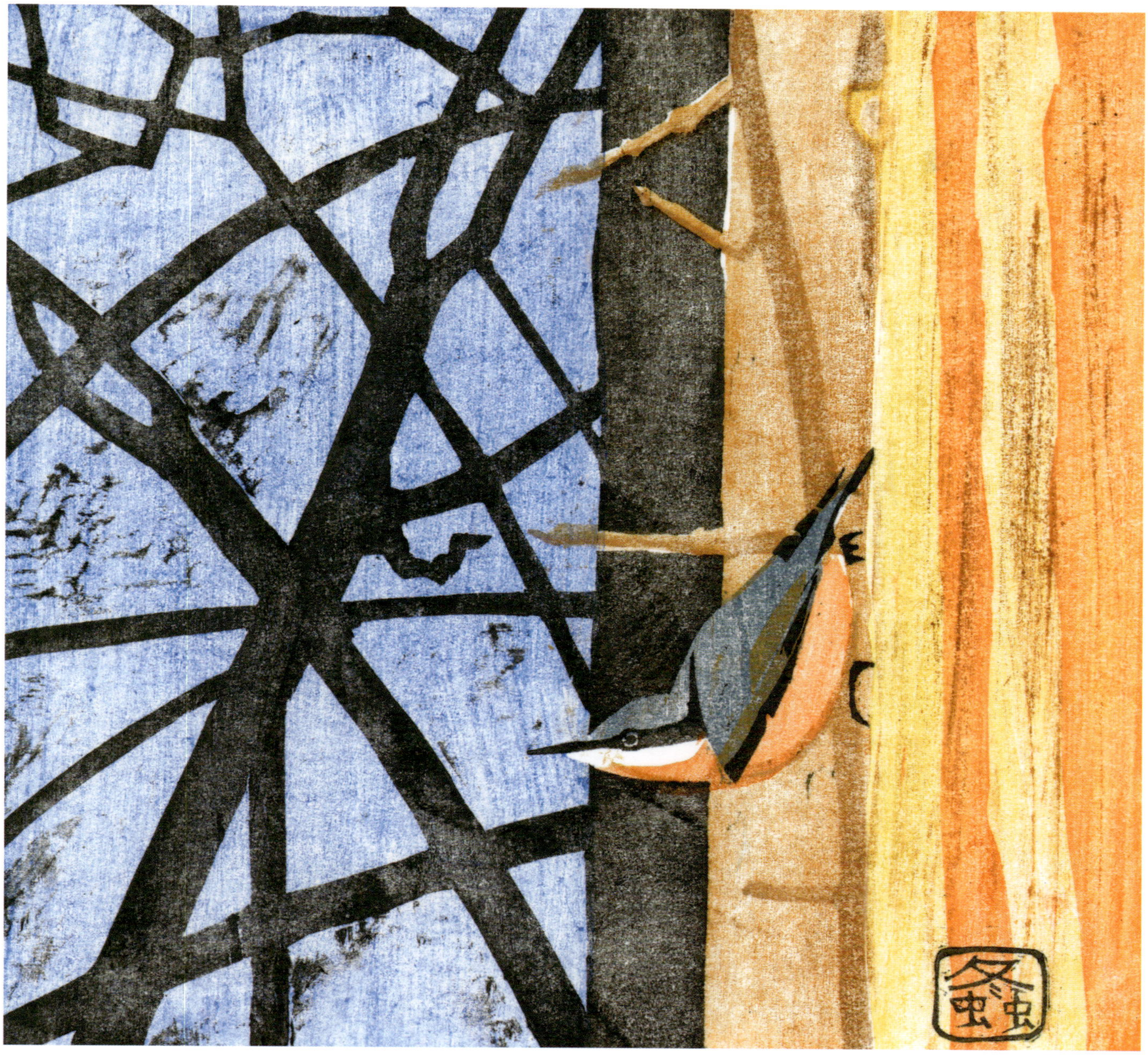

NUTHATCH,
25 cm x 24 cm, 2012

After each colour is printed the paper must be returned to its position in the damp pile. It is essential that the paper does not dry out as it does slightly expand when it is damp, so changes in the humidity of the paper will affect the registration, especially on larger prints. It also affects the transfer of ink – bleeds can happen if the paper is too wet, and if it's too dry the ink will be stippled rather than printing as a solid colour. Over-wet paper is also difficult to maniputate into the kentō blocks, so it is worth exercising discipline over the paper pile.

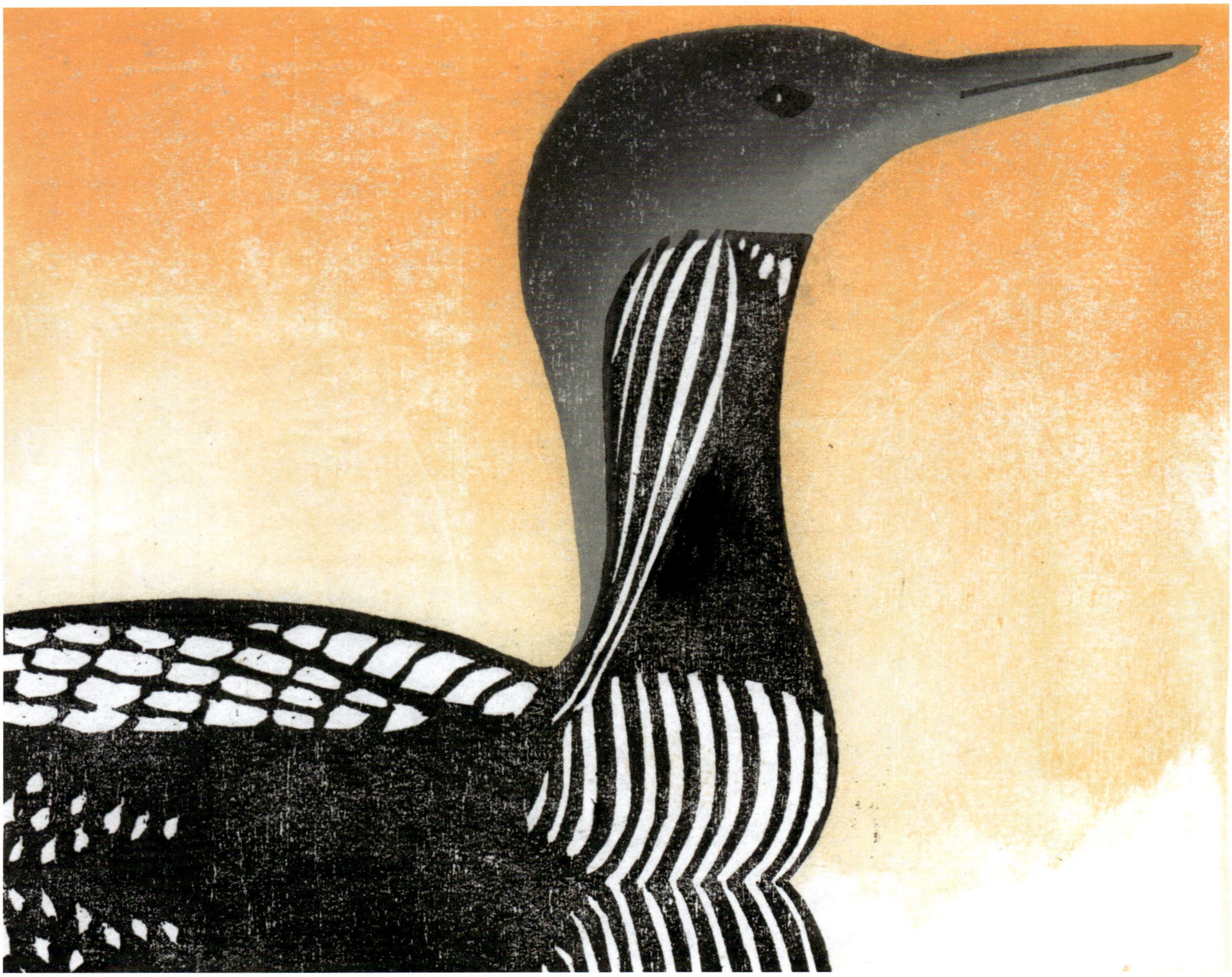

Black-throated diver,
16 cm x 13 cm, 2012

The bokashi background in both diver prints is quite tricky to achieve. The water based colours in Japanese woodblock printing all dry slightly paler than they at first look, which adds to its difficulty.

When all the colours are printed the final prints are dried between blotting paper, under a weight.

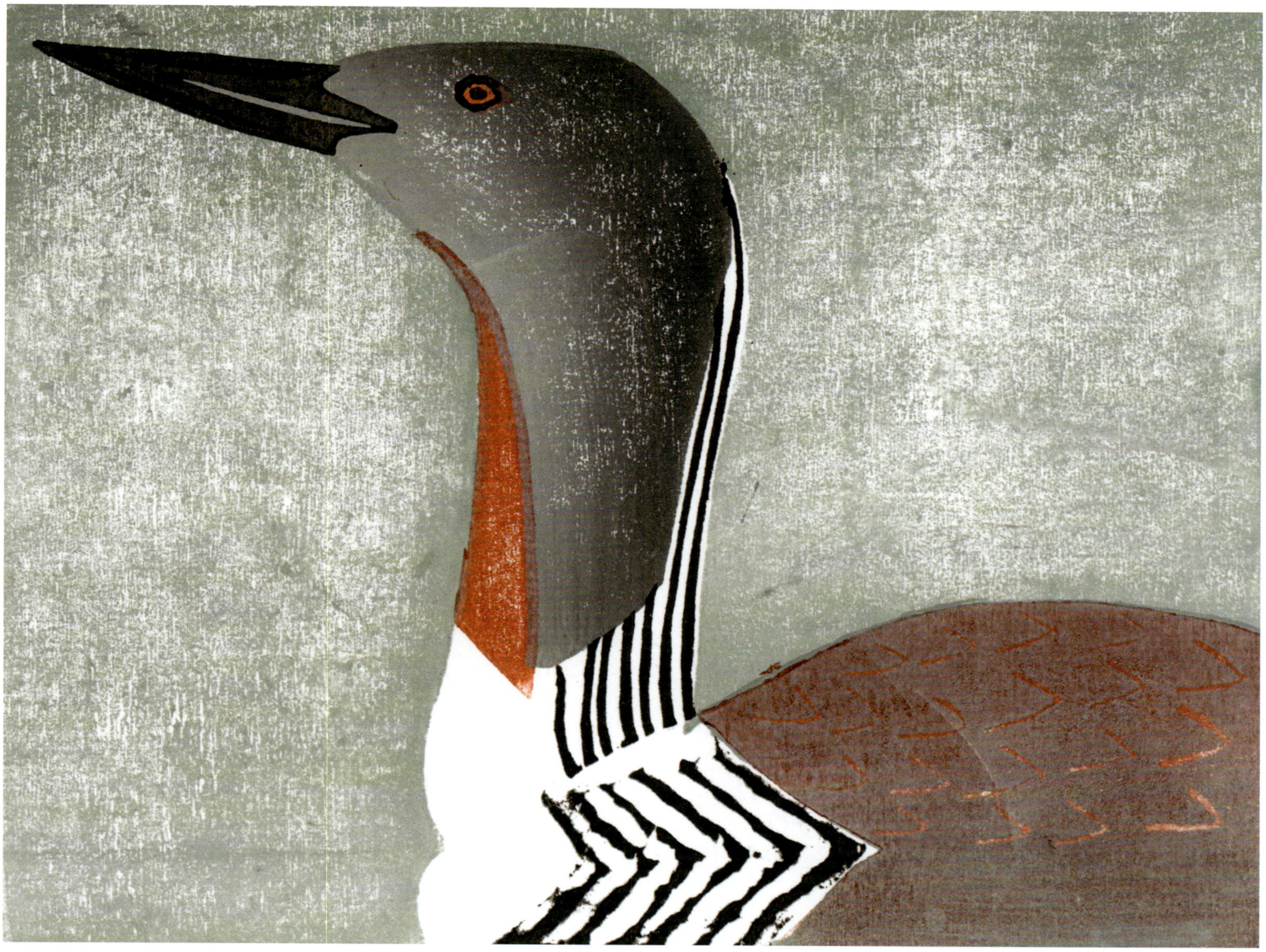

Red-throated diver,
15 cm x 11 cm, 2012

Another seemingly very simple print, which is actually quite difficult to execute.

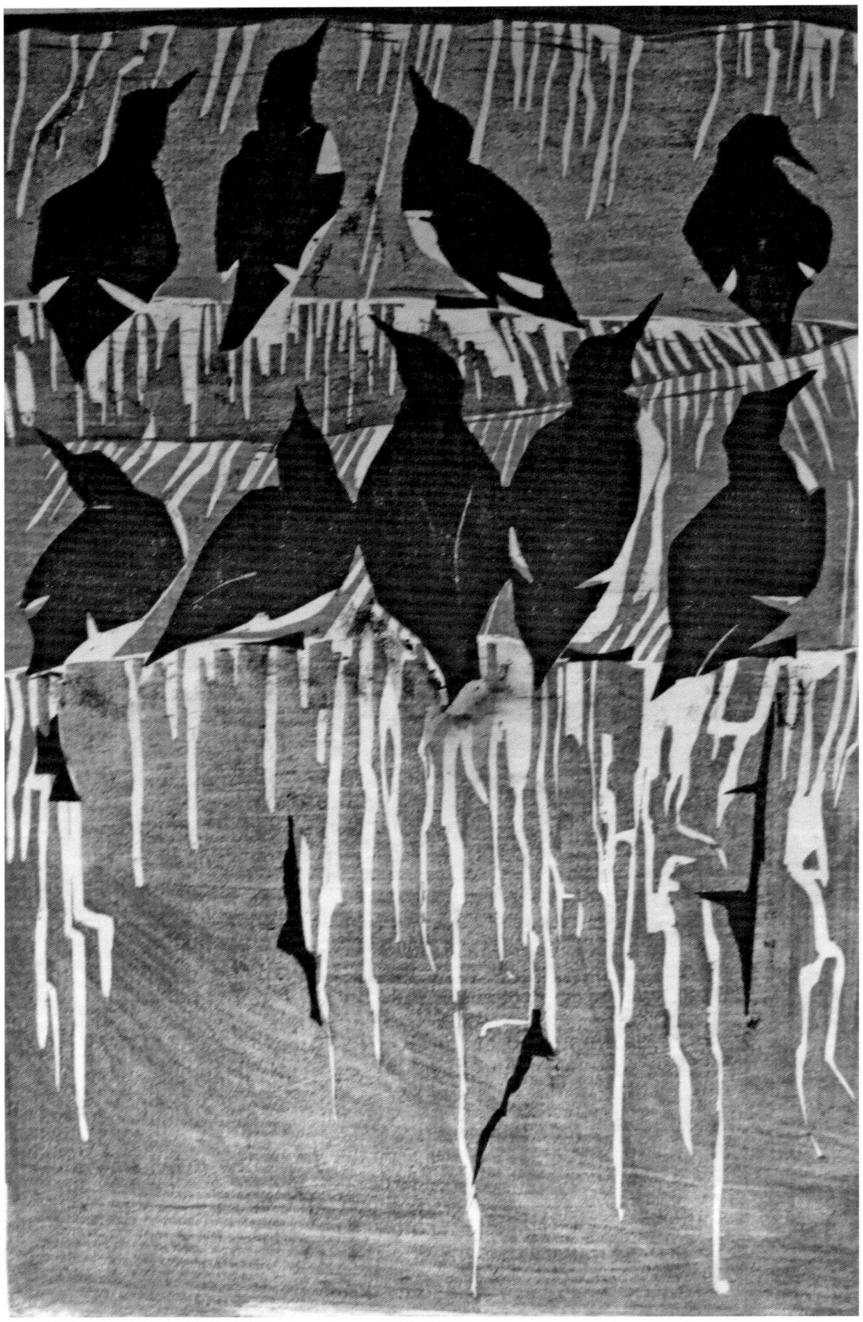

GUILLEMOTS, FARNE,
24 cm x 38 cm, 2012

This was a reworking of an old etching plate design, which I thought would make a more successful Japanese woodblock print.

Mokuhanga is an art form which takes a lifetime to perfect, and I am no more than a novice. This description only hints at the difficulty of making well registered, cleanly printed Japanese wood-block prints. It is in fact very exacting in all respects, and takes a lot of skill and patience. However, the prints have a beautiful, transparent quality, and the process is very satisfying in many ways. In particular, the direct application of the paint to the plate, and the opportunity this affords for blending colours, is a delight to anyone used to struggling with rollers and dabbers to apply sticky oil based inks to wood or lino. Cleaning up and care of rollers etc. is also much easier with water based inks. For me, certain aspects of the technique were so attractive that I now use them with other media: the kentõ registration system, for instance, I now use generally in my work, and the hangitõ cutting tool I also use for any very detailed cutting.

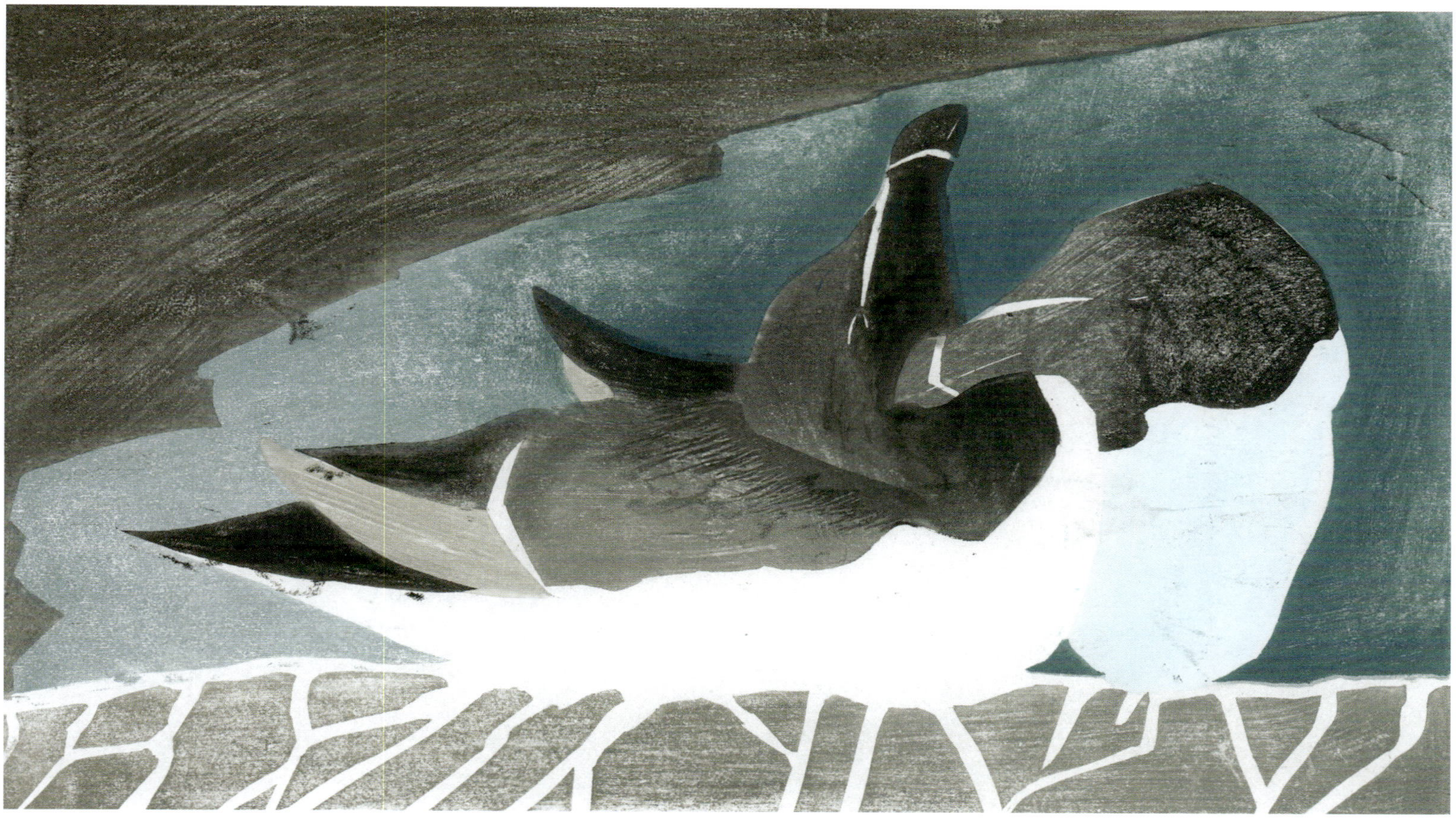

INTIMACY,
30 cm x 19 cm, 2012

Inspired by razorbills on Orkney, this print is an attempt to capture the extraordinary markings on razorbills in a moment of intimacy.

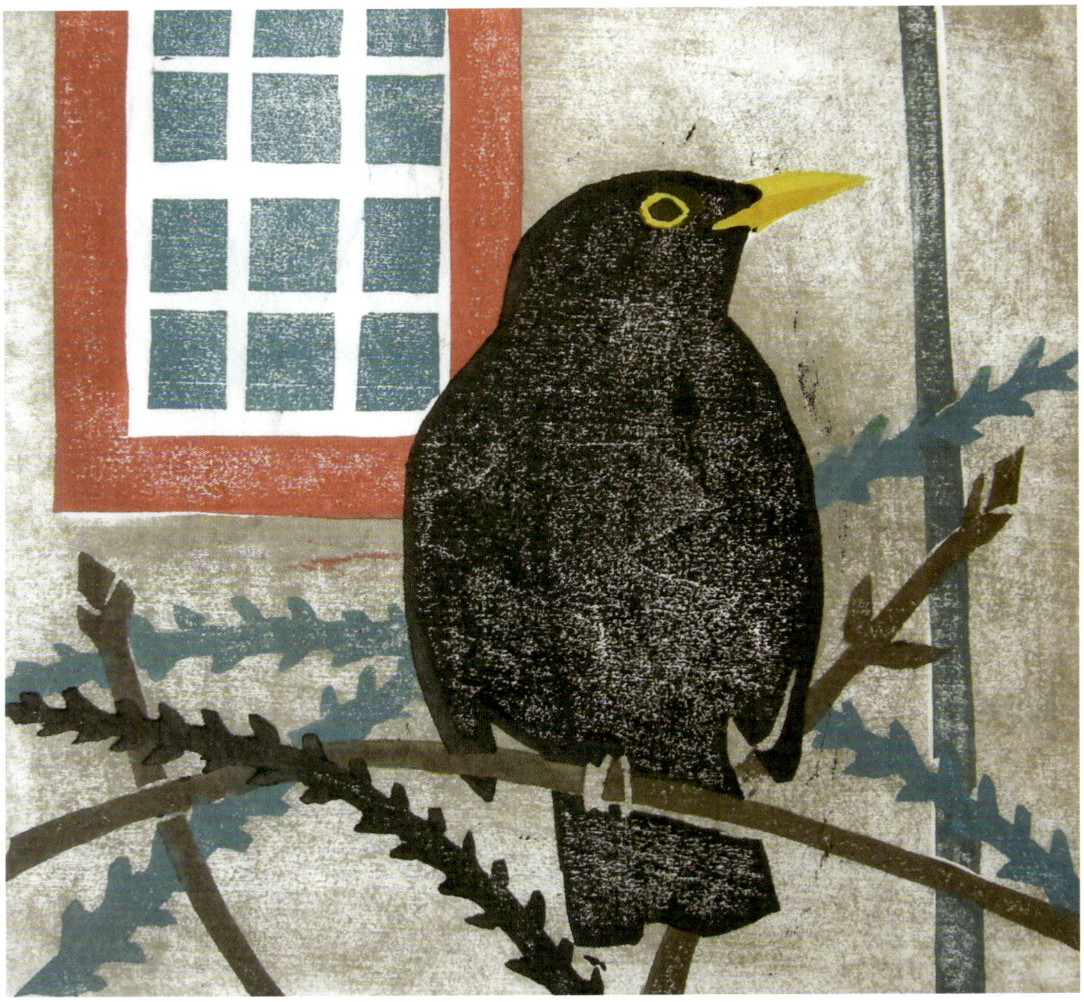

Kirkcudbright blackbird,
16 cm x 16 cm, 2012

This blackbird was singing in some cotoneaster in spring 2012 in Kirkcudbright.

White line woodblock printing

'Originality, Simplicity, Freedom of Expression, and above all Sincerity, with a clean cut block, are characteristics of a good woodblock print'

Ada Gilmore. (Barbara Stern Shapiro, *From Paris to Provincetown*)

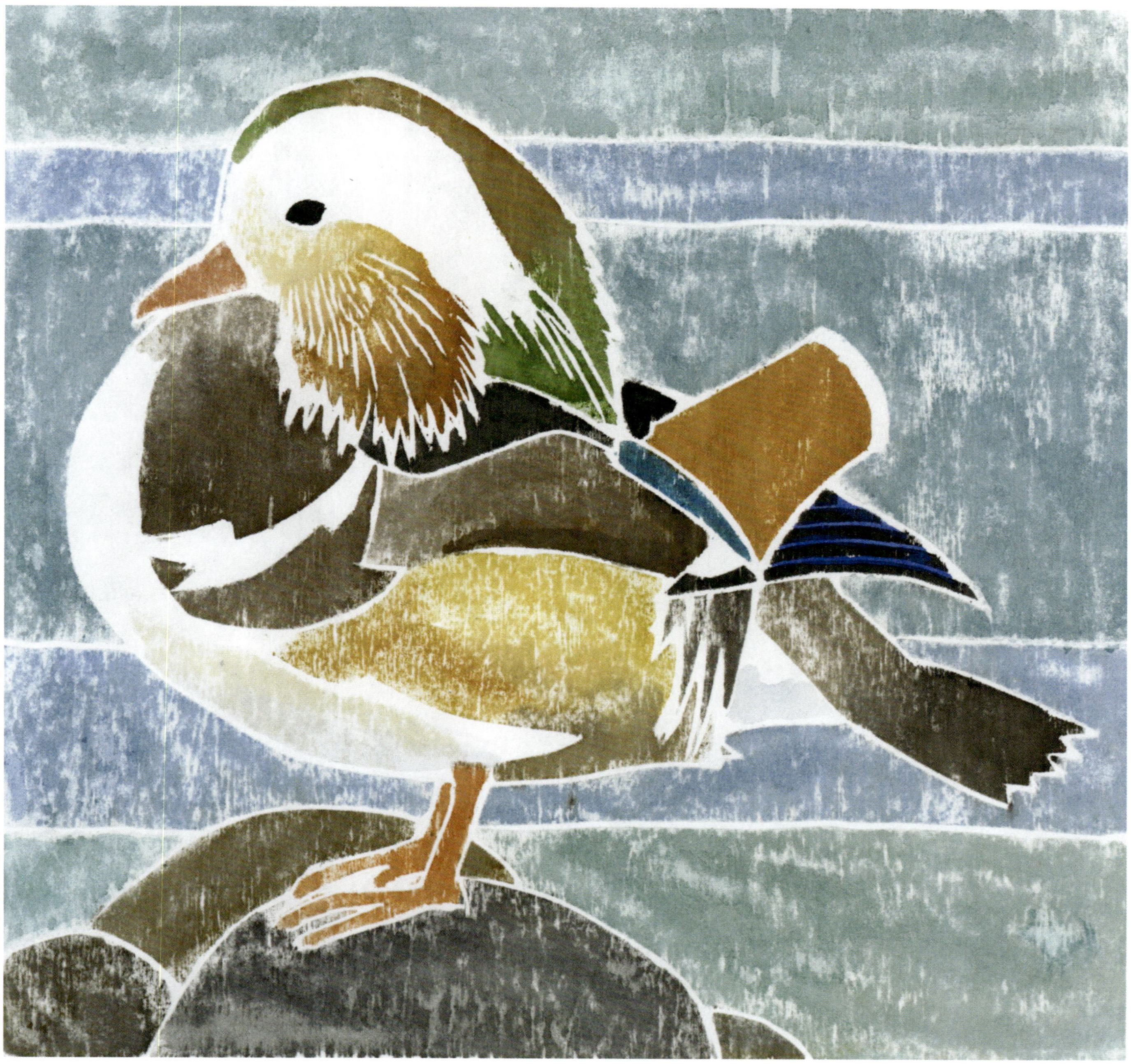

Mandarin duck,
18 cm x 18 cm, 2013

For those who might prefer not to devote a lifetime to the perfection of Japanese woodblock printing, there is a simpler variation of this technique developed by a group of printmakers in Provincetown, Cape Cod, in the first decades of the twentieth century. The wonderful simple prints produced by the so-called Provincetown Printers are much sought after today.

Instead of carving multiple blocks, each carrying a separate colour, just one block is cut using a v shaped tool to separate each block of colour simply. Basically, the outline of the design is cut into the block. Then a piece of Japanese paper is taped to the block, along one edge, making a secure hinge. Finally, watercolour is applied to the dry wood, one area at a time and burnished off onto the paper.

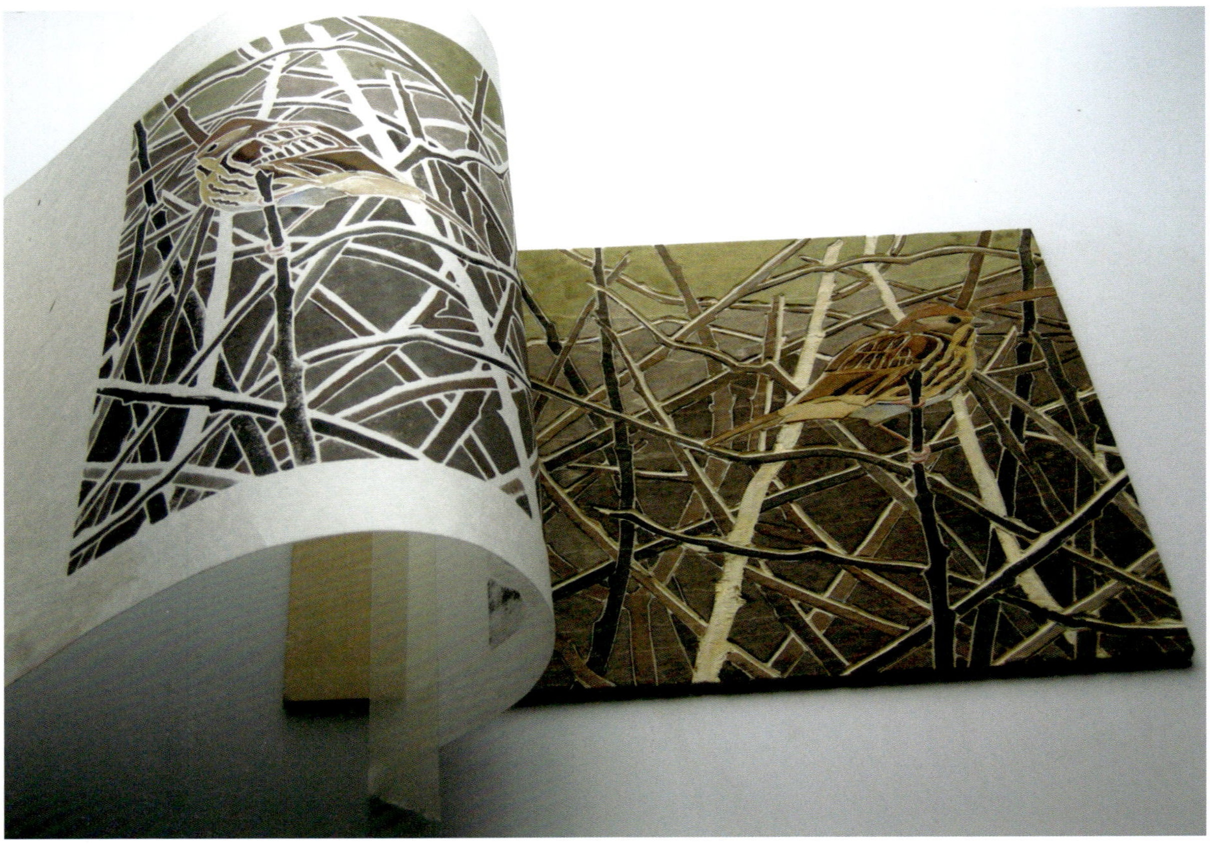

The finished print before it is detached from the block showing the painted woodblock

I was introduced to white line woodblock printing one September morning in Stromness, by American printmaker Jeanne Bouza Rose. I was simultaneously amazed and delighted to find a completely unheard of, new method of printing which was such an obvious and simple development of Japanese woodblock printing. I immediately started to try to devise images with white lines. My first thought was that they might represent frost, which is the intention with the reed bunting print reproduced opposite.

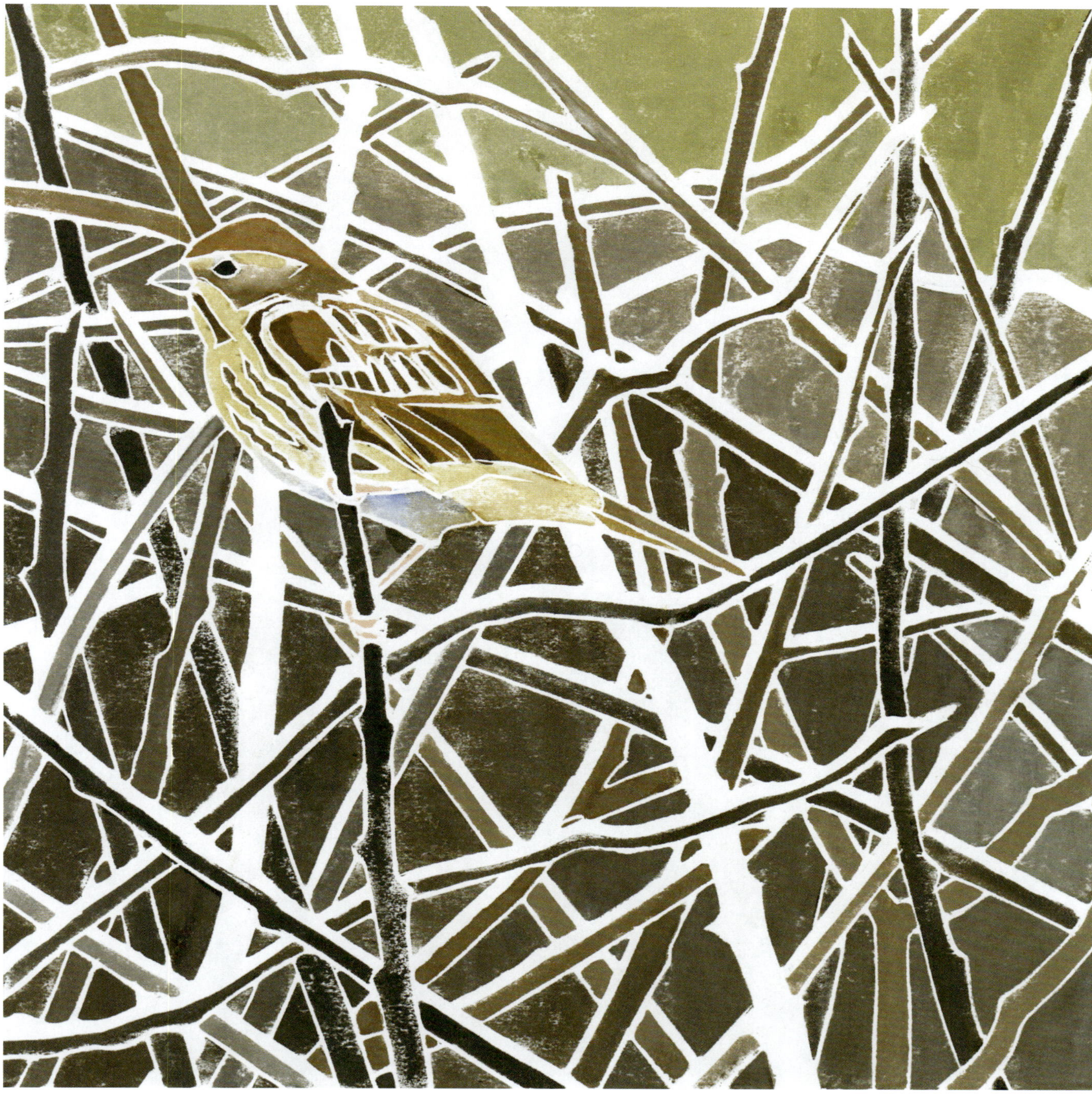

Reed bunting,
23 cm x 23 cm, 2013

This technique has a lot of advantages:

- relatively little cutting is involved so it is easier and quicker to cut the design
- it is very painterly in that a lot of control can be exerted over the colour scheme. You can even re-touch and add shades and blends within areas as you go
- you can make a very large number of prints from the same block
- the block itself is ultimately a very beautiful object as it takes on the colours used in printing
- the paints used are just normal watercolours which are easy to handle and clean up.

The disadvantages are:

- it takes a long time to print each plate. The plate illustrated here of a reed bunting takes about two hours to print
- each print is slightly different as the hand colouring introduces small alterations each time
- you do have to think carefully about the design. Not every design works well with white lines dissecting it.

White line printing is an interesting and rather under-used technique in this country. It provides a good entry point for novice printmakers but is also capable of yielding professional results.

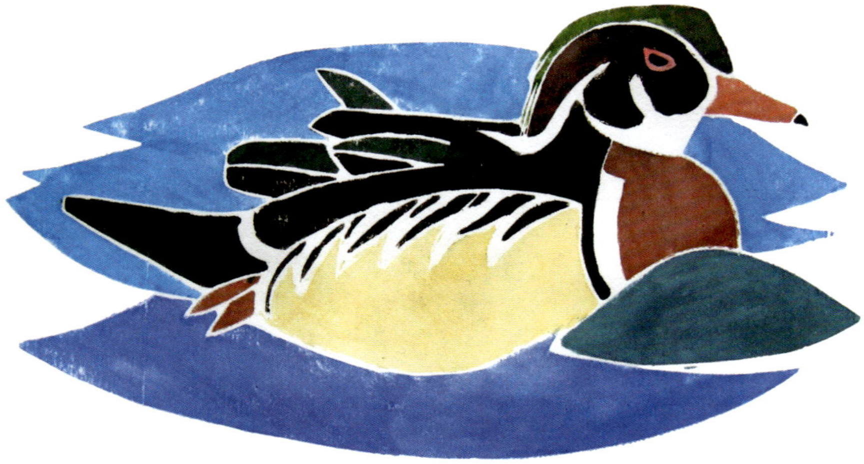

Conclusion

Printmaking and natural history have given me a lot of joy in life. I hope this book, by explaining the former and enthusing about the latter will encourage others to share in it.

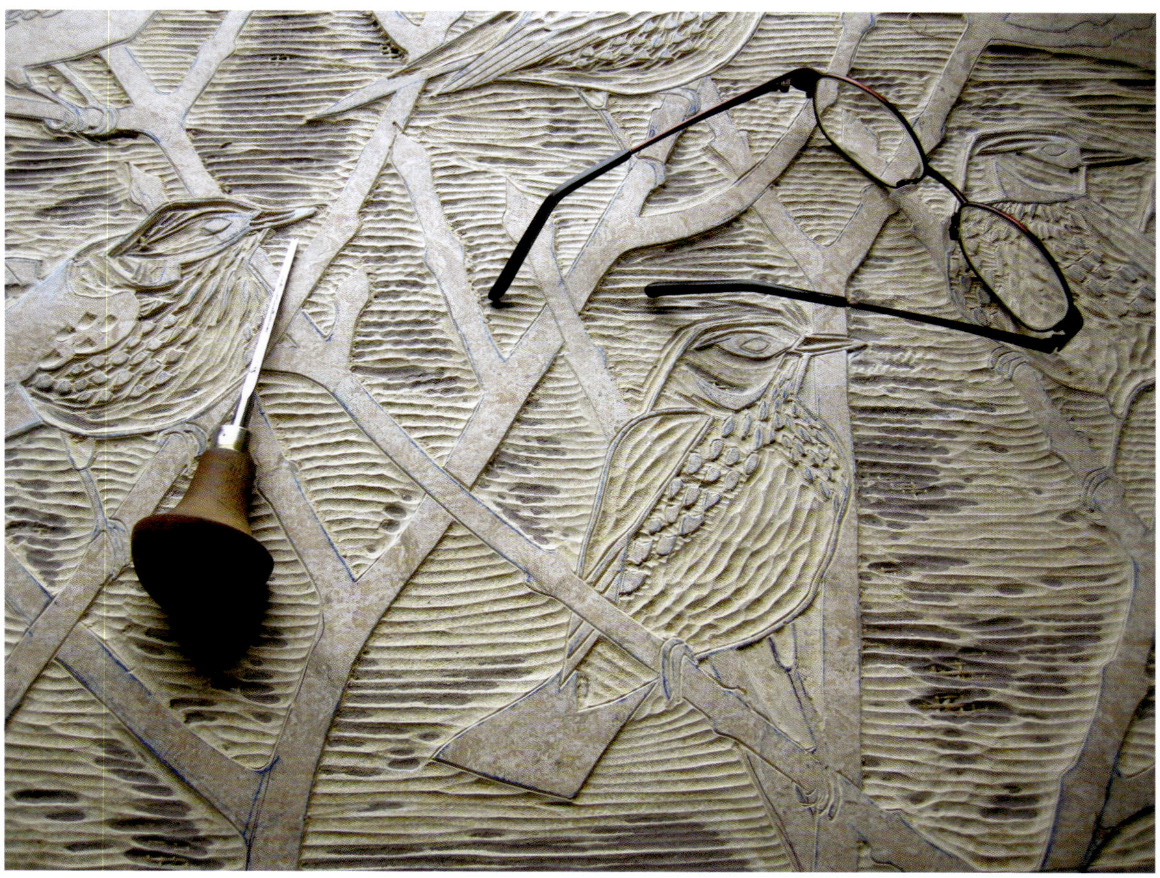

References

Alexander Adams, Printmaking Today Vol. 13, Number 2, Summer 2004

Carry Akroyd (Ed.), *Wildlife in Printmaking*, Langford Press, Peterborough, 2011

Simon Armitage and Tim Dee (Editors), *The Poetry of Birds*, Viking, London 2009

Julia Ayres, *Monotype*, Watson-Guptill, New York, 1991

Julia Ayres, *Printmaking Techniques*, Watson-Guptill Publications, New York 1993

Caroline Bacon and James McGregor, *Edward Bawden*, Cecil Higgins Art Gallery, 2008

J A Baker, *The Peregrine*, Collins, London, 2010

Michael Barratt, *Intaglio*, A&C Black, London, 2008

Jean Blodgett, *Kenojuak*, Firefly Books, Toronto, 1981

Roderick Cave, *Impressions of Nature: a history of nature printing*, The British Library, London, 2010

Walter Chamberlain, *The Thames and Hudson Manual of Etching and Engraving*, Thames and Hudson, London, 1972

Walter Chamberlain, *The Thames and Hudson manual of Woodblock Printmaking*, Thames and Hudson, London, 1978

Robin Cox, *An eye for Dynamic Design, Birds I llustrated*, Spring 2005, Buckingham Press, Lincolnshire, UK. (Article about Thelma Sykes)

W H Gardner, *Gerard Manley Hopkins Poems and Prose*, Penguin Books, Reading, UK, 1963

Jane Glaubinger, *Midwest Modern: the Colour Woodcuts of Mabel Hewit*, The Cleveland Museum of Art, Seattle, USA, 2010

Anne Hayward, *Wood Engraving and Linocutting*, The Crowood Press, Marlborough, 2008

John Irving, *The Hotel New Hampshire*, Black Swan, Great Britain, 1981

Kathleen Jamie, *Findings*, Sort Of Books, 2005

Reva Kern, *The history of the Provincetown Print*, www.angelfire.com/co/exlibris/reva1.html. Article originally posted in “Block and Burin”, Journal of the Wood Engravers Network, (WEN) Ann Arbor, Michigan, 1998

Ewen MacCaig, (Editor), *The poems of Norman MacCaig*, Polygon, Edinburgh, 2005

National Museum of Man, *The Inuit Print*, Ottowa, 1976

Peabody Essex Museum, *Our Land, Contemporary Art from the Arctic*, North Andover MA, 2004

Mavis Pilbeam (editor), *The British Museum Birds*, The British Museum Press, London, 2008

Mavis Pilbeam (editor), *The British Museum Haiku Animals*, The British Museum Press, London, 2010

John Ross, Clare Romano, Tim Ross, *The Complete Printmaker*, The Free Press, New York, 1972 (revised 1990)

Rebecca Salter, *Japanese woodblock printing*, A&C Black, London, 2008

Rosemary Simmons and Katie Clemson, *The Complete Manual of Relief Printmaking*, Dorling Kindersley, 1988

Alan Smith, *Etching, a guide to traditional techniques*, The Crowood Press, Marlborough, 2004

Barbara Stern Shapiro, *From Paris to Provincetown: Blanche Lazzell and the colour woodcut.* MFA Publications, Boston, 2002

Toshi Yoshida and Rei Yuki, *Japanese Printmaking*, a handbook of traditional and modern techniques, Charles E Tuttle Company, Vermont, 1966 (Out of print)

Jane Weir , *Walking the block*, Derbyshire, 2008

Ann Westley, *Relief Printmaking*, A&C Black, London, 2001

Louise Woods (Editor), *Practical printmaking*, Apple, London, 1996

What is an artist's print?

The availability of commercial, so-called, "limited edition" prints from various sources has introduced some confusion over the definition of an artist's print.

I craft my own woodcuts and etchings by hand and I ink them and print them myself on hand operated machinery, or by burnishing. My largest edition size is 50 and I now seldom produce editions of more than 30.

The number in the bottom left hand corner of a print indicates its number in the edition (first or top number) and the edition size (second or bottom number). So 14/30 would be the fourteenth print in an edition of thirty. Some of my prints are marked A/P. This stands for artists proof and in my case refers to early printings of the plate when I am still experimenting with colours and wiping, prior to editioning. Some artists use this term to describe a number of extra prints taken at the end of the edition. Either way they represent a small percentage only of the edition size and are not substandard in any way - indeed some collectors prefer them.

A genuine artist's print may be described as follows, "A mechanically reproduced image which has not previously existed independently of the printing process and in whose production the artist has directly participated" (Alexander Adams, Printmaking Today Vol 13, Number 2, Summer 2004).

Glossary

À la poupée
Technique whereby a small dolly or cotton bud is used to ink specific areas of an etching plate in different colours.

Aquatint
Etching technique for creating tonal areas, using a fine screen as a resist.

Artists proofs
Prints made by the artist prior to finalising colours etc. and producing an edition. They are labelled A/P and there are normally only a handful made.

Baren
Tool for burnishing the back of a print to transfer ink from the plate to the paper in Japanese woodblock printing. Traditionally these are made from a coil of string on a circular support, covered in a bamboo leaf.

Bite
The chemical process whereby an etching plate is eaten away by an acid to produce an image.

Blind embossing
A print made by passing an unlinked relief printing plate through a press, with damp paper, so that an embossing is made.

Carborundum
Coarse, sand like material used to create strong tonal areas on Collagraphs.

Chine collé
By inserting a precut shape, with glue on one side, between the inked plate and the paper, an area of colour is stuck to the print, and overprinted with the detail from the inked plate.

Collagraph
A print made from a collage. It may be printed by surface rolling the plate or by inking the plate intaglio and printing through an etching press.

Copper sulphate solution
Chemical solution used to bite zinc etching plates.

Ground – hard and soft
Resists used in etching. Hard ground provides a robust waxy ground, into which you can draw with a blunt needle. Soft ground provides a less robust resist which may be broken by pressing organic material into it or by drawing through paper onto it.

Edition
The number of prints made from a plate before it is destroyed, excluding proofs.

Intaglio printing
Printing from depressions in the plate. Intaglio prints hold the ink in grooves in the surface of the plate. Surplus ink is cleaned from the top face and damp paper is forced into the grooves by a powerful press, so that the ink is picked up. Etchings and engravings are normally printed intaglio, but collagraphs may also be treated in this way.

Kōzo fibre
Long plant fibres used to make Japanese papers for woodblock printing.

Monoprint
Print made from a plate which is undeformed but which incorporates repeatable elements such as stencils. The image is made by painting or rolling ink onto the plate, then printing, usually through a press.

Monotype
Print made from an undeformed plate such as Perspex or zinc, which is not strictly speaking repeatable. The image is made by painting or rolling ink onto the plate, then printing, usually through a press.

Offsetting
The print is printed onto a non-absorbent surface then reprinted, often onto a new block. This reverses the reversal of the image and is useful for accurately registering a second block.

Plate
Support, the surface of which is etched, cut or otherwise manipulated to form a printable block.

Press bed
The part of the press that supports the plate during printing.

Registration
System for aligning block and paper in multiple plate or reduction prints.

Relief printing
The category of printing which involves rolling or painting ink onto the top surface of a plate and printing from it, so that the cut away areas carry no ink.

Rosin
Ground tree resin used to create a screen for aquatint etchings.

Scrim
Lint free cloth used to wipe etching plates for printing.

Shellac
Organically derived lacquer used to varnish collagraphs to prevent them from sticking to the paper when printing. Soluble in methylated spirits.

Side grain woodblocks
Fruit or other relatively soft woods used for woodblock printing.

Sugar lift
Technique used in etching to apply a resist which is the inverse of the painted areas on the plate.

Woodcut
Print made by cutting a design into a piece of side grain woodblock or ply.

Wood engraving
Print made by engraving marks into a (usually small) plate made from end-grain boxwood.

Zinc plate
Metal support for etching.

Suppliers and other information

Printmaking Today, Cello Press, Oxon.
Quarterly journal on contemporary artists' prints, books and multiples
Principal source of information about open access print studios and tuition

Intaglio Printmaker, London
www.intaglioprintmaker.com
All kinds of printmaking supplies including presses

JPP John Purcell Paper, London
www.johnpurcell.net
Specialist paper supplier

TN Lawrence and Son Ltd, Hove
www.lawrence.co.uk
Wide variety of printmaking and art supplies

Great Art
www.greatart.co.uk
Online artists' materials

Shepherds Bookbinders Ltd and Falkiner Fine Papers
www.falkiners.com
Wide variety of Japanese and other papers

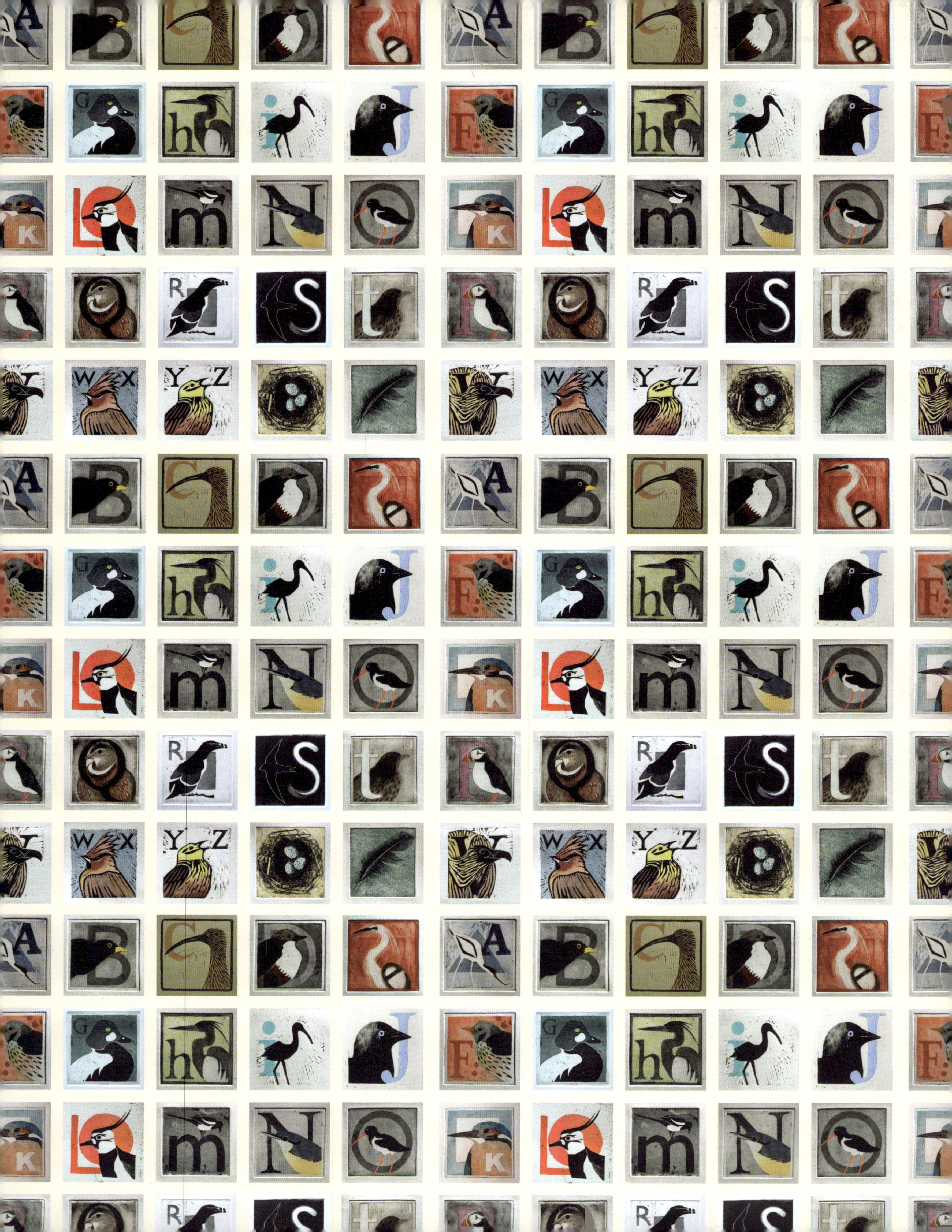